Marching from Defeat

Marching from Defeat

Surviving the Collapse of the German Army in the Soviet Union, 1944

Claus Neuber

Translated by

Tony Le Tissier

Pen & Sword
MILITARY

First published in Germany by
Druffel & Vowinckel in 2014

First published in Great Britain in 2020 and reprinted in this format in 2021 by
PEN & SWORD MILITARY
An imprint of
Pen & Sword Books Ltd
Yorkshire – Philadelphia

ISBN 978 1 39900 003 1

Typeset in 11.5/14 Ehrhardt by Vman Infotech Pvt. Ltd.
Printed and bound in the UK by CPI Group (UK) Ltd, Croydon, CRO 4YY

Pen & Sword Books Ltd incorporates the imprints of Pen & Sword
Archaeology, Atlas, Aviation, Battleground, Discovery, Family History, History, Maritime,
Military, Naval, Politics, Social History, Transport, True Crime, Claymore Press, Frontline
Books, Praetorian Press, Seaforth Publishing and White Owl
For a complete list of Pen & Sword titles please contact

PEN & SWORD BOOKS LTD
47 Church Street, Barnsley, South Yorkshire, S70 2AS, England
E-mail: enquiries@pen-and-sword.co.uk
Website: www.pen-and-sword.co.uk

Or

PEN AND SWORD BOOKS
1950 Lawrence Rd, Havertown, PA 19083, USA
E-mail: Uspen-and-sword@casematepublishers.com
Website: www.penandswordbooks.com

Contents

Publisher's Note

Claus Neuber was born in 1924 in Frieburg, Silesia. In 1924 he passed the Arbitur at the Senior Secondary Modern School there, immediately thereafter being called up by the Wehrmacht as a wartime volunteer in an artillery regiment, and was sent to the Eastern Front in 1943 as a Second Lieutenant of the Reserve.

Following the collapse of Army Group Centre in the summer of 1944 he became a returnee, a soldier seeking to rejoin the fighting troops after this defeat, and was temporarily taken prisoner by the Soviets, but escaped and eventually successfully managed to cross back into the German lines. In 1945 he was posted to a unit in France, where he was captured by the Americans and then released in 1946.

After his release he was employed as an assistant in a chemical factory in Hameln, gaining laboratory assistant status and eventually passing the state pharmaceutical exams in 1954 and becoming a fully qualified chemist. In 1961 he became an active medical pharmacist officer in the Bundeswehr, later rising to commander of a medical battalion and then in 1972 was appointed head of the Reserve medical staff before retiring to Bonn in 1984.

Neuber's manuscript originated in a report written in the autumn of 1944 while the experience of his escape from the collapse of Army Group Centre during the summer months of 1944 was fresh in his mind. This was the greatest catastrophe of the German army in the Soviet Union. The then short report was required from the surviving troops in order to create a detailed account of what had happened. Later amendments and additions were made in light of further research.

Introduction

June 1944 – in just three months the fifth year of the war will come to an end, and in a few weeks, on 22 June, it will be the third anniversary of the attack on the Soviet Union, Operation Barbarossa. Following the fall of Stalingrad on 2 February 1943 and the collapse of our last large-scale offensive near Kursk and Orel in July of the same year, Operation Zitadelle, it was certain that the Soviets would win.

Our armies stood on the defensive everywhere, long since robbed of their full fighting strength in expensive, hard battles. By May 1944, in the southern sector of the Eastern Front, large areas of territory had been abandoned, including the whole Crimean peninsula with its once so hotly fought-over Sevastopol fortress as well as the important harbour city of Odessa on the Black Sea and Kiev, the capital of the Ukraine.

In the north of the front the Soviets had been able to break the ring around Leningrad and push forward as far as Lake Peipus, and in the central sector Smolensk had been lost.

Now at last a pause in the fighting occurred on the whole front. The Soviets used it to prepare their largest operation to date. It had the code name Operation Bagration, the name of a meritorious Russian general in the 1812 war against Napoleon, and aimed at the destruction of the 'Grande Armée' in the fields that in the following weeks would once again become the backdrop to events of Napoleonic proportions.

This operation was against the four armies of Army Group Centre in White Russia (also known as White Ruthenia or Byelorussia), which in the last months, despite continual and extraordinarily strong attacks, had been maintained. From north to south were: the 3rd Panzer Army, led by Colonel General Reinhardt, the 4th Army, under the command of General of Infantry von Tippelskirch, the 9th Army, which was led by General of Infantry Jordan, and the 2nd Army, under Colonel General Weiss. Commander-in-Chief of Army Group Centre was General Field Marshal Busch, who had set up his headquarters in Minsk, the capital of White Russia.

The front line of the army group resembled a gigantic roughly 1,100 km-long semi-circle, which began north-westerly from Vietbsk near Polozk and ended in the south close to Kovel. In the centre of this curve in the front, the most easterly and most exposed section, the so-called 'Dnepr Balcony', ran along the main front line in an area eastwards from Mogilev and Orsha, which in the Wehrmacht reports was described as 'the fighting area between the Dnepr and Tschaussy' and jutted out from there for up to 50km wide over the river. From here it was 400km as the crow flies to Moscow and just over 600km to the East Prussian border.

In order to determine Soviet operational plans Stalin summoned the commanders in chief of the fronts, as the Red Army described them, to him in the Kremlin. They were as follows: Army General Bagramian (1st Baltic Front), Colonel General Sacharov (2nd Byelorussian Front) and Colonel General Tscherniachovski (3rd Byelorussian Front). Added to these were the coordinators at that time of two of these fronts, the Marshals Vassilevski for the 1st Baltic and 3rd Byelorussian Fronts and Zhukov for the 1st and 2nd Byelorussian Fronts, as well as some generals of the air forces and members of the war council.

Beside the military, the Foreign Minister Molotov and Stalin's long-time adviser Malenkov also attended, which indicated the significance of this planned great offensive.

Stalin opened the talks briefly and succinctly with the words: 'You have the task of fighting for the liberation of White Russia. This will begin on the third anniversary of the German invasion of our fatherland.'

When they concluded on 23 May after 30 hours of discussion, the operational plan was confirmed: the Red Army would start major attacks at six widely separated places at short intervals, split up the German defences and take the opportunity to push their forces onto the defence, with the broken up units to be surrounded and destroyed. The operations would be supported by the air forces, the Byelorussian partisans and the Dnepr Fleet.

For this violent undertaking, including reserves, a total of 23 armies comprising 185 divisions with a total strength of 2,500,000 men would be made ready, supported by not less than 6,000 tanks and assault guns as well as 45,000 guns and mortars of all calibres.

It was to be the greatest advance by Russian troops from a sector of the front in history. In addition 240,000 well-equipped and well-organised partisans were to join the operation from behind the German front. They had already made a noticeable impact and would soon play a special role.

Against these enormous enemy forces Army Group Centre had only its four armies with forty partly reduced battle-worthy divisions, including four Reserve divisions and four less battle-worthy security divisions, in all comprising about 450,000 men, to oppose them. Its materiel shortcomings were, especially with the tanks and the artillery, no less wanting. The worst situation, however, was to be found in the Luftwaffe, with a total of 40 German fighters opposing an armada of over 6,000 enemy machines of all kinds, and these 40 fighters could not be brought into action at full strength because there was a lack of fuel.

In addition to these factors there was also a grave lack of judgement regarding the situation, and as a consequence a lack of decision-making at the highest level of command. The Army High Command (OKH) was awaiting the Russian summer offensive not in the Army Group Centre sector, but further south in the Tarnopol–Kovel area in Eastern Galizia with Army Group Northern Ukraine, whose commander-in-chief was General Field Marshal Model. Here, as always during the Eastern campaign, it was important that a concentration of forces should meet a concentration of forces.

The argument in support of the situation evaluation by the OKH was also based on the fact that the Soviets – in a subtly deceptive manoeuvre – were sending a large number of unloaded transport trains into this area which were then apparently emptied at their destination and rolled back again the next day. The idea that a Russian offensive could be expected here was further strengthened by the fact that the enemy appeared to have occupied the town of Kovel which had already been surrounded and after a week-long bitter struggle could be liberated on 5 April.

In any case whatever the reports of the headquarters Army Group Centre, according to which ever more Soviet fighting units were assembling before its sector of the front line, no importance has been attached to them. The troop movements were regarded as diversionary measures in connection with their own forces. Or, even worse, they were quite simply ignored.

With such a view this could be why Army Group Centre on 30 May, only about three weeks before the beginning of the Soviet offensive, transferred the whole of the LVI Panzer Corps with its six divisions to Army Group Northern Ukraine, thus losing over 80 per cent of its complement of vehicles. On top of that one division after another was taken and their panzergrenadier division had to give up 60 per cent of its vehicles, whereby its mobility, and with it its effectiveness, was greatly reduced.

Following these events the Red Army went into action on the morning of 22 June, and fate relentlessly took its course. Army Group Centre's sacrifice is the German Wehrmacht's biggest catastrophe in the war against the Soviet Union. Within a few weeks it would lose almost 250,000 men killed or missing, as well as 90,000 taken prisoner.

Its never to be replaced personnel losses were accordingly as high as those from Stalingrad, which, in addition to serious materiel losses, were considered excessive. And so on to its destruction with all its consequences, from beginning to end, on the whole Eastern Front which became a milestone on the way to Germany's final military defeat.

Many in the homeland first became aware of this catastrophe as the Soviets suddenly appeared on the German eastern boundary at the end of July. Until then people had not been particularly concerned as the current front was still deep within enemy territory. Besides, the Wehrmacht reports on the events in the central sector of the Eastern Front were relatively short and, in view of the extent of the fiasco, were restrained in tone. But soon, once the situation in the lost towns and areas had been looked at on a map, people came to the realisation that something quite different to a 'planned move' was underway.

Apart from this, attention was generally more focused on the spectacular developments on the invasion fronts in the West and in Italy, as well as the events in connection with the assassination attempt on Hitler on 20 July, incidents that were used to deflect attention away from the disaster in the East.

However, with ever more field-post letters coming back home, the situation was becoming unaccountable. One began to grasp what must have occurred between the Dnepr and the East Prussian border. The number of missing was unbelievably high, and some of these had been subjected to a strange fate.

An estimated 10,000 to 15,000 men were involved – their number will never be accurately confirmed – having survived the inferno without being taken prisoner. They originated in the vast cauldron east of Minsk from which they had managed to break out, or belonged to the remains of the many divisions that had already been beaten in the engagements of the Russian offensive near Vitebsk, Orsha, Mogilev and Bobruysk. As always, they were cut off from any unit and without exception had to choose between two alternatives – either to give themselves up with the well-known risks of captivity, or, in the face of of ever present danger, to try to strike through in the rear of the westward advancing enemy and through occupied territory in the hope of somehow getting to the definite front, and from here, after crossing the Russian front line, the last and most difficult obstacle, reaching their own lines.

The overwhelming majority of stragglers chose the latter not realising how long and merciless the journey would be, with most of them sooner or later falling to hunting and search parties or the countless partisans deployed in the vast forested areas of White Russia.

Many drowned in rivers and lakes along the way, vanishing without trace in the extensive areas of swamp or somewhere in woods and fields, going to ground alone and weakened by wounds, illness, hunger and exhaustion.

Many chose suicide, so hopeless was their situation. Some were already close to their ardently desired goal in the enemy's positions and here found their end by killing themselves with their own weapons, or, the most dreadful of all tragedies, when only a few metres from the safe trenches died at the hands of their own comrades because they did not recognise them.

In the end only a very few came back after weeks or even months. By 10 August, when the Russian summer offensive was essentially at an end, some 80 officers and more than 800 NCOs and men had returned, the last of them in late autumn. The experience of these 'returnees', as they were called, who had made the long trek back, can really only be described as incredible.

The following pages describe how, in the hot summer of 1944, a few of us had the greatest luck to see our homeland again and start a new life. But for many soldiers in the front line this was something they could only dream of as they are now included among the countless missing of whom no trace has ever been found.

I dedicate this account to my companion in fate, Georg Maag, who over almost six dramatic weeks became my faithful and reliable companion.

I have to acknowledge at this point with great gratitude and high regard all the men and women in White Russia, and especially in Lithuania, who, despite danger to life and limb, courageously and selflessly provided help. Without doubt the majority of those who fought their way back are indebted to them for being able to reach their goal.

The author was one of the lucky ones. Now let us accompany him on his journey that began on 26 June 1944 in White Russia, east of the Dnepr.

The Route to Catastrophe

Beginning of June 1944

We find ourselves at the observation point of the 1st Battery of Artillery Regiment 18, part of the 18th Panzergrenadier Division, one of the twelve divisions of the 4th Army, which has a 260km-wide sector of the front line, with up to 50km of the so-called projecting 'Dnepr Balcony' to defend.[*] For weeks and months this is repeatedly mentioned in Wehrmacht reports as the 'combat area between the Dnepr and Tschausy' and is at the widest part of the whole front between, to the north, Lake Peipus on the Finnish Gulf and the town of Narva, in the south, and the Black Sea at Odessa.

The 4th Army is combined with the 3rd Panzer Army, the 9th Army and the 2nd Army to form Army Group Centre which, with a 1,100km front line, encompasses about a third of the Eastern Front.

With me in our observation post are Sergeants Meischner and Laska, the telephone operators Senior Corporals Hofmann and Koch, as well as the two radio operators, Senior Corporal Wild and Corporal Glaser. There are seven of us.

Our observation point is some kilometres south of Ssutoki, a big place lying about 35km south-east of the Dnepr and the town of Mogilev, which has about 100,000 inhabitants. This is more than 200km east of Minsk, the capital of White Russia, where the commander-in-chief of Army Group Centre, General Field Marshal Busch, has set up his headquarters.

In order to see as much of the terrain as possible, we have set up the observation post on the forward slope of an almost completely bald mountain range, about 800m behind the main front line, which in this sector is being held by the men of Panzergrenadier Regiment 30 of our division.

---

[*] The front was called this at this point because its shape was a projection similar to a *balcony*.

Just 3km behind us on the edge of Davydovitshi village are the four light 10.5cm field howitzers of our battery commanded by Captain Trost, whose fire we have to direct.

In the past eight weeks, since the beginning of April, nothing much has happened near us partly because of the onset of the muddy season. As in Erich Maria Remarque's novel, one can say 'Nothing new in the east'.

From October to December 1943, however, in the 4th Army's area four so-called 'railway battles' took place and then, at the end of March 1944, massive attacks were launched by the Soviets which resulted in bitter fighting and severe losses against the greatly superior enemy. The last phase of this defensive fighting was particularly praised in the Wehrmacht Report of 3 April, which said:

> Between the Dnepr and Tschaussy, under the command of General of Infantry von Tippelskirch and General of Artillery Martinek, troops have in seven days of heavy fighting foiled the attempt to break out by 17 enemy rifle divisions, one motorised and two tank brigades and thereby gained an outstanding defensive success. The Silesian 18th Panzergrenadier Division under the command of Major General Zutavern especially proved itself.

This was taken as a high honour, but we did not forget to mourn the considerable losses incurred, which, with the constant shortage of personnel, could not be fully replaced.

Now came the temporary quiet that we so sincerely deserved, but while our guns remained quiet, there was a shortage of ammunition. Consequently, in the middle of April, it was ordered that only five shots at most could be fired by each gun each day – only twenty shells for the whole battery. This meant it was difficult to engage a target. At best we could deliver a delayed harassing fire, which would hardly bother those on the other side. Therefore, we save the ammunition for the few, more important targets. This was certainly understood by the infantry, for if in quiet periods we constantly fire in the one area, stronger retaliatory fire comes back on our positions which cannot be challenged. So we do not disturb the peace at all if possible, though this will certainly mean trouble in the future.

Sergeant Meischner, my assistant observer, has taken turns with me with the telescope, exchanging it for an hour at a time, carefully examining the Russian main fighting line and the background. We have observed everything that has happened over there and compiled a report. Such a report by an artillery observer has limited scope, but from time to time it is still a very valuable contribution to the assessment of the enemy's situation.

The telescope remains constantly in use, from early morning onwards, as soon as one can see something – at this time of the year at about 3 a.m. – until darkness. With only 5 hour's sleep, the early morning hours are the most unpleasant, and we can only stay awake by chain smoking. One dare not drop off on any account, for most firing breaks out at this time, but when it stops it is impossible to see where it came from.

Apart from this, in our privileged position a relatively quiet summer is forecast. We wait for a Russian offensive further south on Army Group Northern Ukraine, which is why we have given up some of our divisions to them. On top of this, our 18th Panzergrenadier Division was de-motorised, as was the 25th on the left wing of our 4th Army, and that means that our mobility has been reduced by 40 per cent. As a result, requests were immediately made for: 6 veterinary officers, 35 blacksmith NCOs, 35 animal feeding specialists, 41 men and 75 goatherds! The list reads like a macabre joke, especially when one remembers that the 18th was originally an infantry division and was turned into a panzergrenadier division to improve its effectiveness in the middle of 1943. The title of 'panzer' is, of course, misleading as we did not have a single tank and we were not given any later on either.

It looked as though we were heading up for a 'quiet summer', and that would have been fine by us. But I had a feeling of foreboding.

The time has come for an hour's break. Sergeant Meischner has replaced me at the telescope and I sit down in front of the bunker entrance for a short spell of sunbathing, well protected in the approximately 1.5m-deep communication trench, which leads over the ridge in several places and ends behind it. From here on we can't be seen by the enemy, and a narrow field track leads from there to the firing position of our battery. Our food is brought along this route daily and whatever else is required, including the longed-for post.

A few metres away from the bunker the communication trench bends sharply and runs from here in a zigzag forwards to the front line. The bit on the bend has been constructed for the possible defence of the observation post, and also for defence against reconnaissance or assault troops, which we must always be prepared for. Also here is the machine-gun mounting for our light, captured Russian machine gun, an antiquated model with a drum magazine that takes seventy-two rounds. Unfortunately, we only have one magazine and moreover no suitable ammunition for reloading, so if the worst happens we would have to resort to our machine pistols. However, we hope that because of the defences we have built, a difficult situation shouldn't arise. Another advantage is the primitive mechanism of the operating Russian machine gun. It was said that one could bury it quietly for four weeks in the sand and it would still function afterwards. On both sides of the machine-gun position are rifle firing positions and right next to them, up to 60cm deep in the front-facing trench wall, so-called 'foxholes', which even when one is standing up, offer very good protection, especially against the almost perpendicular falling shots of mortars. We have set up one of these 'foxholes' as a toilet, widening it a little and deepening it and inserting a 'thunder plank', which is always a comfort in front-line situations.

Our bunker can be described as comfortable. It has a high, multilayered raftered ceiling and it is buried deep in the ground. It was thickly covered with earth and, in order to blend in with the surroundings, grass. With careful work we have raised the roof slightly on either side of the crest so the observation post is hardly discernible from the air.

Since we have to set up a screen, which would be fully visible to the enemy while the work is going on, the construction of the bunker has to be done under the cover of darkness. In fact, no one must be seen out of the trench in daylight, as the enemy might aim shots, and whenever an artillery observation post first identifies, or even only suspects, this capability, then can one can take precautions and usually forget about it.

The interior of our bunker has been set up with much love, care and expertise, as always during a quiet period when a change of location is not in the offing. Although there are seven of us, we have assembled three two-storied wooden bunks with six sleeping places, as one of us always has to sit outside at the telescope and at night stand guard over the trench.

The log walls and the floor are covered with planks on the inside like a small ski hut. In the middle, between strong supports, stands a stove which during the winter gives out a pleasant heat. The machine pistols, steel helmets and gas-mask containers hang from the bunks.

In the adjacent observation post where the telescope is mounted there is a small, blanket-covered seat with the field telephone for passing orders to fire to the battery. Like the floor of the living and sleeping section, the observation post is laid out with planks.

Clearly visible in the observation post is the desire for a sense of 'normality'. On one of the supports hangs a small day-of-departure calendar that one of us had received in a package sent to him; this is also an indication of how relatively quiet it has been here for weeks. On the back of each sheet of the calendar is a quotation encapsulating the spirit of the time – and the situation. For example: 'You are nothing, your people are everything' or 'Unending is the thirst of the dead for fame'. There is even a line from Schiller's *Siegefest*: 'In the lives of all good people fame is the highest attribute, for while the body becomes dust, a great name lives on'. I wonder if that will apply to us?

We decorate the bunker's walls extensively with newspaper cuttings, especially pictures of film stars. My contribution is classic photographs of Use Werner and Hannelore Schroth. Most of the pictures come from our front-line newspaper, *Der Stofltrupp*, which we receive regularly in quiet periods. We can live well enough in the bunker out here, and since the present pause in the fighting could soon come to an abrupt end, the watchword is: *Carpe diem*! Seize the day!

Sergeant Laska agrees with me and sits down beside me in the sunshine. He is responsible for the wireless communications and the work of our wireless operator and telephonist, and he brings incredible news with him: 'The invasion has begun, yesterday in Normandy.' That is, on 6 June.

'Great, at last', I reply. We are both strongly convinced that our troops, under the command of two such celebrities as Rommel and von Runstedt, are preparing a hot reception for the invasion force across the Channel and the enemy will be chased back into the sea.

'In Italy everything looks a bit precarious', said Laska. 'A few days ago the Allies marched into Rome, and previously we had to give up Monte Cassino', I replied, and thought of the four months of bitter defensive fighting there by our parachutists, 'The Green Devils', as the enemy respectfully call them. I thought too of how the Benedictine abbey at Monte Cassino, a centre of Western monastic life, had been reduced to an enormous heap of rubble by 229 Flying Fortresses, Marauders and Mitchells. The bombing was carried out even though Abbot Gregorio Diamare had given the assurance that 'at no time were German soldiers to be found inside the walls of the holy cloisters of Monte Cassino'. According to the eminent British military historian, J.F.C. Fuller, the attack on the abbey was 'not so much a bit of vandalism as a clear act of tactical stupidity'. Fortunately, in October 1943, the German Lieutenant Colonel Schlegel had been able to save most of the art treasures in the abbey as well as about 70,000 volumes from its library and archives.

'Listen!' We interrupted our talk and heard the sound of oncoming aircraft. They were two Soviet Rata fighters that unashamedly flew low along the front line. 'They want to see if we are still here', said Laska sarcastically. He was not completely wrong, as for several days more and more enemy reconnaissance aircraft appeared over our sector. They were trying to see whether our deployment had changed and to work out our artillery positions.

'We see absolutely nothing of our fighter planes any more', remarked Laska angrily. 'Probably all of them are at the invasion fronts and over the Reichs territory', I replied. None of us knew that in the whole of Army Group Centre's area only forty fighters were to be found. So, no wonder. With that we stopped chatting and continued enjoying sunbathing. I dream of the possibility of getting two weeks' leave in the near future. My request for leave has been passed on by the chief, Captain Trost, and considering the Russian situation, I think he is likely to agree to it.

The lovely weather really puts one in the mood for leave. How beautifully the sun has shone in the last few days, and today it shines with all its might from the bright, blue sky and it looks like it will be a very hot summer.

Mid-June

Russians are obviously are generally well hidden at the front line and further back. Perhaps they are expecting a German attack and are preparing themselves for it. Or perhaps they want to make us think this and are working instead on the preparations for their own offensive? Whatever, something is obviously going on! Also the usual loudspeaker propaganda, which has no effect on us, has increased. As always, they implore us to run over to them, now with the additional: 'before it is too late!' And something else makes one sit up and take notice: on 10 June there will be a radio address by the well-known partisan Colonel Grishin, in which he will call for the mass destruction of railway lines, and point out that what happens on 20 July will be of special significance.

This doesn't make sense because we know he does not operate near us but further south, in Army Group Northern Ukraine's area. It also seems odd that the partisans should plan to make it more difficult for us to give up a considerable amount of territory.

In the Russian front line and immediately behind it moves have been made with almost a provocative lack of care. For example, I saw four Red Army soldiers bring an anti-tank gun forward by at least 100m over fully open ground to an obviously prepared firing position. And on a stretch of road behind the front line but clearly within effective range of our guns a truck drove fully lit up in both directions as if it were peacetime. All this goes into the daily report, though it is difficult for me not to mention that lack of ammunition means there is nothing we can do about all of this.

In the 4th Army the artillery ammunition supply is now completely inadequate. Major General Trowitz of the 57th Infantry Division was told how urgent the situation was, but couldn't spend time on this because he couldn't solve the problem. Artillery ammunition can now only be used in emergencies. If he wanted to launch an attack, he would have no chance of getting the ammunition required. His division, our neighbour but one to the right, would get nothing.

It has been like this for some time. In the war diary of the 18th Panzergrenadier Division on 5 May 1943 it was noted that: 'The artillery ammunition demands appear very high and there is no understanding of the difficulties of supply.'

I was about to write about this in my daily report when Senior Corporal Hofmann calls across to me, 'Lieutenant, they are bringing you a captured Ivan!' Quickly I leave the observation post and make my way along the trench leading to the main front line in order to bring the prisoner back. I think he looks incredibly well, contrary to what I had been expecting. He has a fresh, calm face, this Ivan, and his uniform is brand new – boots, leather belt, all pristine. The man makes an excellent impression, and he is not an officer – he is a simple soldier. He has the look of a soldier from an elite troop, one apparently intended for things rather greater than a local undertaking with only a few kilometres of ground to gain.

We discover the prisoner belongs to the formidable 50th Army opposite under Lieutenant General Boldin, with which our 4th Army in the winter of 1941/42 had had to fight bitter battles during the retreat from Moscow. Will he attack us again? He will.

But now I want to record what we have been doing on 12 June. Two incidents deserve to be emphasised.

First, the 'de-motorisation' of our division was confirmed, which means 60 per cent of our vehicles vanish by rail and are not seen again. Lots of *panjewagons* and unruly horses, who naturally cannot know their likely fate, fill the gaps left by the vehicles.

Our panzergrenadier division continues to be described as such, but it is now also known as 'Infantry Division 44', and thus is regarded as equivalent to an infantry division. Yes, we are supposed to have tanks, but, as already mentioned, we actually have none.

While these changes were to some extent anticipated, another development was completely unexpected. In a phone call from our chief we discovered that, with immediate effect, leave restrictions have been imposed on all units; for me and many others this is the most deeply disappointing news. We realise the situation must have seriously deteriorated, in particular in the area of Army Group Northern Ukraine, since we have had to hand over our vehicles, one division after another and even the whole of the LVIth Panzer Corps with its six divisions. The 20th Panzer Division is the only panzer division that remains in Army Group Centre, and apparently it is located far behind the front line in reserve; from now on it will only be used as a 'fire brigade' at the critical points. We have to hope there won't be too many of those along our 1,100m front line.

Reinforcements are no longer an option since Hitler stipulated on 3 November 1943, in his 'Directive 51', that in future the armies in the West should have priority in terms of personnel and materiel over those in the East. The Eastern Front must get by with what it's got! But our resources are completely insufficient for successfully fighting a defensive battle and for conducting even limited operations. We can only hope that not much of the 1,100m front line will be given up.

At this time our division commander, Lieutenant General Zutavern, who was already satisfied with the preparedness for action of his two grenadier regiments, GR 30 and GR 51, came to Artillery Regiment 18 to check up on us. Captain Trost called us back from the firing position, saying that a senior officer is going to inspect our observation post, which meant we need to prepare an appropriate reception and make a good impression. The interior of our bunker was tidied up again, and our uniforms too, of course, and the periscope was aimed at a point in the Russian front line. A little later everything was ready. Our much-admired divisional commander, who always took an interest in the welfare of his soldiers, arrived with his escort. I go up to him and report in the customary way: 'Observation Post of the 1st Battery, occupied by one officer, two NCOs and four men: nothing special to report.' He thanked me for the report and then, with an earnest but friendly expression, reached out and shook each of us by the hand. We gained the impression that he was really concerned about us, and this was confirmed when he told us that we were likely to face a serious test soon and he was confident we would act in an exemplary manner as we had done in the past. Then, turning to depart, he said: 'Do your job well, Lieutenant, and the very best of soldiers' luck to you all.'

A strong handshake, a thoughtful, sympathetic glance, then the visit is over. Our bunker and the observation post had not even been looked at. On its own his division lay across the path of the mass of the tried and tested 50th Army, disproportionate in numbers of troops, which was typical all the way along the front line of Army Group Centre. In all 23 Russian armies with 185 fully operational divisions faced just 4 German armies with 40 tattered divisions which were in the process of being brought up to strength – 2,500,000 Red Army soldiers against 450,000 Germans! And these figures don't take into account the weakness of some of our units. At our disposal we still had the IInd Hungarian Reserve Corps with its five divisions, which was positioned behind the 2nd Army in the south of the army group near Kobryn, not far from Brest-Litovsk on the edge of the Pripjet Marshes. They were brave men who understandably would rather listen to the familiar sounds of their homeland than the much-less pleasant clang of the Stalin Organs in the iron-bearing fields of Russia. The important point is that in an engagement we should not expect too much of them.

On 16 June, a few kilometres south of Orsha, a Russian officer was picked up and captured. With astounding openness, as if it was not secret, he reported that the Soviet army would march through here in fourteen days. Through Orsha? This town was not in Army Group Northern Ukraine's area but in that of our 4th Army on the Dnepr, on the highway to Minsk. Not 100km north of my observation post!

Should we believe him? Apparently not. We are absolutely convinced the Russian summer offensive will begin in the Tarnopol–Lemberg–Kovel area, against Army Group Northern Ukraine. Even the most revealing reports from 4th Army's commander about the continuous reinforcement of the already strong enemy units in front of their section of the line fail to alter the assessment of the situation at the highest level. Also at our army group headquarters in Minsk no importance is attached to this threatening development. It is played down or not brought to anyone's attention. The attitude there seems to be: 'None of it is true' or 'Don't speak about it'!

At our observation post we naturally know nothing about this and are full of self-confidence. If the Ivans attack us, we will really show them who they are dealing with! We have already given them a big rebuff, and we want to do it again. This should be possible because at last the 'wonder weapons', which we were told about so long ago, are ready for action. We are full of hope because we have heard that the first V-l was launched against England on 13 June.

Our mood at the moment, despite the enemy offensives and the lack of reinforcements, can in no way be described as pessimistic, even though we are bitterly disappointed and surprised to hear of the Allied landings on the coast in Normandy where they have suffered heavy casualties but are making progress. We believe they will be brought to a standstill in time and then beaten back. We are confident about this because of Rommel's legendary ability. Also, since divisions on the Eastern Front are due to be redeployed to France to counter the invasion, we can't imagine that such a course of action will not reap rewards. So, to use a familiar phrase: 'The morale of the troops is excellent.'

On the Eastern Front we can no longer plan big offensives and, on the contrary, realise that sooner or later further territory will have to be given up. Yet, we are determined to ensure that the Red Army does not get near to the border of the Reich or cross it, as everyone knows well what that would mean for our people, particularly the women.

We are determined to be prepared for action and, as ever, are conscious of our responsibility. We remember our oath to the flag and feel bound to do our duty without shirking. Despite the increasingly irreligious actions of the National Socialist government, many of us are still committed to the current battles against the atheist Soviet Union. The Field Prayer Book says:

> A soldier's honour is loyalty until death, and a soldier should do his duty even in the smallest ways . . . Military duty is honourable . . . Germany's greatness is partly the result of the brave conduct of its soldiers.
>
> Various passages in the Holy Bible confirm that God values soldiers who do their duty. You should feel glad to belong to such a highly valued profession. The call to the flag is God's call . . .
>
> Remember that God, in whose name you have sworn on the flag, has guided you during your service as a soldier!

There is also the prayer: 'Bless the German Wehrmacht and give its members the strength for the highest sacrifice.' These words are inspiring. The same could be said of strongly influential books about the First World War, for example, *In Stahlgewittern* by Ernst Junger, and *Verdun, das grofle Gericht* by P.C. Ettighoffer and *Douaumont* by Werner Beumelburg, where the last line is: 'that from the bones of the dead a generation grows, as true, brave and manly as ever; that is our prayer'. But at the moment, our primary motivation is, by every possible means, to keep the Red Army away from our territory.

In view of the seriousness of the current situation there are seldom cases of desertion. Those that do desert are then sentenced, and particularly reprehensible is the abstruse notion of erecting memorials to the 'Unknown Deserter' on the basis that such individuals merely made poor decisions.

Until now hardly anyone – at least at our level – has expressed the opinion that the war is already lost. We do not believe this can happen, as we still trust in Hitler's much-praised skill as a strategist, thanks to his victories in Poland and France.

We are also waiting for the new 'Wonder Weapons', which will change everything for the better. Many of us still believed that we would march under the Brandenburg Gate in a victory parade before the jubilant population. Of course, many others would be satisfied if the war came to a timely end before the German borders had been crossed and the Red Flag was raised high on the Reichstag building.

The morale of the troops is as strong as ever. We are not depressed because, although the situation has become difficult and the enemy is increasingly efficient, we still feel that we are evenly matched. In the 'Dnepr Balcony' Soviet activity on the ground is resuming as is their unopposed air reconnaissance, and recently they launched a night assault with troops dressed in black camouflage uniform. Then in the early morning of 18 June a stronger group penetrated our main front line in woodland near Davydovitshi which was not far from our firing position. But by midday the advance, doubtless a reconnaissance mission, had been thrown back by Grenadier Regiment 30, which counterattacked. We observed increased activity in both directions in the trenches connecting with the enemy front line as if a relief was taking place, and noticed that the incoming Red Army soldiers were carrying assault packs. Therefore, we expected a local attack, probably with the aim of tying us down here when the offensive against Army Group Northern Ukraine started. But we did not understand why they were bringing in assault packs.

The remainder of the day passed without anything unusual happening. I went to my bunker, where Senior Corporal Wild and Corporal Glaser were working on their radio pack 'D', known as 'Dor-Aparatus'. This consists of two heavy packs. One contains the radio apparatus and the other the accumulator as well as the earphones and other equipment. Unfortunately, this radio does not perform very well. Its range is only about 5km. While this is sufficient for general use, sometimes in hilly country contacts can't be made or can only be made at short distances. Sergeant Laska has been given the task of testing it. If there is a big battle telephone cables are often broken by artillery and mortar fire, whereupon radio has to be used. If the radio isn't working, the communications people have to repair it, often doing so under enemy fire, and this always leads to casualties. How many fault finders have not come back? But their task is essential as without radio communication the 'eyes' of the artillery are blind and the battery remains ineffective.

I had finished my daily situation report, when my eyes fell on the page in the calendar for the previous day. On the back is a quotation: 'The last word Wisdom ever has to say: he only earns his Freedom and Existence, who's forced to win them afresh daily', J.W. von Goethe, *Faust*, Part 2, Act 5, Scene VI. This quotation was the subject of an essay at school in the Lower Fifth. At the time I recall that I thought the word 'daily' in this context was an exaggeration. But now, given our predicament at the front, the word 'hourly' seems more appropriate.

On 19 June we got to the observation post earlier than usual. Although the enemy was quiet – because they had already completed their preparations – we did not take our eyes off him for a moment. We felt that something was going to happen. I had prepared a sketch of the terrain using the telescope and brought it to the observation post; on the sketch everything we could see was plotted. First came our own front line, then a section running through this front-line sector known as the 'Panzer Position', then the Russian line, the rest of Grasivez village and finally the hinterland. Ranges for opening fire on all prominent and important points have already been calculated, so that we can fire back quickly if we need to.

Today General Field Marshal Busch goes on home leave. That appears to be a remarkable decision in view of the tense situation, but leads one to believe that that the situation cannot be as serious as we thought. If the commander-in-chief of Army Group Centre can take leave, then we can breathe more easily again, even though the ban on leave continues for us.

I cannot get to sleep and so shortly before midnight I go back to our position in front of the bunker, where Senior Corporal Hofmann is on duty. He tells me he has 'nothing special to report', which at that moment is still correct. As on previous days, we look up at a starlit sky. 'Nicely warm again tonight', remarks Hofmann, 'and not a single cloud.' Suddenly we hear muffled growls of thunder to the rear, far behind us to the west. 'Funny, a storm in this weather', says Hofmann, and I am of the same opinion. When we turn around, we see on the horizon a black-grey cloud which is accompanied by further claps of thunder, rising slowly and forming a gigantic mushroom. 'That is no storm, that must have been an ammunition or fuel dump flying up into the air', I say, and Hofmann adds: 'Surely that was Genosse Grishin [partisan leader] back at work.' And he was right. But it turned out that it was not just Genosse Grishin who was responsible. On the night of the 19/20 June, 240,000 partisans at 10,500 locations in the hinterland of Army Group Centre between the Dnepr and the Beresina and even still west of Minsk blew up or otherwise made unusable railway lines, airfields, bridges, supply depots of all kinds, radio and telephone installations, electricity plants and other important sites. This had serious consequences for us.

It is difficult to understand why the biggest partisan action of the war, which was aimed against Army Group Centre, did not indicate to our commanders that the Soviet summer offensive would be directed at us, not at Army Group Northern Ukraine. In addition, in an intercepted radio message on 10 June Grishin had said that his activities would be of special significance on 20 June. He had done his job on time, as had all the other partisan units, following Stalin's 'Order of the Supreme Commander No. 95', which was issued on the twenty-fifth anniversary of the Red Army on 23 February 1943. Part 3 stated that:

> The flames of the partisan battle in the rear of the enemy are to be made even stronger, the communication routes of the enemy are to be destroyed, the railway bridges blown up, the despatch of enemy troops as well as the delivery of weapons and ammunition are to be thwarted, the army camps blown up and set on fire and the enemy occupiers overwhelmed; . . . The attacking Red Army is to assist with all forces and by all means. Long live our famous Red Army, our heroic navy, long live our brave male and female partisans!

The 'brave male and female partisans' had thus performed brilliantly, and they would continue to make a contribution to the catastrophic events that came upon us all too soon.

20 June

It remains relatively quiet in our division's area on the 4th Army's right wing. But in the left-hand sector on the boundary with the 3rd Panzer Army, the enemy took action against the 78th Assault Division and our 'de-motorised' 25th Panzergrenadier Division. Their reconnaissance probes were all thrown back.

The 3rd Panzer Army soon became more involved. Three days ago there was heavy fighting around Vitebesk – for example, the village of Sharki changed hands several times. The Ivans were reported to be fighting to the last man! This had frequently happened before, but this time undoubtedly the recent intense political indoctrination of the troops had had an impact. In every company a small team of political organisers ensured that the soldiers 'knew what it was all about'. Before the attack was launched, stirring exhortations from the commander-in-chief were read out to the troops, and every man had to put up with it.

While all this was going on to our left, nothing of any importance had disturbed us. Yet we continued to observe the enemy with as much attention as before. Hardly anything moved in their main front line and their artillery was completely silent. Apparently they do not want to reveal their firing positions because they know we have very effective sound-ranging and flash-spotting equipment that can precisely locate a battery in action.

So we have enough time to read what has been happening in *Der Stoßtrupp*. We are the first in line for news of successful operations on land, on water and in the air. Less pleasant news is treated with some reserve. The successful acts of sabotage recently carried out by the partisans are not featured at this time.

Besides the military, political and cultural news, important sporting events are reported. One prominent article describes a German Football League game at the Olympic Stadium in Berlin in which Dresdener SC convincingly beat the Luftwaffe Sports Club Hamburg (which later became HSV) 4–0. On the Dresdeners' team was Helmut Schön (the former manager of the national team), an outstanding player and goal scorer who was enthusiastically applauded.

'It is really terrific that in Berlin at a time like this a football championship can be played', said Glaser, and Meischner wondered what would have happened if, during the game, a couple of bombs had struck the Olympic Stadium! 'That has already happened in Hamburg', said Laska, thinking of the British bombing raid known cynically as 'Action Gomorrah' which caused a fire-storm at the end of July 1943 that killed almost 45,000. "The Dresdeners don't have to worry that their beautiful Florence on the Elbe will be attacked like that', I threw in. 'There is no important war target there', said Wild. None of us at that moment envisaged that the most frightful tragedy in the history of air terror would be visited on Dresden, the German Hiroshima.[*]

Today is unusually quiet for us, apart from frequent flights by enemy planes, including some of American origin. But the 3rd Panzer Army in the Vitebsk area was caught up in heavy fighting again. The title 'Panzer Army' is of course misleading since its divisions have no tanks whatsoever. Instead, it is equipped with assault guns which look similar to tanks but do not have revolving turrets so are more like artillery on self-propelled gun carriages.

In addition to keeping conspicuously quiet, the enemy was maintaining an absolute radio silence, which is highly suspicious. Is this the lull before the storm? The timing of an attack would be appropriate because tomorrow is 22 June and on this date three years ago the war against the Soviet Union – Operation Barbarossa – began.[**]

22 June

Since 3 a.m. I have been intensely observing the enemy front line. Absolutely no movement; unnatural silence. Then at 4 a.m. the expected Russian summer offensive begins. The initial attack wasn't made against our 4th Army, and the 9th and 2nd Armies on our right, nor was it aimed at Army Group Northern Ukraine. Instead, it was launched against our Army Group Centre, and then the 3rd Panzer Army in the general area around Vitebsk.

---

[*] Rudolf Augstein, editor-in-chief of *Der Spiegel*, wrote on 7 January 1985 that: 'According to the standards set at the Nuremburg war crimes trials, the victors too should be hanged . . . Truman for the completely unnecessary bombing of Nagasaki, if not for Hiroshima before that, and Churchill for ordering the bombing of Dresden at a time when Germany was already shattered.'

[**] It is worth remembering that Russian historians have documented how Operation Thunderstom, the pre-emptive strike by the Soviet Union against Germany and the West, was planned, and was brought forward by two weeks. The historian Ernst Topitsch, a professor at Graz University, wrote: 'If the Red Army had rolled over Europe, then the Americans would have had to liberate France not from German but from Soviet troops.' By 22 June 1941 the Red Army had deployed over 4 million men with the intention of conquering a continent already weakened by war. Therefore, Operation Barbarossa was in no way an unprovoked 'surprise attack on the peaceful and unprepared Soviet Union', as politically correct historians claim.

No less than 6,000 guns and mortars opened fire supported by a deployment of air-force units that was stronger than we had ever seen before. The 1st Baltic Front under General Bagramian joined the attack, reinforced by part of the 3rd Byelorussian Front. Given the overwhelming size of the Soviet force and following the massive artillery preparation and air attacks, they probably expected simply to march through without meeting any opposition, but there was some resistance, albeit on a small scale. Of course, they broke through at various points in our line, but there was no great concern at this early stage.

Field Marshal Busch had returned in haste from his leave to his head-quarters in Minsk, where the big attack northwestward of Vitebsk seems to have come as a complete surprise. The commander-in-chief of the 3rd Panzer Army, Colonel General Reinhardt, had repeatedly expressed his growing concern, pointing out that the Soviets in front of his sector were constantly reinforcing and sooner or later an attack with overwhelming force could be expected. Yet, all such warnings were waved aside with brusque remarks like: 'It cannot be true' or 'Don't mention it.' During the winter and in four rapid battles the Soviets had overrun the area around Vitebsk and the town itself, making it an obvious focal point, and then they had increased the number of reconnaissance missions and brought assault troops forward.

And now here it is, the great attack, Operation Bagration, and fate takes its inexorable course!

During the rest of that day hardly anything of significance occurred in our sector. We had no news of events around Vitebsk, and the thunder of the guns could not be heard at a distance of 200km.

23 June

On this day the strongest of the four Soviet 'fronts', the four armies of the 3rd Byelorussian Front, under Colonel General Tscherniachovski, took the offensive at Vitebsk and overcame the 78th Assault and 25th Panzer-grenadier divisions which were on the left flank of our 4th Army. The Soviet force consisted of over 1,800 tanks and self-propelled guns, more than 7,500 guns and mortars of all calibres and almost 2,000 aircraft.

Towards 5 a.m. we heard from the far north a muffled rumbling as if a storm was approaching. At this moment both the Wurtemburg divisions were subjected to a 3-hour drumfire. The bombardment was so intense that even at our observation post 80km away a light vibration of the ground was detectable. A massive ground attack followed which pushed our men back along the great Smolensk–Minsk road to Orsha, where a complete breakthrough could only be prevented with great effort.

Three hours later the three armies of the 2nd Byelorussian Front, under Colonel General Sacharov, attacked our 50th Army at the critical point where our position in the 'Dnepr Balcony' extended furthest to the east. The enemy achieved a deep penetration and the situation slowly became critical for us as their advance was clearly aimed at Mogilev, which lay only 35km to the northwest of us. In the area held by our 18th Panzergrenadier Division, which was not on the main line of the advance, the enemy action was limited to a reconnaissance with weak forces which were opposed at Vetrenka by Grenadier Regiment 51 and Grenadier Regiment 30, behind which was our observation post.

The enemy was able to make a breach in the much too thinly occupied front line, and we watched through the periscope how they moved towards us in small groups. We were unable to open fire as they were so close to the front line that there was a risk that, adjusting of our periscope, we would bring our own people under fire.

I had our captured machine gun brought into the position and all the firing points were occupied. But an exchange of artillery and small-arms fire with the enemy never came about because the leader of the enemy reconnaissance troops rose to his full height, looked around and then gave the signal to his men to withdraw, pointing eastwards with an outstretched arm. Once the front line had been crossed a decision had to be made about whether it was worth exchanging fire with the captured machine guns. So, for a time, peace returned, but we were still concerned because our feeling of superiority had been diminshed by the movement of the enemy behind our lines. There was no further action during the day.

24 June

The main Russian attack came early in the morning at 3.30 and 4 a.m. in two places. The heaviest artillery fire hit the 9th Army on our right. Then the 1st Byelorussian Front, supported by elements of the 2nd, a monstrously superior force, went into the attack. If the 2nd Army, which as yet wasn't engaged, is included, this meant that Army Group Centre was now fighting against the Soviet summer offensive on a front almost 800km in length. Breaches were made in our lines at several points, including the sector held by the 9th Army, which could only be partly eliminated.

It was now clear to us that the enemy's superiority in men and materiel was much too great to resist. What use is it for a regiment to defend against 100 attacking tanks, putting 10 or 20 out of action, only to be run over by the remainder before being torn apart?

The enemy broke through and our resistance was futile. While our losses could not be fully replaced, the Soviets had enormous reserves at their disposal that could be immediately committed to action, closing up all the gaps in their advance before being thrown into breaches to widen and deepen them. That is precisely the situation we found ourselves in.

The Red Army is also advancing on the 'strongpoint' towns of Vitebsk, Orsha, Mogilev and Bobruysk – or is already standing right in front of them. In each of them a division has been selected to defend it 'to the last man and the last bullet', even if the red tide should break over them.

Towards midday the food carriers arrive, bringing news that on the left wing of our army 'a big foul up' has occurred. 'The Ivans have broken through, broken through everywhere!' They are referring to yesterday's attack on Orsha and the breach in the line of the 337th Infantry Division in the direction of Mogilev. This is the first time we have heard about this, and we don't know what has happened since then.

The attacks on Orsha and Mogilev could have been blocked by committing elements of our two Reserve divisions, the 14th Infantry Division and the Panzergrenadier Division 'Feldherrnhalle'. The latter is replenishing just behind the front line west of Mogilev. Apparently, because it had recently been given a famous name (previously it was simply called the 60th Infantry Division), it has received some highly prized equipment from the 20th Panzer Division, our 'fire brigade'. Now it is the only division in Army Group Centre with tanks – eleven – and the only panzergrenadier division that has not been 'demotorised'.

In addition to the 11 tanks of the 'Feldherrnhalle', our armour can be reinforced with the 40 tanks of the 20th Panzer Division and the 29 Tigers of Heavy Tank Detachment 505 which are available as army reserves. But even though the Tiger is an exceptional tank, there are not many of them! The Soviets on the other hand have deployed against Army Group Centre at least 4,000 tanks, not counting self-propelled guns.

Let us return to the day's events with the 9th Army. What happens at the boundary with the 4th Army is of special interest to us because, if something goes wrong here, our right flank will be in danger. Where the 57th and 134th Infantry Divisions are positioned is one of the hotspots and it looks like the enemy will break through there – and no wonder!

Major General Trowitz, the commander of the 57th Infantry Division, had urgently requested more ammunition, but was told he would get some as soon as he attacked. Well, he is now under attack and he got nothing. His division's situation is made more difficult by the fact that only a short time ago, on 18 February, after considerable personnel losses and the sacrifice of all its heavy weapons, it broke out of the cauldron of Tscherkassy. Its current position has not been properly prepared and its replacement personnel are not fully trained.

It is also unfortunate that a few days before the beginning of the Russian offensive several regimental and battalion commanders in the 134th Division were moved to the Western Front, and the divisional commander, General Schlemmer, had been given a new role. His successor, Lieutenant General Philipp, formerly commandant of the Artillery School, was efficient and capable, but had inadequate front-line experience and before the beginning of the offensive there was insufficient time for an orderly handover of the division and for him to settle into his new role. This had been allowed to happen because of a completely false assessment of the situation at the highest level. The result was that both divisions, after offering stiff resistance and suffering heavy losses, had to give way before the advance of the massively superior Soviet forces and the 4th Army risked being outflanked on both sides and surrounded. The 20th Panzer Division, which was lying in reserve west of Bobruysk, was brought into action. This was the only panzer division in Army Group Centre's area. But the mobile elements of this force must have been moved to a danger point near the town of Paritshi, south of Bobruysk. From that position the 'fire brigade' couldn't deal with the fire either in the north or in the south and finally itself perished in the flames. The situation of the 9th Army was critical, and the 3rd Panzer Army, immediately to our left, was also threatened. The LIII Corps now stood at the centre of events. In order to better understand what happened, I should point out that this was the only complete army in the 3rd Corps which contained six divisions in all.

The LIII Corps, with its four divisions, had set up a defensive ring around Vitebsk, which was a 'strongpoint' and, in accordance with Führer Order No. 11, had to be held to the last man. This city of 160,000 inhabitants on the Diina River is the best known and largest in Army Group Centre's front, and it is a prestige target. Its loss would have a serious propaganda effect. It was also feared that our ally Finland could break away if Vitebsk and other parts of the occupied territory in the north were relinquished. Apparently this issue was deemed more important than the survival of these four divisions, and now they were in grave danger. The Soviets had broken through on both sides of the city. The LIII Corps was divided, the IXth in the north and the VIth in the south, and the Soviets were now in the process of surrounding Vitebsk where the LIII Corps was based.

Colonel General Reinhardt, the commander-in-chief of the 3rd Panzer Army, asked if these divisions could be given permission to break out of the encirclement but, as expected, this was refused for the reasons I've just explained, and this decision was a tragedy for the troops involved.

Against our 4th Army the Soviets had achieved further success, which allowed them to outflank the well-fortified Dnepr position. In response a proposal by the army commander, General of Infantry von Tippelskirch, was rejected by General Field Marshal Busch. The situation of the 4th Army was not seen as serious, but yet again the divisions involved in the fighting had to accept considerable losses of personnel and materiel. The 337th Infantry Division, for instance, had been forced back in the direction of Mogilev, losing three-quarters of its artillery.

Our 18th Panzergrenadier Division, which with the 267th and 57th Infantry Divisions formed the XII Corps on the right, hadn't been affected by the main attacks. It had the good fortune to lie between two of the six focal points of the Russian offensive and had suffered relatively few losses, but now it was in danger of being circumvented on both sides.

25 June

From early morning until dusk I had been taking turns with Sergeant Meischner to keep a lookout. No signs of an immediate attack were visible on the enemy's main front line. Nothing was happening behind the front line either – the guns were silent and there was no harassing fire from the light artillery. Absolute silence reigned, an unnatural strange quiet. One got the impression that the enemy, at least for the moment, had no interest whatsoever in putting any pressure on us. On the contrary, they want us to stay here quietly just as we are. The longer we do so, the better for them because the breakthroughs on either side of us will get larger and our situation will get worse with every hour. At the same time around Mogilev and especially Orsha they are making increasingly threatening progress. On our left flank in the sector held by the 3rd Panzer Army, the badly stricken VI Corps has long since lost the connection with the LIII Corps near Vitebsk and its remnants are now supporting our

4th Army. As a consequence, there is a yawning gap in our line through which the tanks with the red star storm through to the west meeting hardly any resistance.

The four divisions of the LIII Corps in and around Vitebsk were surrounded yesterday and overrun a little later. Today at last, much too late, the surviving units receive permission to break out, but only a few isolated groups manage, with a lot of luck, to get back to our lines; 10,000 soldiers of all ranks walk into captivity and 20,000 dead were buried by the Soviets while thousands of the missing receive no burial at all. The 3rd Panzer Army has been reduced to a limbless torso.

Things do not look good for us in the 9th Army around Bobruysk. Here too the enemy is advancing everywhere and closing in on the city from all sides. What happened at Vitebsk could also happen to us, for we are still sitting in our old positions deep in the east, in the 'Dnepr Balcony'.

26 June

The field telephone sounded at the observation post in the early hours of the morning. Sergeant Meischner, who was already sitting at the periscope, called me: 'The chief wants to speak to you.' I went across and was eager to know what Captain Trost had to tell me at that time of the day. 'Can you hear me?' 'Yes, I'm listening', I replied and then he told me slowly and in a muffled voice, 'A-1-p-e-n-v-e-i-1-c-h-e-n v-e-r-m-i-e-t-e-n, have you understood?' 'Understood, Alpenveilchen vermieten.' 'Good, end.'

I grasped the code book in which the most important orders were given a code name. The list is secret and is replaced every day. 'Alpenveilchen vermieten' means 'prepare for change of position'. So I know that things have gone seriously wrong. I shout out the news to my people and all of us are surprised as this hasn't happened before. We are used to hearing messages like 'gigantic foul-up' and 'Ivan has broken through', but from distant units – we haven't been affected by them. On this occasion, though, Senior Corporal Koch realises something drastic has occurred: 'Now chaps, the shit must have really hit the fan!' But, as usual, none of us knows anything definite.

A little later another call comes in, this time in clear text: 'All super-fluous equipment immediately back to the firing position.' So everyone packs their private belongings first and then the two telephonists begin to dismantle their equipment. I organise all the other equipment that has to be retrieved and then everything was carried through the communication trenches behind the high ridge to a VW-jeep that was waiting to take it to the firing position.

The situation on the Dnepr is getting desperate. Orsha is surrounded on three sides and is about to fall. South of the town the enemy have reached the Dnepr and crossed it at several points, and north of Mogilev, which was being defended by the 12th Infantry Division under Lieutenant General Bamler, they have reached the river. Clearly it is high time that we pack up our post and retreat – and it may already be too late.

Beforehand we had had plenty of time to wonder what this sort of situation would be like, but there was no point in thinking about it now – we had to concentrate on what we had to do.

Over in the Russian lines nothing moves, just as before, yet clearly they are ready to attack at any moment, and certainly they will attack when they see that we have begun to retreat because then we will be in a weaker position.

Towards midday the chief rings again and tells us we have an allocation of 400 rounds to bombard the Russian front line. The hope is that this shelling will keep them back and allow us to make an undisturbed withdrawal in the evening. 400 rounds is only a twentieth of the number previously allocated, so we go back to work in order to finish our task hoping to keep our losses to a minimum and thinking to ourselves that the longer the enemy waits, the better it is for us.

So we go back to work in order to finish our task, hoping to keep our losses to a minimum and thinking to ourselves that the longer the enemy waits, the better it is for us.

As I said before, I had made a sketch of the terrain, marking the important feaures. One of these was the solid-looking 'two-loophole bunker' which was a conspicuous feature in the enemy front line. The bunker was an obvious target, but because of insufficient ammunition we had had to hold back from taking action against it.

The worn-out barrels of our howitzers scatter the shells and so, as a precaution, we have to increase the range by several hundred metres and then gradually bring the aim closer to the target. Of course, this means we use up our ammunition faster, but this is the only way we can reduce the risk of short shots, the nightmare of every artillery observer, and maintain the confidence of the infantry.

Now though for the first time there is sufficient ammunition at our disposal and so the fate of the 'two-loophole bunker' is sealed. Soon it receives a direct hit which sends roof-beams whirling though the air, and smoke, accompanied by flickering flames, billows out of two firing slits. Usually this is something you can only dream about, I say to myself. The next target is what I called the 'three-cornered village'. It is the sorry remains of Grasivez, which the Soviets had incorporated into their front line and fortified. We started to shell it, but after about half of the allocated ammunition had been used we had to stop. Also thick smoke over the Russian front line prevented any further observed fire.

After a while the smoke drifted far enough away for us to start firing again. This time the rear of the front line was the target, in particular the communication trenches. One location where two trenches ran towards the front line looked significant because troops could be concentrated here. So I gave the firing order and immediately heard the muffled sound of the guns. Seconds later the shells roared over our observation post and a moment later I saw two medical orderlies with their stretcher running right into the position that I had picked as a target. If I could have held back the next four rounds, I would have done, but they were already on their way, and I could only hope they missed their target and the two stretcher-bearers were able to throw themselves under cover in time. At that moment the shells landed close to but not actually in the trench, and at the last second the two stretcher-bearers disappeared like lightning. I was very relieved, thinking that the two unarmed stretcher-bearers were surely on their way to a wounded comrade. If they had been killed, I would have been very unhappy about it, and we would all have reacted in the same way. Instead, we could have said 'c'est la guerre' or compared it with the frightful incident at Lysovka on 2 September 1941 when the Red Army attacked a field hospital. The main dressing station was shot up by tanks and then all of the wounded, doctors and nursing staff were squashed into the ground. Russian sick and wounded were also being cared for there, and the villagers, acting on instructions, tried to take away their countrymen before the attack.

There was also the massacre in the local hospital at Feodsia (Crimea). Following its recapture on 18 January 1942, the horribly mutilated corpses of hundreds of wounded who were too ill to move were found and more bodies were discovered in the Black Sea – they had been thrown into the freezing water while still alive.

Countless partisan attacks on ambulances, hospital trains and Red Cross facilities could also be mentioned, but I could not afford to think about such things. Attacks on medical stations were unknown on our side.

Contrary to all our experience, so far during the whole day the enemy had not responded with a single shot. Towards evening the first elements of Grenadier Regiment 30, which had been deployed in front of us, left their positions without provoking any enemy action along the communication trenches coming from the main front line and went slowly past our observation post. They waved at us, some of them smiling anxiously. Perhaps they were asking themselves why they had had to leave their well-constructed positions when there seemed to be no necessity to do so. They, like us, had no concept of what had happened to our neighbours, the 3rd Panzer and 9th armies – they did not know that they had long since quit the field!

Once the last shell had left the barrel we prepared to leave. I went through the bunker again to check that nothing had been forgotten. It was not easy to abandon it after it had protected us for months, and we had put so much work into the construction of the interior. There was no point in trying to make it unusable, especially as explicit orders had been given that we were not to use any explosives in the front line or in the area immediately behind it that might indicate our withdrawal to the Soviets. Also, the bunker would not be of much value to the Soviets as an observation post because it was on a reverse slope and looked towards the east.

I was about to go when my eyes were drawn to the pinups of filmstars on the walls. No, I tell myself, Ivan is not going to get you and so I rip them down – pictures of Use Werner, Marika Rokk, Hannelore Schroth, Kristina Soderbaum, Winnie Markus, Elfi Meyerhofer, Paula Wessely and the lovely La Jana in *Tiger von Eschnapur*. I screw them up into a ball, go outside and shove this in a hole in the trench wall, which I close up with earth. A 'funeral with military honours' comes to my mind, a strange thought, but everything was strange now – and '*Honi soit qui mal y pense*' ('Shame on him who thinks ill of it').

Finally we are all ready, and off we go in the direction of the firing position with one final look back. There is no reaction from the enemy, but soon I expect the first Red Army soldiers will appear and occupy our lovely bunker. Perhaps, of course, they will pass it by.

From the other side of the hill, and hidden from enemy sight, we were taken by a waiting truck to our battery. On reaching the firing position we find that everything has been packed up to go and, no longer at full strength, we drive off to our detachment's collection point. (An artillery regiment at the time was divided into three detachments, each of which contained three batteries. Our 1st Battery belonged to the 1st Detachment, which was commanded by Captain Schubert.)

Later we went on to the regiment's assembly point in Tshervony-Ossovez. Everywhere small groups of infantry had been posted to prevent a quick pursuit by the Soviets, who had now begun to fire a light barrage with mortars. Lieutenant General Zutavern, our divisional commander, was on the spot to oversee the redeployment. No one thought of a full retreat at this time.

The division had been given the task of crossing to the west bank of the Dnepr, 20km away near Dashkova, south of Mogilev, in order to take over the defence of the strongly built 'Barenstellung' (Bear Position). The night drive, in the divisional formation, was completed without any major incidents. But we overtook long columns of extended units, which again and again brought the march on the narrow road to a standstill.

In the distance the sky is red from burning buildings. Lone aircraft are bombing the villages through which we will have to pass. The 'Sewing Machine' – the Polikarpov Po-2 bomber (U2) – is back at work. This machine has several nicknames. Because of its characteristic engine noise it is also referred to as the 'Coffee Mill' and, since it operates almost always at night and at the same time, it is sometimes known as 'The Duty NCO'. In addition, some troops scornfully call it the 'Runway Crow' and the 'Fog Crow'.

The number of nicknames shows how popular this aircraft is with us. It is an old single-engined double-decker which is used for liaison and as a maid of all work. Since its nightly bombing attacks are made at very low heights, it is well armoured underneath against shots from infantry weapons – so well protected that it is also known as the 'Iron Gustav'. Shortly before it drops its bomb, the motor is switched off so the aircraft makes a rustling sound that can be clearly heard and induces a fearful psychological effect. Everyone takes serious notice when the engine is switched off, knowing the bomb is coming and hoping it will not fall nearby.

This one strikes close to us but, because of the noise of our truck, we did not get the usual warning. A fully occupied VW Kübelwagen receives a direct hit and flies into the roadside ditch and catches fire. No one gives the occupants any chance of survival.

This long column's journey goes on until the early morning, surprisingly without any further enemy interference.

27 June

With daybreak the silver gleaming band of the Dnepr comes into sight, and the wooden bridge of Dashkova. Our sappers built it a long time ago – it is a very solid and effective piece of work and it looks good to the eye. It is a shame that it will not remain so for much longer. Before the beginning of the Russian offensive it was damaged several times by air attacks but was immediately repaired again. Today it is in full working order and we are able to cross the river without any problems.

Explosives have been set at several points, and when the news is passed on that all the vehicles and the infantry rearguard have crossed, it will be blown into the air. Our battery takes up position on the edge of Dashkovka. I am tasked with going to the 'Barenstellung' as forward observer.

A forward observer is always inserted directly with the infantry in a front line so that in an enemy attack he can call for fire more or less close to his own lines which, given the deployment of the guns, often involves considerable risk. In addition, he engages known targets in the enemy front line and, in specific instances, behind it as well. During our own attacks he accompanies the infantry and directs the fire by radio according to his judgement of the situation and in cooperation with the troops around him.

The objective now is to prevent enemy units from crossing the river and, in cooperation with the infantry, to destroy those that manage to reach the west bank.

With Sergeant Meischner, my trusted assistant observer, Radio Sergeant Laska and Corporal Glaser, we settle into the 'Barenstellung'. Since the terrain is hilly it is difficult to establish radio contact, and this is a problem because laying a cable would take too long and the enemy might appear on the scene at any moment. Straight away shells strike unpleasantly close to us, but the bombardment soon stops. The shelling may also have been aimed at the Dnepr position, though it wasn't hit.

At least the defences in the sector we find ourselves in make the right impression. A trench runs along the forward slope of a ridge almost at neck height. Several very solidly built bunkers can be seen as well as numerous firing positions. There is even an observation post for us, although without overhead protection, and close by a large semi-circular bunker, similar to a tank turret, in which we can take shelter in an emergency. The ground in front drops gently to the river bank about 300m away and is completely without cover so there is an ideal field of fire. If we had conducted a tactical retreat, abandoning the 'Dnepr Balcony' – which tied up so many of our men – before the Russian offensive in order to take up better positions about 100km in length on the west bank of the river, then things could well have turned out quite differently. Now, though, once again, it is much too late!

A 7.5cm gun has been brought into position a few metres from our observation post, and a bit further on the demolition squad have set themselves up with their equipment in order to be able to blow the bridge lying to the left of us at the right moment.

At the same time my radio operators have set up their apparatus and are trying to make contact with the firing position – and, to our surprise, they succeed. In such a situation an artillery observer has a really important task even if he hasn't as yet caught sight of the enemy. We have also received a specific order that, due to the lack of ammunition, we can only open fire if the enemy attacks and attempts to cross the river.

It turns out that we have been spotted by the Soviet artillery. Well-aimed fire comes down on our position from a 12.2cm battery and, as the shelling appears to be concentrated on my observation post, we have to evacuate it. We immediately bundle up the wireless equipment and the telescope and head for the nearby concrete bunker. A machine-gunner in front of it has been badly wounded by shell splinters and is carried off by two comrades. Among the infantry there is a medical orderly who is tries to calm down the badly wounded youngster, who calls for his mother, then dies.

The Russian battery is firing remarkably precisely, and a shell explodes right on the concrete dome without breaking through it. The sound is deafening as if a gigantic bell had been struck. When the shelling ceases a little later, we immediately reoccupy our observation post. Sergeant Laska and Corporal Glaser set up the wireless equipment in another corner and try once more to make contact. This time they succeed, even though the reception is not as good as it should be, and there is an audible sigh of relief!

Although our battery is now ready for action, firing on the east bank of the Dnepr has been stopped by a standing order and because there is a risk that we might hit our infantry rearguard, which has just come in to sight. They emerge in small groups and sometimes one by one from a patch of woodland several hundred metres from the river bank and run as fast as they can towards the bridge knowing that it might fly into the air at any moment. There is another reason for their haste – suddenly Russian infantry in company strength emerge from the wood, very quickly cross the open ground to the river bank and establish themselves on either side of the entrance to the bridge. Surely the bridge has to be blown up now.

The Soviets are aware of this risk too, as none of them have dared go over the bridge to the west bank. Perhaps they are also waiting for the tank that is now emerging from the wood. It is one of the new T-43 Stalins, which rolls up to the bridge at great speed. Probably the crew are already thinking they will receive the 'Order of the Red Banner' for their heroic action, but they don't get it because the first shot from the 7.5cm anti-tank gun, which had taken up a position near us, hits it. The tank swivels some 90 degrees – probably this was a final reflex reaction by the driver – then stops dead, blocking the approach to the bridge. The successful anti-tank gunner hurries happily over to us in order to get conformation of the kill, which we gladly give, although we are surprised that he should think of such formalities in this situation.

But then I look across to the place where the demolition squad had been stationed and see signs of panic. The equipment seems to have failed – the crank on the detonator is being turned again and again, but nothing happens.

The situation is critical – 'Hannibal is at the gate'! Since at any moment the enemy might cross the bridge, it is obvious that the only way of destroying it in time is by artillery fire. Immediately we give the firing order to the battery. Thank goodness the radio contact works because our position would have been desperate if it hadn't, and seconds later we hear the guns and the shells rush over. Almost simultaneously the bridge comes under fire from another battery and unexpectedly it flies into the air shortly afterwards with a mighty explosion. Beams are hurled high like matchsticks, and once the smoke clouds clear, we can see that, apart from the remains on the riverbanks and numerous, shattered pieces of wood drifting downstream, the bridge has disappeared. A shell must have hit one of the interconnected demolition charges, causing all the others to explode, as even several hits from our light field howitzers could never have achieved such total destruction. Everyone is relieved because a quick enemy crossing at this point is no longer possible.

Using the periscope I scan the east bank for signs of further Soviet activity. A heavy Maxim machine gun has been wheeled into position there. The machine-gunner is only a short distance away and I can see every detail of his movements. In order to stop him, I must report his location precisely. Judging by his controlled and self-assured actions I presume he is an experienced soldier who is confident that he is making a useful contribution to the Soviet attack. Without exposing myself to any danger, I am able watch him closely, and he makes a thoroughly sympathetic impression. He could easily be one of us and in no way is he the 'Jewish-Bolshevist sub-human' as portrayed in *Der Stürmer*, the inflammatory anti-Semitic newspaper published by Julius Streicher.

We regard movements like his as 'enemy attacks' and send a few shells over. Those Ivans still on land dive for cover, while those already in the water become victims of infantry fire. Those trying to reach the west bank have no chance of succeeding.

Late in the afternoon we had to abandon our positions much more quickly than I expected because the Red Army had crossed over at various places on both sides of the Dnepr.

The Orsha 'strongpoint' on the river had already been taken by the Soviets during the morning and from Mogilev, a similar strongpoint on the Dnepr, came a last radio message: 'Can only hold the town centre.' Then there was silence.

Before we continue our march, a hurried conference takes place in the detachment headquarters. Captain Schubert summoned all the officers and gave a short situation report, passing on to us as much information as he could about the enemy's advance. The news was not exactly encouraging. Among other things he said that, according to orders, civilian cars are to be destroyed after their fuel has been siphoned off. The fuel is then to be distributed so that the batteries can cover a distance of about 150km. 150km? That is as far as the Beresina! Clearly the defences so far back must be incomplete, but we expect to establish a new main front line when we get there. As we are dispersing Captain Schubert comes up to me and, as his youngest officer, puts an arm on my shoulder in a fatherly gesture and says to me in the most thoughtful way that now the most difficult part of our lives as soldiers is about to begin. He was certainly correct!

With decidedly mixed feelings we destroy the vehicles as instructed, then set off towards the next river, the Drut, a tributary of the Dnepr about 40km away.

The journey through the night goes comparatively well, even though lone enemy aircraft drop bombs on burning villages on our route. They were able to do this without hindrance as our Luftwaffe is nowhere to be seen.

28 June

After the rapid march at midday, only a short distance from the Drut there is a sudden halt – we don't know why. Perhaps there was a risk of enemy resistance close to the bridge or the bridge itself was impassable, which wouldn't be a surprise.

The hours pass without any contact with the enemy, at least for us, and unbelievably we are spared from air attacks. Things are quite different for our neighbours on the right, the 9th Army, in particular for the 134th Infantry Division which forms the junction with our 4th Army. Immediately before the beginning of the Russian offensive the division had gone through a series of personnel changes including the divisional commander. Then his successor, Lieutenant General Philipp, had had a breakdown. He had not been able to cope with the destruction of his division and taken his own life, as Varus once did when his legions were destroyed in the Teutoburg Woods by Arminius, and Philipp would not be the last commander to resort to this. 'Varus, give me back my legions!' complained Caesar Augustus when he was told of the disaster, and today instead of 'legions', German 'divisions' would be more appropriate.

The situation around Bobruysk was catastrophic. Threatened by encirclement, military units of all kinds, after destroying their heavy weapons and numerous vehicles and in a state of near panic, streamed towards the strongpoint then poured into it, whilst other units sought to fight their way out to the west. In the town itself, which was under continual attack from Russian bombers and fighter aircraft, there was a chaotic standoff.

The hopelessness of the situation is illustrated by the war diary of the army high command which noted that: 'the 9th Army has as a fighting unit practically given up. It no longer has any units capable of going into action'. It looked as if our neighbouring armies – including our 4th Army – were thoroughly beaten, but had not yet been 'cut down to the ground', as someone put it.

At this critical moment Army Group Centre said farewell to its commander-in-chief, General Field Marshal Busch, who was replaced by General Field Marshal Model, who maintained command of his Army Group Northern Ukraine. 'That man knows an unbelievable amount and now he is our only hope', declared Lieutenant General Krebs, the chief of the general staff at the headquarters of Army Group Centre.

He also had a good deal of self-confidence. As he arrived at his new headquarters in Lida on the night of 29 June – Minsk was no longer safe enough – he was asked what assets he had brought with him, and he replied briefly: 'Me!' But it was too late for him to make a difference. The fate of Army Group Centre was already sealed and he could not prevent the situation from getting even worse.

But what was going on at headquarters was far away from us in our camp near the Drut. We were happy enough because we were left alone for the rest of the day, though towards evening some suspicious-looking civilians were picked up and detained until the march continued.

It really was a quite unexpectedly quiet day. We took the opportunity to wash and shave ourselves as best we could. Our cook prepared a wonderful warm meal for us and then we slept undisturbed as there were no incidents during the night. Yet, somehow we had the feeling that we were losing a lot of valuable time – in fact we had lost time that couldn't be recovered.

29 June

After we had released the arrested civilians – men from two nearby villages who might have been partisans – the march was resumed in the early morning. I took my place on the co-driver's seat of one of the trucks that towed the battery's four light field howitzers.

We had only been driving for a few minutes when suddenly the engine stopped with a loud, metallic screeching sound. 'What is wrong, Petersen?' I said, turning in shock to the driver. He knew straight away what was wrong: 'Shit, damn it, the camshaft – we must have pulled off the casing!' There was no simple solution to the breakdown, and the gun couldn't be abandoned. Since we couldn't afford to lose any more time, the howitzer was hastily attached by a cable to one of the 5-tonners so it could be pulled along.

A little later the long column of vehicles stopped at the Drut. The wooden bridge there had been badly damaged – presumably by partisans – and our sappers are making rough repairs.

The constant interruptions in the journey make me nervous. We must get on as quickly as possible because we imagine the Soviets are on our heels and could appear at any moment. Suddenly there are excited, horrified shouts. 'The Ivan is coming! The Ivan is coming.' Some of the drivers lose control, swerve out of the column and race like madmen over the fields on both sides of the road. Panic threatens to break out. Immediately we get our battery into positions on either side of the road in order to counter any attack with direct fire. But nothing happens – Ivan does not come. Finally, it is announced that a false alarm had been given and soon the vast line of vehicles has reassembled on the road in good order. However, some vehicles have stuck fast and have to be blown up or set on fire. They burn in the fields.

While we were waiting there ready to continue our march, unmolested by the enemy, a drama unfolded in Bobruysk that was even worse than the one that occurred at Vitebsk. In 3 waves almost 100,000 men – elements of 11 divisions of the 9th Army – sought to break out of the wide encirclement.

Incredible things took place. In the town's citadel, in which a large field hospital had been set up, over 5,000 wounded had had to be left with their nursing staff. When the Soviets penetrated Bobruysk and the citadel they stormed into the rooms of the field hospital and shot the wounded in their beds with machine pistols. Only two escaped this massacre, one of whom was found in the cellar of the hospital and described what had taken place.

In another field hospital with 700 untransportable wounded only 100 survived as several Red Army soldiers in oil-smeared uniforms broke in and emptied their machine pistols indiscriminately into the beds. Apparently this was done by tank crew who were taking revenge as, in the fighting for the town, the Soviets had suffered unexpectedly high losses of tanks.

In a similar incident 200 anti-aircraft gunners were cruelly killed because their 8.8cm guns, which were equally effective against tanks and aircraft, were particularly feared by the enemy. After being taken prisoner these unfortunates were made to lie down in two rows, head to head, at tank-track intervals. Their heads were then crushed flat by the tracks. One of them was lucky enough to escape and reported this unbelievable episode.

More than 500 seriously injured soldiers were also killed by partisans in a field hospital near Svilotch, not far from Bobruysk. A lieutenant with a wounded lung had hidden at the last moment under a fir tree and then escaped. Unable to intervene, he had to watch a band of partisans, some wearing bits of German uniform, shoot down the helpless wounded or hit them with spades or other tools.

Our division was still waiting to cross the River Drut. The Soviets were harassing us with light artillery fire, but no infantry appeared. They seemed to be following us in a hesitant way, as if they did not want to engage in any large-scale fighting at that time.

During the afternoon, after several hours of delay, the bridge was roughly repaired and one vehicle after another rolled across it in single file. As it is very narrow and slopes down right to the surface of the water, the tow trucks and other heavy vehicles have to go over with great care and at walking speed.

As our truck's turn comes I have cold sweat running down my back, but the crossing is carried out accurately and goes well. I didn't dare to think about the consequences if both the tow trucks, along with the guns, had fallen into the water.

At any moment we expect to come under air attack, but not a single aircraft appears. It is simply unbelievable!

After we have successfully crossed the bridge it is blown, but unfortunately not completely. It lies there very sharply tilted, half in the water. It is no longer passable for vehicles but soldiers can get across.

Our battery then has the task of securing the bridge area against the enemy who are following us closely, and we take up a firing position in a field on the edge of a village about 2km from the west bank. I receive the order to set up an observation post near to the river bank and to fire into the battery as quickly as possible.

As time is so pressing and my radio operators are occupied unloading and assembling their equipment, I go forward to seek out a suitable spot in this completely coverless terrain. I am lucky and soon find a firing point that could well have been established for the sentry guarding the bridge. I quickly set myself up and observe closely the terrain on the other bank, and especially the edge of a bit of woodland several hundred metres beyond. Nothing is moving there. But where are my radio operators? Surely they know that they can find me near the bridge!

I begin to work out firing orders for the terrain between the river and the edge of the wood. According to the map it is about 2,200m, but in view of the variations among our gun barrels, it seems advisable first to lay them at 200m. If the situation becomes desperate, of course, I could end up giving the order 'fire at my position', since I am located close to the bridge. In that case I should be all right since my observation post is quite well protected and a direct hit would be unlikely, particularly as only four field howitzers would be firing. Nothing, though, can be done till my radio operators finally appear, damn them!

The minutes rush past. Around me there is complete silence, only now and again broken by the explosion of a Russian shell. Still no sign of the two of them! At any moment the Russians could come out of the wood, just like the day before yesterday behind the Dnepr bridge, and I'll be sitting here without radio communications! I find it incomprehensible that these usually reliable guys have been unable to find me, and in such open terrain. I conclude that my situation is ridiculous – and puzzling – and that I can't continue with my task any more. Swearing, I pack my things together and make my way back to the firing position. On the edge of a field of grain several men, women and children crouching in holes look silently at me. They had not been there on my way in.

If there are partisans nearby, they could easily be getting ready to attack me as I seem to be the only German on the west bank of the Drut. I give the people in the holes a cautious look as I pass, but they show no sign of anxiety and remain there without moving. Apparently they are inhabitants of the village on the edge of which our guns are standing and they are hoping to stay safe when the fighting starts.

When I reach the village I cannot believe my eyes. The square where the battery had been was empty, and no one is to be seen. I stand there astounded. It cannot be true! For a moment I think I must have gone to the wrong village, then, when I get closer, I spot the track marks of our artillery tractors on a field, and I know instantly what has happened. I run off like a wild thing with giant strides in the direction of the retreat. There, already kilometres away, is a large cloud of smoke rising into the sky where the division is rolling westwards! Damn it! They have completely forgotten me and made off. Immediately I understand what the consequences will be for me.

I tie on my machine pistol more securely and run, feeling desperate and hopeless, along the road behind the cloud of smoke. I realise how pointless this is. The sweat runs in rivulets down my glowing face. Soon I slow down, but thoughts rush through my mind. I'd set myself up in the position by the bridge, determined to stay there to the last minute, and instead I'd been abandoned – I'd been hung out to dry. It is unbelievable, simply unbelievable! Then I blame myself: damn dog! Why did you go off alone, and in such a hurry? It was all for nothing – absolutely nothing!

Gradually, I began to think more clearly and quietly and to come to terms with what had happened. I realise I am now in Russian territory. The first thing I must do is get away from the road because they are likely to travel along it in their advance. Near the road there is a cornfield and I run along its edge. Countless poppy flowers are blooming there, very lovely to see, absolutely peaceful, almost unreal, and at this moment I remember the well-known song '*Roter Mohn, warum denkst du denn schon*' ('Red poppy, what are you thinking of now?'), sung by Rosita Serrano in her typical Latin style. At such a moment it is odd that this song comes to my mind – I can almost hear it – and it must have been a reaction to the strain of the awful situation I found myself in. Soon, though, I face up to the grim reality again, yet now with a feeling of hope that perhaps I can get out of safely.

Suddenly, I near the noise of an engine in the distance. 'That's it', I say to myself and throw myself down in the unfortunately sparse corn, the machine pistol ready for firing. I am fiercely determined to sell myself as dearly as possible – I couldn't stand to be taken prisoner. Surely it is only a weak vanguard without tanks, I tell myself, and I reach for both my magazines. A vehicle passes by. So perhaps I can't been seen after all! Then the sound of an engine gets louder – there are no tank tracks, thank God! Wrapped in a thick cloud of smoke, a motorcycle combination draws near. If I shoot the Ivan and rush off on the motorcycle, I can get away, I tell myself, for I firmly believe the vehicle is Russian.

But then I realise the machine might be a 750 BMW and, when it comes closer, I become convinced it is, and I see the rider is wearing a German steel helmet. I jump up, wave and shout like crazy, to stop him from driving on, as it is quite clear that this is absolutely my last chance. Finally, he notices me, slows down and stops the machine. It is Senior Corporal Scaffrath from my battery, our motorcyclist. Indescribable mad joy! I crush his hand and thump him on his back with both fists like a madman. He shows no sign of embarrassment, and that is when I come to my senses.

'Tell me what's happened?' I ask. Quickly he reports that the battery has already changed positions again, that the road back is clear and the division is moving on quickly. The chief has given him the task of waiting for me near the abandoned firing position, assuming that, in the absence of my two radio operators, I would soon reappear. Then a military policeman turned up on a motorcycle and told him to leave immediately as the Soviets could appear at any moment. But he stayed where he was, determined to do his job, until the policeman came up again and ordered him to go. So he had driven back a few kilometres to a patch of woodland where he had hidden. He let the policeman drive past, then turned back to find me.

'I simply could not leave the lieutenant', he said in his self-confident way. Quickly I climb onto the Sozius and clap him on the shoulders, expressing myself more emphatically than I could with words, and I am certain he understood. Once again, this man demonstrated the reliable, self-sacrificing character of our soldiers who faithfully do their duty however difficult the situation. Often soldiers like this senior corporal are described as the 'backbone of the army', and so they are.

We roar off and reach our battery in half an hour. Everyone greets me. My radio operators wave happily at me and get no ticking off. Now we can laugh and be happy about something, and it is a great feeling being back with the 'old gang'. Sixty-four days later, almost 500km away from this spot, I was even luckier, but no one from our battery was there to share my pleasure and by then such a moment of joy was inconceivable.

The heat is intense, as it has been every day since the beginning of the retreat, which no longer looks like a 'withdrawal'. Tired and fought out, our infantrymen, who have again and again saved our lives by fighting rearguard actions, are pulling back on both sides of the main road. How lucky we are to be in our vehicles. We take on a couple of completely exhausted grenadiers for a while so that they have time to revive themselves until their comrades come along.

Now and then some enemy scout planes can be seen in the distance, apparently checking on our line of march which can be changed so quickly. Where is our Luftwaffe now? There is not a single fighter to be seen.

Late in the afternoon there's a storm – the clouds burst and torrents of rain pour down. The air cools, which is fine for us, but the roads are quickly flooded which seriously slows down the column. The enemy has given us time to draw breath, but then nature turns against us and places us in a grave situation. This is immediately apparent. Shortly before nightfall, as we feared, the long column of trucks can no longer make any progress. All the batteries of our regiment have to take up positions on the muddy and water-logged fields on both sides of the road, and in these conditions we can hardly be described as being ready for action.

The march must resume as soon as possible, but the vehicles are so firmly stuck up to their axles in the mud that it is only with the greatest effort that we can get them moving. Many are so deeply sunk into the morass that they can only be hauled out by our artillery tractors. Again and again the wheels and tracks are smeared from top to bottom with the mud, and we know that at any moment through the night we might be attacked. Such a lot of valuable time has been lost! Our pursuers must be battling against similar problems with their vehicles, but apparently their tanks can get through even in these conditions.

And so this eventful and physically and psychologically demanding day comes to an end.

30 June

We have to wait until morning before we can get moving again, but then we become bogged down in a swampy wood. The road, which narrows here, is no longer passable for ordinary traffic – only the tracked vehicles manage to churn their way through. The wheeled vehicles, especially the big trucks, are soon hopelessly stuck, with howling engines struggling to make any progress along the road. The chaos is complete. The situation is absurd, and time is so pressing!

We are given the task of helping to pull the trucks through. There is nothing else we can do. We don't dare to ask how much further we will get with our supply of fuel, but realise that the 8-tonners are consuming an immense amount.

The heat of the day is increasing as we extricate vehicle after vehicle from mud which is so deep in places that two traction engines have to be harnessed together before any progress can be made.

The long drive through rough terrain overloads the engines. We pray they will hold out because if we lose any more vehicles we will have a very serious transport problem.

The heavy, muddy tracks come off one of the tractors several times and only with great effort can they be put back on again. It is unbelievable what the drivers have to put up with today! Since the beginning of the retreat they have had hardly any rest, and now they must cope with this very difficult situation.

Many *panjewagens* have gathered with their horses in the wood on either side of the road. Apparently they are part of the baggage train of the 31st Infantry Division which is our neighbour in the Dnepr Balcony. I get the thankless task of holding them back until all the vehicles have got through this stretch of swamp. This order is given with the greatest reluctance, as everyone wants to get through as quickly as possible towards the West. It is immediately clear to me that it is unrealistic to expect to make much headway. The column is so noisy, and even the most drastic measures are unlikely to succeed. So I calmly try to make clear to the men that their fate depends on their ability to keep moving and on their willingness to fight. Finally, they also see the sense in this and I am relieved to have got the message across, but the impression remains that gradually everyone is beginning to look out for themselves.

Many soldiers are lying totally exhausted in dry places on the side of the road and in the wood, and some of them are already so apathetic that they don't take any interest in what is happening. Others are restless and nervous because at any moment the Soviets might appear and we all know what a catastrophe that would be. Again and again scouting aircraft with red stars on their wings cross over the wood. The pilots would have to be blind not to see us.

The first serious doubts about this retreat having a happy ending have arisen. A radio message, which circulates quickly, says enemy forces are on both sides of us and they are advancing on Minsk. They are already 100km ahead of us, and Minsk lies exactly on our line of march. Between us and Minsk is the Beresina River. This is our next objective and it may be the site of our new main front line – we can't be sure. Several of us are reminded of Napoleon's disaster at the Beresina in the winter of 1812, and perhaps also recall the *Fluchtlied* song that Friedrich August wrote soon afterwards, which begins with the words 'With man and horse and wagon . . .'.

Even though our immediate situation is difficult, no one realises that the position of the whole of Army Group Centre, with its four armies, is critical. Two of the armies – the 3rd Panzer Army and the 9th Army – that are our neighbours, have been wrecked. Their survivors have dispersed and are hunted and repeatedly attacked as they try to fight their way out to the west.

In order to distract the soldiers from their gloomy thoughts, I set them to work on improving the road and building defences. Because of the enormous strain of the last few days I find it difficult to concentrate and my morale is low. I desperately need some encouragement. Once the vehicles that were still in good enough condition to continue the march have been selected, the men with growing enthusiasm uproot small trees and break off branches and throw them down on the boggy spots so the vehicles can get through. The mood among us becomes confident once more.

Late in the afternoon there is a short but heavy barrage from a Stalin Organ which hits our vehicle assembly point. The tree bursts cause casualties, but fortunately only a few men are lightly wounded in our battery. Probably we have been spotted by the reconnaissance aircraft which often pass over and they have reported our position.

We have to stay where we are during the night and our uncertainty and apprehension grow, but the time passes without disturbance.

1 July

The march was at last resumed in the early morning. All the equipment that could not be moved had to be put out of action so the enemy weren't able to use it.

After a few kilometres we left our proposed return route with the aim of reaching the main road to Minsk which ran between Pogost and Beresino. We planned to cross the Beresina there. On the main road the mood of the column was calmer and we made quicker progress, or at least we thought so. But what an error this was!

The closer we got to the Beresina, the more shocking were the scenes we came across. The shot-up and burnt-out vehicles of the various divisions which preceded us were piled up along the road, and an enormous amount of equipment of all kinds was strewn across the area. At one point we drove past a column several hundred metres long of overturned *panjewagons* along with the bodies of the horses that had pulled them. It looked as though a major incident had taken place there.

As we made our way full of misgivings through this chaos, I was stopped by Colonel Gunther, the commander of our artillery regiment, and given the task of finding the command post in Pogost. Then, early the next morning, I was to go on to meet Reconnaissance Detachment 118, which had been ordered to secure the river crossing at a bridgehead east of the Beresina for the many divisions assembling there. Well, I'll be damned, I say to myself, how on earth did I get this high honour, and from the regimental commander in person! I am even allocated my own vehicle which, loaded with all the necessary equipment and myself, Sergeant Glaser, my trusty assistant observer, and the reliable radio operators, Glaser and Wild, takes us off. First, we drive on further with the battery which is to take up a position on the east bank near Beresino with all the other regiments. Then we report to our chief, who wishes us the best of luck with a look that says a lot.

Even before Pogost we come under light artillery fire and have the feeling that tomorrow will surely be a dangerous day. Finally, we reach the little village unscathed and report to our regimental command post, which is located in the living room of a well-maintained farmhouse. A depressing, stress-laden atmosphere pervades the small room. I suspect that everyone there has already received lots of very unpleasant news and they know much more about what is going on than they are prepared to tell us. But we have no time to spare and also don't feel it is up to us to give them further details. Instead, we concentrate on our task for tomorrow. Among other things we are informed that we need to reckon on a maximum firing range of about 7km. I object, saying that at this range a radio link couldn't be maintained, but got no response other than an irritable remark by the signals officer.

After the discussion we quickly got our heads down but, given the unrest in the room and apprehensive thoughts about the coming day, we could not really sleep.

2 July

The morning was grey and gloomy, almost dark. We were tired and depressed. We carry out a quick complete check of our kit – map, compass, periscope, machine pistol. Everything is there, so we head off to the reconnaissance detachment, which is located north of Pogost 'somewhere on the highway'. At first we drive down a side road and then go through a completely burnt-out village. Several heavy Maxim machine guns and an anti-tank gun lie destroyed on the village street, and we wonder how fighting with Russian infantry could have taken place here already. Meischner thinks the weapons were almost certainly left by partisans, as they are active everywhere in the area.

The main road we are going to take soon comes into sight, and we are surprised by the sight of the kilometre-long column of vehicles running alongside it. Judging by the identification symbols on the mudguards the vehicles belong to elements of the Feldherrnhalle Division which have been shot up by fighter aircraft and perhaps by tanks that have broken through.

As the main road is blocked with debris and wrecked equipment of all kinds, and we are not far from our destination, we get out of the vehicle and send the driver back, continuing on foot. An indescribable scene comes into sight. What a disaster had occurred here! The dead lie or sit in their vehicles, and some hang half out of the doors. Drivers have fallen forwards onto their steering wheels, others are sitting upright as if waiting to drive on. More corpses lie on the road and in the fields, mowed down by the guns of the fighter aircraft as they shot up the highway.

I had been following the course of events with growing concern over the last few days, but now, confronted by these scenes, I could see we were caught in a trap from which we would only escape with a lot of luck and God's help.

Many dead horses are lying around too, with their big staring eyes and shrunken bellies. A frightful sweet smell of corpses lies in the air. A few Russian shells explode nearby, but we don't dash for cover – instead we put our heads down and trot on without a word, disheartened and thoughtful.

Too many divisions were converging on the Beresina, and the overcrowding was only going to get worse.

As we go forward, we see more and more abandoned materiel. Mounds of washing and bits of uniform lie in the roadside ditches next to guns and piles of ammunition which include the latest anti-tank weapons. Beside a brand-new tractor there is a large wireless, a model I'd never seen before, which has lots of delicate glass valves and resistors. The casing has been smashed in and the cables and wires are hanging out. Clearly, the division was equipped with the best and most modern equipment, as we see abandoned here things that we could only dream of.

But where is the damned reconnaissance detachment? We have already been on our way for almost an hour but there is no sign of it. 'Perhaps they have already cleared off, while we keep going forward just like Ivan!' says Glaser in a worried voice. Fortunately, we don't have much further to go and a short time later we finally reach our goal. Close to the highway is a flat, sandy hollow about 100m wide which, in this otherwise almost flat terrain, offers good cover. Here about thirty men have set up a defence. On the edge of the hollow immediately next to the highway I am relieved to see a wireless truck which has been given to us in case our equipment doesn't work.

The first thing I do is report to the commander of the reconnaissance detachment, who formally introduces himself as *Rittmeister* (Captain) von Lyncker. With an encouraging smile he shakes hands and says that he is so pleased to meet us that for a moment he can forget how vulnerable we are to enemy attack in this bridgehead east of the Beresina.

But then we get straight back to the task in hand. We assemble our radio equipment, call through and switch to 'receive', but nothing happens, a clear demonstration that the equipment won't work at this range. I go over to the wireless truck which has a more powerful set. There I am delighted to be greeted by Lieutenant Wagner, who is well known to me. He has already made contact with our regiment and this is exactly the right moment to do so because we observe a few hundred metres away from us the first Soviet units establishing themselves on the edge of a wood. Immediately they begin to work their way around our right flank and towards Pogost. For a while we hold them back with salvos from our batteries, but when our ammunition starts to run out we can only manage harassing fire.

This allows the enemy troops to advance more quickly, and they get close to the hollow. Apparently we have been spotted, or at least assume so, as suddenly we receive unpleasantly well-laid mortar fire and we hear the sound of light anti-tank guns. The firing becomes stronger and we can only lie still and hope not to get hit.

Nearby a soldier jumps up, leaving his foxhole like lightning. He drops down beside me, his whole body shaking, completely at the end of his tether. 'Come on, calm down, everything is OK', I say, and it is good to be able to speak a few words and not be alone. Seconds later a grenade explodes right in the hole that he had just left. Wordless he stares at me. Clearly, he must have sensed this in advance, and that is why he had been so agitated. In the winter of 1943, as an artillery observer in a supporting position near Staraja Russa on Lake Immensee, I had a similar experience. I was passing through a trench when suddenly an inner voice told me to stop immediately, and shortly afterwards a grenade hit exactly where I would have been had I gone on. Afterwards I remembered the line in *Hamlet* where the protagonist says: 'There are more things in heaven and earth, Horatio, Than are dreamt of in your philosophy.'

Finally, the heavy bombardment eases off, and then stops completely. We know the infantry attack will follow and we don't look forward to it, but maybe it is better than lying helpless under the shelling. Then somebody shouts: 'The Russians are going around us!' We are forced to abandon our position at once and break through to the rear. We jump out of our foxholes, firing our machine pistols and shouting 'Hurrah!' wildly, and withdraw a few hundred metres. My two radio men, crouching under the burden of their heavy boxes, manage to keep up, but don't join in the shouting.

While we are establishing a new defensive line, two assault guns and a tank appear unexpectedly in front of us and cover the now-hesitating enemy with their fire. Their presence makes all the difference. I feel confident now because I cannot imagine that these heavily armoured vehicles can be knocked out. During this brief moment of respite, we try to make radio contact, but again without success. The distance is still too great.

Possibly the batteries which have almost run out of ammunition have already moved from their positions and are crossing the Beresina; all the divisions assembled here have to complete the process by evening. Bearing this in mind, I don't think there is much point in staying where we are, and I don't want to expose my men to unnecessary danger. Also I don't want to risk losing the radios which will be especially difficult to move if we are caught up in an infantry engagement, as we know all to well our apparatus's deficiencies.

So, I seek out the commanding officer to tell him of my decision and to take my leave. He understands what my men have gone through but pleads with me to stay – he needs every man he can get. For a moment I really don't know what to do, but when I see his imploring look I simply have to agree to his request. Without speaking he shakes my hand and I am convinced I have to help him even though this is an unfamiliar role for my men. The news that we are going to stay was taken hard by Meischner, Glaser and Wild, and Meischner throws me a harsh look as if to say: 'We will need lots of luck now'. Before we go we glance back at the area of the bridge, about 6km away, where tall, dark clouds of smoke can be seen caused by the heavy shell fire.

In addition to the divisions assembled here, there are units from other formations, mainly from the 31st and 267th Infantry Divisions as well as the Panzergrenadier Division Feldherrnhalle. They are tasked with constructing and manning the defences around the important bridgehead on the Beresina.

For a while we hold on well, but then under ever-increasing pressure from the enemy, we have to gradually give way. They penetrate Pogost at about noon.

We reach the wreckage left by units of Feldherrnhalle, taking shelter among the many destroyed vehicles along the highway, and we manage to prevent the Soviets from advancing more rapidly. As yet not all the divisions have crossed the Beresina. We know how significant the bridge at Beresino is, and all of us would very much like to cross to the other side of the river.

Despite the severity of the fighting for the bridgehead, I wonder why the Soviets are not attacking this important objective more energetically. They haven't launched tanks against us, for instance. If they had, we could not have stood up to them.

But the light anti-tank guns and the feared *Ratschbum* – 76.2mm guns – pin us down on the highway. One exceptionally unpleasant thing about the *Ratschbum*, which – with appropriate ammunition – can also be used against tanks, is the speed of its shot, for the sound of the gun going off and the impact of the shell are practically simultaneous. Hence the name *Ratschbum*.* As a consequence we cannot get under cover in time, and the Soviets fire at anything that moves. Many comrades fall victim to this firing, increasing the number of dead lying in and around the destroyed vehicles. In the intense heat the smell of putrefaction, which we had become aware of in the early morning, became even more penetrating and depressing, especially as we have long since emptied our water bottles and there is no water anywhere to reduce the smell of death.

A pressing problem is posed by the wounded. Those that cannot walk must as a rule be left behind and experience teaches us they have a slim

---

* The Germans called the ZIS-3 76.2mm gun the '*Ratsch-Bum*' because of its sound. When being shelled, first came the buzzing noise of the shell ('*ratsch*') and then the sound of explosion ('*bum*').

chance of survival. Only in isolated cases can the seriously wounded be saved, as a medical orderly service which would carry them to safety is impossible to organise in this situation.

There is a shortage of ammunition, even though some reserves can still be found in the confusion on the road, and the effects of this are becoming more and more obvious. I have already set my machine pistol to fire single shots. This makes sense as long as the enemy remains at a distance and for a time he does so in order not to come under his own artillery fire which has been reinforced with a 12.2mm battery.

The assault guns and the tank have, after firing to give us support, driven on and not returned because they are also short of ammunition.

Late in the afternoon we reach the burnt-out village through which we had passed earlier in the day on our way forward. At the edge of the village we came across a well and immediately threw ourselves greedily on the cool water. Nobody asked whether the water was drinkable and we ignored the danger from the 12.2mm shells landing close by. We had reached the point at which a mouthful of water is more important than anything else. How refreshing it was, and what a relief in the stifling heat! Once we have quelled our burning thirst we tip the water over our heads and glowing faces and then concentrate again on the events going on around us.

It is really impressive to see how readily the men, in such a precarious situation, return to their task. They cannot possibly know, and would regard it as absolutely inconceivable, that later on they would be defamed, by people who have no fear of the consequences, as 'murderers in a murderous organisation' and even described as only slightly different from those who served in concentration camps. In consideration of the dead moreover, also a third disparagement of the memories of the dead! They were abused then and are ostracised even today, although they served loyally in the most difficult conditions and only survived the war if they were lucky.

As we leave the village after fighting a delaying action, I unexpectedly meet Captain Hannig, the commander of our third detachment. From him I learn that the regimental headquarters is only about 2km away in a wood on the east bank of the Beresina and that some batteries have already crossed the river. I take this as a reason for reporting my departure to *Rittmeister* Freiherr von Lyncker. We shake hands – for the last time because, only two days later, like so many of the others, he would be killed in the big cauldron before Minsk.

A little later I met the commander of the second detachment, Major Waldschmidt, who is also making his way in his vehicle to regimental headquarters. We drove on together and soon reached our destination. The headquarters is full of activity, as Colonel Gunther had just issued orders for a change of location. The bridge had to be reached immediately and the river crossed. On the west bank I hope to find my battery, so I jump onto the running board of an overladen truck and away we go over a narrow track right through the wood. The nearby village of Beresino is lying under heavy shell fire at that moment, but the shells are exploding at a safe distance from us.

We see the bridge in the distance and the road that leads to it. As we approach we get a view of the destruction around it which we hadn't been able to see before. There are many wrecked vehicles, some of which are still burning, that have been hit by artillery fire and strafing aircraft. How many dead and severely wounded must still be lying in the wreckage, and who is attending to them? Where should one start searching and helping in this chaos? All the time we have to reckon with the next burst of shell fire or air attack, and every unit is concerned to cross as quickly as possible – and often there are delays.

On the east bank in a small area at the edge of woodland there are a number of heavy and super heavy tanks, including some Tigers. They have been put out of action, then abandoned because the badly damaged bridge would be unable to take their enormous weight. There they lie useless now, these steel monsters. They represented our greatest hope if there was a test of strength or if we had to break out using every available means.

Our sappers have repaired the bridge. This is exhausting and highly dangerous work for them because of the heavy shell fire, and they have had to do it several times. The landscape around the bridge is pitted with numerous shell and bomb craters.

As most units have already reached the west bank, to our great relief the queue goes forward comparatively quickly and we begin crossing the 100m-wide river. The repaired sections of the bridge, several of which are metres long, have to be crossed with great care. The wheels of our vehicle thump noisily over the wooden planks, and the tension is high as at any moment the artillery fire might be resumed or a fighter attack occur. But we are lucky and reach the other bank, beyond which there is a well-constructed trench system.

For the last few days we've assumed that our new main front line will extend from here and that it will stop the Soviets – and stop them for a long time. But it is already too late because the enemy is attacking on both sides of us and is already across the Beresina, making rapid advances.

Work had already started on defensive positions as part of a plan made by Army Group Centre known as the 'Big Solution' (in contrast to the 'Smaller Solution' which only covered the Dnepr Balcony). This allowed for the withdrawal of the front line to the Beresina which could have been carried out successfully if it had begun before the expected Russian offensive. The plan would have reduced the length of the front by 160 km and would have released around 6 divisions – in all 60,000 men – to reinforce the front line and form a reserve. General Field Marshal Busch had presented the plan at the Führer Headquarters on 20 May, just five weeks before the commencement of the Russian offensive, but – as was feared – the 'Smaller Solution' as well as the 'Big Solution' were abruptly rejected by the Wehrmacht's commander-in-chief. At the time Busch made the scathing remark: 'Until now I hadn't realised that you are the same as the generals that always only look behind them!' Yet, the field marshal had swallowed this affront and had obeyed Führer Order No. 11 which insisted that the soldiers should hold on. (Perhaps he was thinking 'we'll see what comes of this'.) Towns lying near the front line of Witebsk, Orsha, Mogilev and Bobruysk were selected as strongpoints. At the same time orders were given to complete the defences that had already been started in the rear areas, including the Beresina.

It seems pointless now to speculate on how long the Beresina line might have been held. Certainly, another course of action should have been taken to avoid the catastrophe that faced us. Then perhaps the retreat to the Reich's borders and the tragedy that then occurred in the eastern provinces might have been prevented.

As one of the songs about the French retreat in 1812 has it: 'commanders without brains, gunners without guns, escapees without shoes, nowhere rest and quiet . . .'. Hardly anyone anticipated that the words 'escapees without shoes' would soon apply to us.

We were very relieved to have crossed the Beresina, even though we had suffered enormous losses, and were driving slowly along the main road towards Tscherven, which was about 30 km away. Minsk was about 60 km beyond that. If anyone had asked us at the time for an assessment of our situation, most of us would have replied with 'serious, but not hopeless". We were convinced that on this good road we could make rapid progress during the night and, if the enemy air attacks diminished, we could reach Minsk. There we believed we would be able to stop the Soviet breakthrough and establish a firm defensive front line. At Velikie-Luki, Demjansk and Tscherkassy, for example, we had done this, even though our casualties had been severe. Why shouldn't we succeed again now?

So we were 'full of confidence and the will to break out', as Lieutenant General Vincenz Muller said when he reported at 6.45 p.m. to Army Group Headquarters in Lida that his divisions had crossed the Beresina. These included XII Army Corps to which our 18th Panzergrenadier Division as well as the 57th and 267th Infantry Divisions belonged. In addition, there were elements of our 4th Army as well as the remains of the subordinate VIth Panzer Corps of the 3rd Panzer Army. This conglomeration of troops had been amalgamated and given the title Muller Group.

Our confidence would have been dampened if we had known that during the previous afternoon Russian tanks and infantry had taken the village of Tscherven and flattened it on either side of our retreat route. This was the reason why our journey from the west bank of the Beresina, which we had begun so hopefully, took a different course after only a few kilometres. We left the road to Tscherven and turned north into an extensive forested area, travelling along tracks that were among the better woodland routes. There were many marshy areas and – even more unpleasant – some very active partisans to contend with, but we had no choice as there was no other way out.

The Minsk partisans, who are well organised and reinforced and led by members of the Russian army, are a dangerous and cruel enemy. Anyone who falls into their hands has to be grateful if he gets a quick and painless end from the bullet and is not tortured in the most horrible way. It is difficult to describe the precise details of these atrocities, and it is also difficult to understand how people who are otherwise quite normal and peaceable can commit such crimes.

Even if in fact there are only a few of these deplorable cases, one shouldn't jump to conclusions, for possibly this way of conducting warfare is not only officially tolerated but is consciously supported with the aim of provoking increased countermeasures. Then the population, which in general is very friendly and helpful, will be driven increasingly into the arms of the partisans, and that will lead us to impose even stricter controls.

This policy and its consequences were promoted through heated tirades by Russian writers and journalists, in particular by Ilya Ehrenburg who played a leading role in the Soviet war propaganda. In a leaflet circulated with the front-line newspaper *Krasnaya Zvezda* the Red Army soldiers and partisans were told, among other things, that:

> The German soldiers are not people . . . The German soldiers are worse than wild animals . . . they are worse than beasts of prey . . .

they shame women . . . torture children and rape girls. As soon as you hear the the word 'German' you should load your gun. We will not talk, we will not upset ourselves, we will kill. When during the course of a day you have not at least killed one German, then that is a lost day for you. If you have killed a German, then kill a second one. For us there is nothing more amusing than a German corpse. Don't count the days, don't count the kilometres, count only one thing: the Germans killed by you!

We will never forget his savage writing and that of his fellow authors. Their perverse work encouraged Red Army soldiers and partisans to kill many German soldiers in a cruel fashion during some of the darkest chapters of the war. Then, when the Soviets conquered and occupied the German eastern provinces they committed widespread crimes against the civilian population which in their brutality can only be described as unique. The well-known Russian author Lev Kopelev commented in his work *Aufbewahren für alle Zeit!* that 'commissars, journalists and writers – like Ehrenburg and Simonov and hundreds of thousands of other agitators . . . were preachers of holy vengeance'.

If similar perfidious propaganda had been directed at us, we would have rejected it. As for the so-called 'Commissar Order' issued by Hitler, by which all Soviet political officers were to be treated as non-combatants and were to be shot immediately upon capture, it was withdrawn because it was challenged and only followed occasionally. Although since the war the order has been given lots of publicity, often the commanders responsible did not pass it on to the troops because shooting prisoners went against the German soldier's sense of honour. A few did not feel like this, but they did not belong to the army's elite, and we firmly distanced ourselves from them. Front-line soldiers were usually reluctant to pour oil onto the fire and when they came across such actions in the rear areas they were very concerned about it, especially as it tended to antagonise the civilian population who were then less willing to cooperate.

On 5 October 1941 *Evangelical Germany* reported:

German soldiers are helping the populations in the areas freed of Bolshevism by restoring their churches and retrieving crucifixes, vestments and other sacred objects from godless museums. In churches which for years have been misused as cinemas, car workshops, and so on, the first church services are now taking place once more. The bishop of a cathedral church, Archimandrit Boris Jokubovski, has expressed his thanks for such help to the commander of a sapper battalion: 'How lucky and happy we were when the mighty German Army released us from the yoke of Bolshevist rule! It was the will of the Almighty that you the population . . . after long years of godlessness helped bring about this revival and re-established church services. You have earned our endless and heartfelt thanks because, as a highly respected commander, you opened our cathedral in a friendly manner and stood aside and allowed your engineers to recreate a church worthy of God out of what had become a Bolshevist military camp. In the same way we thank you for the manufacture of six crosses as well as the cleaning of the exterior of the cathedral which, like the interior, has been restored to a worthy condition.

This particular example shows what could be achieved – and have a serious impact – in these circumstances. In addition, the SS Sondercommandos and Einsatzgruppen were carrying out their activities behind the front line.

Yet when Reserve Captain Theodor Oberlander reported on the failed policy in the occupied eastern territories, Admiral Canaris, head of the intelligence service, dismissed his criticism,

Directly from Führer Headquarters often came the simple instruction: 'To spread every horror that alone is frightful, to take every pleasure in being obstructive.'

At first the villagers greeted us with traditional bread and salt as liberators from the yoke of Stalinism. They hoped for freedom and understanding and hoped to enter our service in their hundreds of thousands. But they were soon deeply disappointed by us, and embittered, and eventually ended up supporting the partisans.

While the events here strongly remind one again of those of 1812, so does Napoleon's order of the day to his army at the beginning of the war which, with remarkable realism worthy of note here, stated: 'White Ruthenia is not to be handled as a conquered country but rather as fellow member of the league.'

Also the outstanding Major General and military writer Carl von Clausewitz (1780–1831) commented in his work *Der Russische Feldzug von 1812*, in which he had participated alongside the Tsar as General Chief of Staff of the German-Russian Legion: 'that so great and wide a country with European culture is not to be conquered by any other means than a fight!'

The significance of this understanding was a given, and allied with the fact that the Western Allies, during the for us so successful opening phase of the war against the Soviet Union, had reckoned with the quick and inevitable collapse of the Soviet Union – especially the highest party, governmental and military officials, as well as the Diplomatic Corps, who were already being transferred the 800km to Kuibyshchev – and consideration had been given to how the Russians could carry on the fight without them.

The world-renowned philosopher Georg Friedrich Hegel (1770–1831) had been correct when he sarcastically stated: 'The only thing that we learn from history is that the people do not learn from it!' And that evidently applies to the here and now!

This was also relevant to the partisans, especially in 1943, as the superiority of the Soviet army began to increase and expanded in size and incorporated other elements of the population. They could have offered their services to us and operated once more in the Soviet sphere of influence, or done so soon, but must now fear being turned into collaborators and liquidated. Even minor jobs like kitchen work, wood cutting or snow shovelling counted as 'helping the enemy' and were punished accordingly. To avoid this danger – also when one was not certain whether the collaborator could be interrogated or denounced – if whole groups of the civilian population shut off our withdrawal movements and if they came into contact with Red Army units or partisans they were killed thoughtlessly just like the escorting soldiers. Such incidents occurred especially during the fighting in the area of Bobruysk, which has already mentioned.

During unbelievably brutal and devious ambushes, which are contrary to international law, they have not openly and predominately worn civilian clothing, or even captured German uniforms, but have appeared quite clearly as partisans. This has influenced the Haag land warfare orders of 18 October 1907 regarding increasing legitimate retaliation measures, which under the current circumstances are unavoidable and occasionally excessive, especially if the incomprehensible acts of cruelties have been carried out in daylight, which is a step too far. Inevitably, this generated further hatred and the battle on both sides was now conducted with increasing harshness. 'Partisan warfare opens the gates to Hell' remarked appropriately the Duke of Wellington (1769–1852), and what Schiller in his play *Die Piccolomini* cited is also relevant: 'That is precisely the curse of the bad deeds that they draw attention to so that even worse ones have to behave!'

Meanwhile, we were stuck in the marshy wood on the west bank of the Beresina, where we had retreated after discovering that the route via

Tscherven near Minsk was closed to us. We were about 60km south of the spot where Napoleon on 26 November 1812 crossed the river on his way back to France with only 11,000 men, the miserable remnants of his Grande Armée which had once numbered 500,000 soldiers. On the long journey from Moscow in icy cold weather the enemy fell on them again and again 'like a swarm of eagles', and on 13 December, when the survivors reached the Memel River, just 1,600 were left. Only a small number of men without weapons were saved. What a precedent for the experiences that lay ahead of us!

Although for a moment everything remains quiet, we stay where we are and soon it begins to grow dark. There is no trace of my battery, but it would have been pure coincidence for me to have come across it in this impenetrable wooded area. Tomorrow with daylight I hoped it would be possible to find it.

On both sides of the road are numerous bits of equipment thrown away by units that have passed through. Since so many vehicles have been lost, transport is scarce and equipment can't be carried. I got out of my vehicle to see if I could find things I could use. Nearly everything there is intact. I find a mosquito net that would be useful in the swamps and then a brand new uniform shirt still in its original packaging, a 'day shirt' as it is called. I am delighted by this and immediately put it on. My own shirt, which hasn't been changed for a week and is therefore dirty and sweaty, I throw in a high curve into the nearest bush. What a delightful feeling to be dressed again in a clean and dry shirt! Of course, at that moment I didn't know how long it would be before I could wash myself again in a river, never mind change my clothing.

After several hours of waiting around we finally set off in the darkness and so come to the end of an eventful day. Later, exhausted but happy to have survived and trusting things will work out well in the end, I fell asleep within minutes.

3 July

During the night elements of other units join our column and, in a line of vehicles with an assortment of badges, we move ahead. The withdrawal now looks well organised and, now we have reached western territory, I hope it will continue like this. Early in the morning we reach without incident a wooded area near Mikulitshi and Kalita, about 20km north-east of Tscherven, and we come across a sign saying: 'Increased Vigilance – Danger of Partisans!' After a short sleep I prepare my machine pistol to fire and hold it out of the vehicle window. Several smaller, more mobile vehicles, including mine, deploy themselves as a vanguard under Colonel Gunther, then, 50 to 100m ahead of the rest of column, we drive with a sense of foreboding into the hazy wood.

'Typical partisan wood', says a comrade next to me, and I am thinking the same thing when the shooting starts.

We get shot at from both sides – rifle and machine-gun fire. The driver puts his foot down in the hope of getting through the ambush more quickly, but then the leading vehicle comes under heavy mortar fire and immediately afterwards rockets from a Stalin Organ hit us. We have driven into a partisan barricade, and the use of artillery indicates the partisans have been reinforced by regular troops. Some soldiers jump out of their vehicles to look for cover on the edge of the wood. Colonel Gunther is wounded by a shell splinter in the chest, and as a result the column falters and comes to a halt. The vehicles at the front turn round on the narrow road with unbelievable speed – speed that can only be achieved in desperate situations like this.

We turn around too, and so does the vehicle behind us, and we race back in wild flight through the wood. Soldiers who have been lying in cover on the edge of the wood, some of them wounded, get up and run towards the oncoming vehicles and try to jump onto them, using the last of their strength. Some fall back and, if they can't roll back fast enough, they are driven over as if they were dead bodies that have been left on the road. One of them lifts himself up by a few centimetres before the wheels run over him. Anyone who remains alive here will never be seen again. The partisans will make sure of that and all of us are aware of this.

We drive back quickly into the wood we had just passed through without any problems and in which most of our column is still to be found. In these circumstances an organised march won't succeed because we could be attacked at any moment by Red Army regulars. If we were only opposed by partisans we would not have anything to fear as they almost always avoid an open fight.

Colonel Gunther, although visibly wounded, gets to work. He presses his left hand to his breast and is understandably agitated, but seems to be thoroughly in charge of the situation, and he gives a first lieutenant and myself the order to occupy the wood on both sides of the road. The first lieutenant takes over the northern and I the southern sector. My 'company' consists of soldiers of various units and arms of the service who don't know each other – certainly I don't know any of them and they don't know me. There is no bond between us and none could be expected. A mood of listlessness and indifference is evident and, for the first time, a sense of resignation. Some of the men take cover under the trees but remain close to their vehicles, hoping they can get back into them at the earliest opportunity. I tell myself that, if I am going to carry out my task – a task I had been given by the regimental commander – I must act quickly without making any fuss as obviously there are no laurels to be won here.

First, I allocate individual soldiers to their places in the position, and most of them dig out a few centimetres for themselves or at least cover themselves with rough and ready camouflage. Then I collect spades and shovels from the vehicles so that temporary shelters can be created. 'Sweat saves blood' is an old soldier's saying, and the men seem to understand this as they get started on the entrenchments. Most of them are older and they have been working on supply lines and in other rear services, so the demands being made of them are unusual.

Several times I searched vehicles on the edge of the wood for ammunition for the rifles and machine pistols, then I asked the men whether they had sufficient bullets and how many they would need. My endeavours seemed to cheer them up for, one by one, hand grenades, rifle grenades and some panzerfausts are obtained and several light machine guns brought into position.

At first my efforts as a 20-year-old youngster were regarded with some scepticism. But now all were digging eagerly to form their defences, making their weapons ready for action and testing their machine guns, and here and there some wag found his sense of humour again. I kept on going through the position – which could now be described as such – telling them how important our actions were and seeking to lift their spirits where necessary. Once I heard by chance that they were talking about me as 'our lieutenant' and I was content to have been left there with them and pleased to have been given the task of leading them.

But our defences were not tested – there was no attack. A reconnaissance party thrust forward to the position in which our vanguard had been surprised and turned back without making contact with the enemy. The reconnaissance party commander reported he hadn't found any of our fallen men. As usual the partisans had taken them in order to acquire, among other things, their uniforms so they could pretend to be German soldiers and carry out their actions behind the front with reduced risk.

In our column I hadn't found anyone from my artillery regiment. The only gun available to us is a captured Russian anti-tank gun with just sixteen rounds which is being towed by one of the other units. Although we didn't appear to be in immediate danger, I had the gun brought into a firing position as a precaution, quickly making myself familiar with the aiming mechanism and pointing it over the road at the spot where the partisans were most likely to emerge.

Late in the afternoon we learn that the column is going to be reorganised before the march continues. It would be reinforced with three tanks and six assault guns. I wonder how they are going to get here so quickly, but then I see they have already arrived, and they give us a feeling of fighting strength.

The column of march is rearranged. At the front is a strong leading group, consisting of the three tanks followed by a truck with an open back. Behind them are three assault guns, then another truck with an open back, and the other assault guns. The tail of the column is formed by all the remaining vehicles, predominantly trucks with enclosed rears.

Before I let my men go to their vehicles, I tell them what is happening and encourage them by saying how much our situation has improved. Then we waited, full of confidence and the will to break through, for the order to march off. The men make an impressive sight as they stand there, among the tanks and assault guns and on the open trucks, with their weapons ready to fire in any direction. I can see their determination and how relieved they are to be going forward again.

We wait for a while, but no orders come. To hell with this, time is running out and soon it will begin to get dark. The crews of the tanks and assault guns are increasingly restless, as their deployment is completely senseless if they cannot see, and also the soldiers on the trucks are getting ever more twitchy.

Then Colonel Gunther, who is still in command despite being wounded, loses patience. Since there is no radio communication, he drives off to see the divisional staff – at least that was what we thought because orders to march must come from them.

Slowly it becomes dark and nothing happens. We have been standing idle for so long that the men's eagerness for action has dwindled and the tank men are absolutely fed up.

Finally, at about 11 p.m., Colonel Gunther returns with the news that our march has been called off. We are bitterly disappointed, although it so late at night that the decision may have been a sensible one. But the hammer blow comes with the second order – that all the trucks were to be destroyed immediately once their fuel had been removed. At this moment everyone senses that the situation must have got much worse.

And indeed it has deteriorated – dramatically so! Early in the morning of 3 July the Soviets took Minsk from two sides, so the ring around us has tightened. But this had been anticipated and the necessity of breaking out from the Minsk area had already been discussed at the Beresina.

But another development took us by surprise. The Soviets were not content with simply conquering Minsk, the capital of White Russia, and surrounding us, which was a major success. No, they wanted much more, and so their tanks on both sides of Minsk went straight on to Molodeczno, 65km north-west of it, and in the direction of Baranowicze, 130km to the south-west.

Both towns are important railway junctions with connections to Diinaburg, Vilna, Grodno, Bialystok and Brest-Litovsk. And they took them quickly – Molodeczno was already in their hands by 5 July. 'Don't give them any peace! They did it near Bobruysk and now, as quickly as possible, they must take Baranowicze', Marshal Zhukov, who was coordinating the Southern Front (1st and 2nd Byelorussian Fronts), had told Lieutenant General Batov, and so on 8 July the Red Flag fluttered from the top of all official buildings of the severely damaged city, which had been bombed by more than 500 Soviet planes.

Of course, at the time we don't know about this and our commander, Lieutenant General Vincenz Muller, has another more immediate concern. This came in the form of a radio message despatched at 2.35 p.m. to the commander-in-chief of the 4th Army, General of Infantry von Tippelskirch. This said that he was coming into the fortified position with his divisions and that Gruppe Muller could no longer be regarded as a combat-worthy unit. Because of acute traffic congestion on the routes available to us and the vast numbers of stragglers, it would no longer be possible to organise the infantry and artillery so that they could launch attacks quickly and with sufficient ammunition. He had therefore decided to order the breakout, taking with him all the soldiers who were fit enough to fight. They would carry the 'lightest armament' and aim to pass south of Minsk on their way to the west.

He himself would fight his way out of the cauldron and, with his most dependable troops, head for the west. In fact – something I would not have thought possible – he was soon negotiating to become a prisoner of war. He then joined the National Committee for a Free Germany which operated in the Soviet Union and he took part in actions against the retreating troops of Army Group Centre.

But I must return to the harsh reality of the present. We had to destroy at once everything we didn't need to carry and, despite strong objections, smaller vehicles that were still in good working order. I was dismayed about this decision as my vehicle was included. But it was made because the engines of the smaller vehicles use a lot of fuel and cannot carry many passengers. So, in bright moonlight we empty the fuel tanks by boring a hole in them and letting the valuable fuel run into reserve canisters.

Afterwards comes the destruction of the selected vehicles. Angrily we cut off the tyres using hacksaws, then wreck the engines with a few heavy blows. It is a desperate business! We had started the day full of hope and ready for action, expecting to continue our march quickly, but we have been stuck here since early morning without having advanced a single step – and now we have been told to destroy many of our perfectly good vehicles! We are so angry that we take it out on the vehicles – we smash the lights, windscreens and dashboards, rip up the leather upholstery and even cut up the canopies and hoods. Once this depressing destructive orgy is over, we divide up all the equipment we have taken from them.

I have the great good fortune to share the driving of a sidecar. This should increase my chances of finding my artillery battery again because with a motorcycle it is much easier to get through difficult terrain and past hold-ups. Also, one can overtake convoys and search through them at the same time. Tomorrow at daylight surely we will be off again!

4 July

Shortly after midnight we were ready and got moving, although not in a westerly direction as our original route of retreat was certainly blocked. Instead we turn back eastwards for a short distance, then took another road on which we had a chance of getting through.

As I've already said, there were very few roads, but some of them are ignored by the partisans so uninterrupted progress was possible to a limited extent. After a few kilometres we come across a road junction near a small village where we plan to make a turn, but then the march stops. The drivers are instructed to switch off their engines and headlights. The night is intensely muggy. I leave my uncomfortable sidecar and take a walk alongside the vehicles.

Most of the men appear to have sunk into exhausted sleep and some of those who have been squeezed into overcrowded vehicles have spread out their tent halves and blankets on the roadside and stretched themselves out so that they won't have to sleep sitting upright which has happened so often during the retreat. But a few can't rest. I see the glow of their cigarettes and, here and there among the vehicles, hear conversations in subdued voices, and I get the impression that unpleasant things are being discussed.

A few aircraft can be heard buzzing in the distance. Then silently they hasten towards the tracer spurs of some anti-aircraft guns, one after the other, almost like a string of pearls. A few seconds later they disappear after a burst of short flashing light. These must be roaming enemy aircraft because we have not seen any of our own since we left our positions east of the Dnepr nine days ago. We can't expect anything else. Since the beginning of the big Russian offensive Army Group Centre, which had a front of 1,100km, had just forty fighter aircraft. Fuel shortages meant that they were unable to take to the air even once and some of them must have been lost in the course of the fighting. So, in the coming days we don't see any machines marked with the Balkan cross in the sky, but many with the Red Star, incredible numbers.

After about 3 hours, almost at nightfall, we start off again. I had just been told Lieutenant Meyer, the orderly officer on our regimental staff, had been killed. He must have been a victim of the attack on our vanguard, as we had not seen any further enemy activity since then.

My driver is a skilful lad who has the motorcycle sidecar firmly in hand and is surely a good enough rider to take some liberties with the machine if he has to. Just the right man to have by me! We roar past our line of vehicles and have soon left them behind. It is a wonderful feeling to be able to drive like this in such a free and unhampered way. I think back to the marvellous weeks of motorcycle training that I had had as a recruit at Oppeln/Obeerschlesien where I passed the course on the same 750 BMW motorcycle combination as we are riding in now. I would love to be sitting on the saddle that the driver clearly likes so much!

Theses happy memories are unfortunately soon dampened as on both sides of the road and on the edges of the woods we see the wrecks of so many vehicles that had been destroyed by the units coming through here because of lack of fuel. There are many VW-Jeeps, amphibious vehicles and tracked cycles, caterpillar tractors and various special vehicles that needed fuel and were hardly suitable as troop transports.

We search some of the abandoned vehicles for useful items, above all fuel and things to eat, but there was virtually nothing left. We stand every empty petrol can we find upside down and let the last drops run into our reserve can. Most only contain a few cubic centimetres, but a few have a little more. We collect a small supply in this way. The mixture may be a hazardous, but it is better than nothing.

In an abandoned radio truck we find two packets of crispbread and immediately tuck this valuable booty into one of the motorcycle's saddlebags.

Apart from that we find a groundsheet, which one can always use, some repair for the tyres and eventually a mosquito net which I immediately press into the hands of my driver as I already have one that I had found in a wood behind the Beresina. There is also a small pocketbook with anecdotes from stage and film – something that will distract us from our situation will do no harm – and finally a map of Russia. We take everything with us except the map. What we would not have given for that little piece of paper a few days later!

A few hundred metres from us a convoy is on fire, sending a thick yellowish-grey cloud of smoke up into the sky. The sun, seen through the smoke, looks like a bloody red ball. We come up close to the column, then drive slowly alongside, hoping to make out on the dust-covered vehicles the yellow stripe with the slanting bar, the tactical sign of our 18th Panzergrenadier Division, but in vain. The column is the remains of another division in our army group that is trying to get out to the west. Incessantly the wheels and chains whirl the dust around, sometimes so violently that the vehicles appear ghostlike. Soldiers, rigid-looking, stand or sit there. Sweat runs in streams over their tired, dusty faces and around the whites of their eyes, and their teeth seem to stand out. If any of them had opened their dry lips to speak or even to shout, we would not have understood a word because of the heavy roar of the engines and the rattling of the caterpillar tracks.

Disappointed by our unsuccessful search, we leave the marching column behind us and are happy to get away from the masses of dust. The glowing heat and the dust, even when there isn't any fighting, is an enormous strain, and if it rains here again after this long dry spell, the conditions would be even more demanding because these 'roads' would turn into an impassable muddy waste such as we had experienced in the past.

Then, almost in an act of defiance given the scene around me, I begin to leaf through the pages of the pocketbook I've just found, reading with growing pleasure some really exquisite stories. For a while I can can make time such things, partly because for at the moment the enemy has left us alone.

Also there is less chance of partisan activity here since we are on a side road and passing through territory that is not so thickly wooded. But as everyone knows one should not praise the day until the evening!

Another marching column comes up and this time there are some vehicles from our division within it. A bit further on we glimpse, surrounded by thick clouds of dust, trucks towing light field guns. 'Man, we have done it!' I call out to my driver for there in front of us is our 1st Battery which we have spent such a long time searching for.

Over the last few days the battery has shrunk. Of the twelve vehicles that started the retreat, only seven are still present. One truck and both the VW-Jeeps had had to be destroyed because of the lack of fuel. A defective artillery tractor had been left standing on the east bank of the Beresina, and Senior Corporal Schaffrath, who saved me at the Drut through his perseverance, had had to throw his motorcycle into a ditch because of engine damage.

I then report to the chief who is delighted and surprised to see me as no one had expected me to return.

Since there aren't many places left among the trucks and artillery tractors I decide to stay on the motorcycle combination. Early in the afternoon we reach a small river in a densely wooded area. The bridge is surprisingly undamaged, but hardly have we got over it when we are stopped in a wood by anti-tank and rifle fire. Fortunately, during the river crossing the column had become further spaced out so that the individual vehicles could accelerate when they crossed the stretch under fire. My driver turns the throttle to full speed and we race forward along the road with our bodies bent right forward. This time the dust helps us as it makes it impossible for the enemy to take careful aim and so we get through, it seems without casualties.

The next hours passed without incident, but the heat and the dust nearly drive us to despair. How parched are our throats and our faces glow as if we have a fever. We lie down for a short rest in a village where at last we find water. Bucketful after bucketful is brought up from the well by the old rattling pail. The field flasks and mess tins are filled with the precious liquid and are drained in big gulps. The ice-cold water is wonderful and we don't care that it also tastes a little bitter and mouldy. When everyone has washed the sweat and dust from their dirty faces, we jump up, feeling fully refreshed, into the vehicles. Then, with a roar, the heavy engines start up again, making a monotonous song.

A little later we bump into elements of various divisions, including the remains of the Feldherrnhalle, which we are obliged to join, as overtaking on the narrow road is completely out of the question. The speed of the column is much reduced and again and again there are blockages and interruptions as some vehicles ran out of fuel.

We have another confrontation with partisans in a wood. At first there are a few insignificant shots, then the firing becomes so intense that we are obliged, in spite of possible losses, to leave the vehicles rapidly and take cover at the edges of the wood on either side of the road. We have to pick out each of the gunmen individually in order to put them out of action. As I've said before, the partisans seldom allow themselves to be drawn into an open fight – they only do so if they are surrounded and have no alternative. On this occasion they have nothing to fear and can withdraw quickly into the darkness of the woods.

Although our position seems to be safe for the moment, we stay where we are. Slowly the day comes to an end. I rejoin my battery and let the experienced motorcyclist go so he has time to get back to his old unit. While we are waiting there Captain Trost tells us to park our vehicles under cover on the edge of a small clearing near the road. Our cook immediately prepares a hot meal out of the last of the supplies which in the circumstances is a remarkable achievement.

Suddenly we hear noise on the road. Around the rear of a large truck a crowd has formed and it gets bigger and bigger as more men rush in from all sides. I leave our clearing to find out what is happening. When I get closer I see that near the truck is a supply vehicle that has been shot up in the attack or stopped because of lack of fuel. Its valuable load is being thrown off and grabbed by the unruly soldiers in the crowd. As our supplies have practically run out, I struggle to get hold of something in the wild confusion and emerge with a sack of peas, a can of sauerkraut and a bag of ersatz coffee. The butter or margarine had already been taken and some items had been trampled in the dust, so the men must have gone off in high spirits.

I return with my booty and give it to the highly delighted cook. He has already prepared our meal. Then he cleared everything away, including the cooking implements. This was our first hot meal in a week and, although we didn't know it, we would not have another one for a long time.

Towards evening we and the other batteries receive the astonishing order that we should immediately destroy the two artillery tractors with their guns, as well as all the disposable equipment and baggage. In these circumstances no one who was fully aware of our situation had expected an order of this kind and we asked ourselves why should our heavy weapons be sacrificed when they would surely be urgently required in a breakthrough attempt, especially as most of the tanks and assault guns were lost at the Beresina. But the order has been given and, although everyone is visibly surprised, we start to sort out our packs.

The chief tells us that only so much luggage can be kept because we may have to march on foot and we can only carry a comfortable load. Marching on foot?

Everyone has a different point of view about this and different expectations, but no one anticipated what marching on foot would be like and realised how few of us would get through. All of us dig around in our packs and soon the clearing is brimming with blankets, coats, tent halves, washing kit, bits of uniform, drilling tools, boots, shoe polish, socks and all sorts of bits and pieces. It looks as if someone had thrown the contents of a whole department of a medium-sized warehouse into a heap.

Finally, the battery equipment goes onto the heap: telephone apparatus, drums of cable, azimuth circles, my periscope – yes, even two of the expensive radio sets and much else that instead of being carefully tended to and handled has to be disposed of. They fly in high curves from the vehicles and are made unserviceable with hacksaws and spades.

With bitter irony. I remember that I, as a younger and still inexperienced soldier, was given three days' detention because I hit my sidearm on a nail without realising it and was committed to prison for 'damaging Wehrmacht property'!

Everything that appears to be burnable is carried to an substantial heap, richly sprinkled with cartridge powder and then set on fire. As we have already lost one of the artillery tractors, we only have one to get rid of. The first of the two howitzers that has to be destroyed is pulled to a spot deeper in the woods, then the vehicle turns back and picks up the second gun. We interrupt our depressing work in the clearing and watch the guns until they vanish between the trees never to be seen again. Shortly afterwards there is a flare of flames, then the dull detonation of an explosion. Among us there is an icy silence; no one dares say a word, but our faces speak volumes.

A little later the demolition team returns, along with the driver of the artillery tractor. He carries a canister containing the fuel from the vehicle that has been destroyed and shares out this incredibly valuable fluid between the two remaining vehicles.

Although we have dumped most of our equipment, there is not much space for all of our men in the vehicles – luckily our battery's personnel losses have been few until now. But finally everyone finds a place, however limited, and I squeeze into the driver's cabin of one of the vehicles next to the driver.

The march goes on and soon it begins to get dark. Behind us we leave a smoking field of wreckage from which now and then weak flames dart out from the smouldering heaps.

The night is extremely muggy as on the previous days. I suddenly feel ill. My body is freezing despite the warm temperature and I have a maddening thirst. With this comes a severe, cramping pain in my belly and also a fever.

From the head of the column faint sounds of fighting can be heard. Almost certainly partisans again, I think, but at that moment all I want to do is to lie down. The firing peters out after a few minutes and the column stops, so I leave the vehicle and, with leaden limbs, stretch myself out on the carriage of the gun we are towing. The pain diminishes a little, but I cannot sleep. When I close my eyes everything goes round in a crazy whirl. I wonder what the problem is. Was there something wrong with the cool spring water I'd drunk or couldn't my stomach cope with the sudden chill? As yet I don't realise I have dysentery.

5 July

Midnight passes and there is no sign that we will soon be moving on again. Instead of being impatient to keep going, I am quite happy to stay lying there even though sleep is impossible. The pain is intense and I tell myself that at any moment I will have to summon up my last reserves of strength.

During the early morning hours nothing much happens – there is no movement or fighting.

The silence is uncanny. It is the calm before the storm. The sun is up and burning unmercifully again, and the thirst is unbearable.

The field flasks we filled up yesterday at the village are completely empty and there is no water to be found. My tongue sticks to the roof of my mouth – it really does – and the fever seems to be increasing. Medical assistance is not easy to come by in this situation and tantalising thoughts of a field hospital are straight out of the realm of fantasy.

Towards midday something seems to be happening, as the order is given for the battery to deploy. We pull the two guns remaining with us further forward and position them ready to fire in a patch of open ground between the wood and the road. Immediately afterwards wild shooting breaks out at the head of the column and we are told to bring one of the howitzers forward.

Captain Trost comes over to me and says quietly and unobtrusively, 'This is a suicide mission!' Then he hurries to the artillery tractor to set an example – as in many other dangerous situations, he intends to lead from the front. In such circumstances I feel I have to go along with him, though in my condition I long to remain where I am. But since I've tried hard to conceal my illness, no one in the battery would have understood if I had let the chief go off on his own into such danger. Also, I know that if I stay put, I could never again ask for full commitment from my subordinates.

Everything is quickly prepared and then we drive forward with the howitzer's crew and two machine-gunners who will provide cover using their light machine guns.

This stretch of road is a bit wider so that we, with our gun tractor and howitzer, can get past the convoy and quickly reach the chosen spot. Not far from the road the wood opens up into a large clearing on the edge of which the Soviets have firmly established themselves, preventing us from going forward. Several of our leading vehicles have already fallen victim to their fire.

The howitzer is set up in incredible haste, unbelievably quickly, between the trees in an open position, and immediately begins to fire at the enemy. While this is going on one of the two machine guns gives covering fire and I race with the gunner of the second machine gun across the road and go further into the nearby wood. We throw ourselves into the undergrowth between the first trees and then spray the edge of the wood where the enemy are positioned with short bursts as we cannot fire continuously because of lack of ammunition.

Then two armoured reconnaissance vehicles take up supporting positions on either side of us and join in the fight. The Soviets soon become aware of this and reply with mortar fire that quickly increases to a strength similar to that at the Beresina bridgehead three days ago, but here there is much more tree damage. After only a few minutes the reconnaissance vehicle on our left gets a direct hit and breaks apart in a gigantic jet of fire. We wait for the cries of the wounded, but nothing is heard, and we conclude there are no survivors. One quickly puts such things out of one's mind at critical moments like this one, especially when one is distracted by illness, pain, fever and thirst.

The enemy fire is so intense that it seems nothing living could possibly come out of this witches' cauldron. We were facing not just partisans but army detachments which had been flown in with the aim of encircling us. By constructing barricades they are delaying us and at the same time they are seriously reducing our strength so that we have little chance of breaking through the ring.

An obvious sign of our dwindling fighting ability is our a lack of fuel, the increasing need for heavy weapons and transport vehicles, and a shrinking stock of ammunition of all kinds. Our supplies have been used up and cannot be supplemented any more – neither a litre of spirit nor a single bullet can come in. Air-drops have stopped and nothing has reached us by land for a long time.

My brave machine-gunner inserts his last belt of ammunition and throws me a short, but significant glance. If the Soviets attack, our defence will depend on our machine gun, and so every action must be calculated, but the mortaring has lessened noticeably, perhaps from the effect of our rifle fire. As if everything depended on me personally, I jump up and rush through the wood across to the road in the hope of finding ammunition in one of the destroyed and abandoned vehicles. The road is overlooked by the enemy and therefore I have to go very quickly over this stage, ignoring the dust raised by the mortars.

I search through the first vehicle in haste, without success, but then I discover two cases on the back seat of a VW-Jeep. Without delay I pull them out and find something incredible: the ammunition is already belted and the belts are full. I have been really lucky. With effort I lift the heavy ammunition boxes over the side of the vehicle, put one on my left, the other on my right and then drag them along the floor of the wood behind me, as I am exhausted and lack the strength to carry them.

When I get back to the machine gun in one piece, the gunner looks at me for a moment as if I had personally brought him his Christmas present, grasped one of the belts and, shaking his head, turned back to the edge of the wood and brought it back under fire.

Soon afterwards other men begin calling for ammunition. I look around and see between the trees one of the gunners hurrying to a damaged gun tractor further from the edge of the wood, in which he was hoping to find some shells. If his search is successful he would at the most only be able to take two, so I decide to help him. My luck with the machine-gun ammunition encourages me, but I also know that everyone here has to do what has to be done – whatever is immediately necessary – no matter his rank.

I found twenty-five rounds in the vehicle, not a lot but certainly better than nothing. Working together we manage to carry another two shells, as quickly as the heavy load allows, across the road and put them down on the edge of the wood.

At first everything goes well but then the Soviets open fire with a machine gun as we can see from the spurts of dust on the road. The first vehicles try to get through the barrage at full speed and at big intervals, partially hidden by the whirling dust.

The mortar fire has greatly diminished, and even more vehicles are racing past us. As the firing finally dies away we realise with relief that we have got away with it yet again, but we begin to grasp the magnitude of the task that awaits us if – perhaps tomorrow – we have to break through the considerably stronger ring that encircles us.

Our morale is not improved by our army commander. He had sent a moving message to us by radio when we were at the Beresina, saying he was following 'our route with a warm heart', before he had driven away. He went on to say, 'We are doing everything we can to help with our limited resources.' But from then on we received no assistance and we felt ourselves abandoned, perhaps already written off.

If only we had been sent a few aircraft carrying indispensable fuel and ammunition and some fighter planes so that the 'Butcher', as the notorious Soviet Ilyushin-Il-2 Sturmovik ground-attack aircraft is known, could be kept well away from us – it always had a considerable impact.

We had just left the woods when six black spots appeared in the sky on the horizon and seconds later the feared Sturmoviks flew low over us firing with all their guns. Some soldiers jumped out of their vehicles and ran flat out into a nearby patch of woodland, but even before they reached their goal, one after the other they were hit and collapsed. Immediately the 'Butchers' turned in a great curve and attacked us again, but by now the crew of a 2cm anti-aircraft gun has reached their post and suddenly one of the machines bursts into flames and explodes in a yellow-red ball of fire. In a continuous somersault the two crewmen whirl through the air and the burning remains of their aircraft flatten them into the ground. Everyone cheers and after that the other five machines fly off.

Partisans have made the route of our retreat impassable by destroying stretches of the road across this swampy strip of land, but army units that have gone through ahead of us have used planks, beams, empty ammunition boxes and petrol cans to fashion a rough bypass so we can go around the swamp, moving with great caution. Two dead horses lie there in front of their overturned cart. They have half sunk into the black-brown morass and give off a beastly stench. Any vehicle that falls off this makeshift path can't be recovered.

In order to get back to the old road after this stretch of swamp, we must climb a steep slope and, while the halftrack vehicles have no problem with this, the heavy trucks go uphill with steaming radiators and their engines straining to the utmost, laboriously, metre by metre. Some fail to make it and slowly roll back again in order to make another attempt, again without success. So, yet again we have to assist them with the artillery tractor.

Shrouded in grey-brown clouds of dust we roll on in the glowing heat. We are north-east of Ssmilovitshi. Small, gently sloping and mostly wooded hills alternate with meadows and fields, and here and there we see settlements of a few wooden houses – a really beautiful part of the world. But we have neither the time nor opportunity to enjoy the countryside because suddenly a whistling noise cuts through the sound of the engines. Seconds later something crashes between our artillery tractor and the truck which is driving in front of us in a cornfield next to the road and lets fly a whole swarm of splinters.

'That was a big one', says the driver next to me pressing down harder on the accelerator. Another shell hits, throwing up a giant fountain of dirt, fortunately a bit further away. 'I don't like the look of this!' I murmur and then turn to say loudly to my driver: 'Have you worked out where they are coming from?' 'From ahead, half right!' he shouts back and points in that direction. Minsk is over there, about 30km away. 'Damn, now they have us in a sack!' I call to him and he dumbly nods.

At the time we didn't know that the Soviets had occupied Minsk two days ago and that the sack we are caught in is already enormous.

Once we have got that stretch of road successfully behind us, we stop for a short rest by a clump of bushes. The vehicle is driven as close as possible to the undergrowth, and quickly camouflaged from aerial view with a few branches. These rests in the shade are such a relief, especially as I feel sharp pain in my belly and urgently have to find a nearby bush. I throw my field blouse, webbing and pistol on my seat, taking only my machine pistol with me as we have to carry it at all times. Now I understand why I am unwell. But there is no time to think about the possible consequences because suddenly the sand squirts up high from the track, immediately followed by a ripping-bellowing bang. 'Pak!' shouts somebody and already the crew of the artillery tractor – except me – have taken cover behind the steel wheels and caterpillar tracks. Another shell strikes nearby. The fire is coming from a light anti-tank gun in a bit of woodland about 500m away and it is accurate. The next shot goes straight through the tarpaulin into the cargo space and kills the gunner who is the only one there. Perhaps completely exhausted, he had not got out. From behind my bush I see him, through the open back of the vehicle, topple forward and fall with a thump on the wooden planks.

Captain Trost rushes up, shouting out: 'Go, drive off, go, go, go!' and jumps into the driver's cabin, taking my seat. In seconds the driver has climbed in behind the steering wheel and immediately he gets the vehicle moving. I run behind like a crazy person and at the last moment, with extreme exertion, jump on to the gun carriage of the howitzer. Apparently no one else has come with us, as the artillery tractor was open at the rear between the caterpillar tracks and jumping up in front of the overhanging gun when it was moving would be exceptionally dangerous.

To avoid a further bombardment, we race along the road. When we run into a traffic jam, the driver turns on to lower ground in order to find better cover, but immediately afterwards a tremendous blow shook the artillery tractor, which stopped immediately as if nailed down. I felt I had been thrown up by a gigantic hand, then dropped. An awful rush of air took my breath away for a moment and a hellish incandescent wave hit me in the face. A heavy anti-tank shell has hit the driver's compartment.

With flattened hair and half-covered in dust I slowly climb down from the gun carriage and stagger forwards. I feel a frightful presentiment. Smoke is whirling out of the driver's cabin and I look down into it to see if it is empty. Of the driver, on whose side the shell had hit, there is no sign. He has simply gone, vanished together with his steering wheel. But what has happened to my boss? I climb onto the running board in order to see better. The leather cushion of the bench seat is burnt, smoking a little, and tatters of my battledress tunic are still recognisable next to the misshapen remains of a corpse, and beyond that, a head. Captain Trost stares with torn-open eyes past me into infinity.

Appalled, I jump down from the running board and dash across the road, away from this horrible sight. I must have seen much worse things during the war, but this was simply too much to bear. What had happened had gone beyond the boundaries of what I could accept – beyond reason. Normally I want to live life to the full, but the shock of that awful moment is so deep that I feel I don't want to go on living.

While still stunned by this experience, I pull myself up onto a passing vehicle and looking inside recognise the commander of our IInd Detachment, Major Waldschmidt, who had taken me with him in his vehicle three days ago to the Beresina. I tell him that Captain Trost is dead and at the same moment I realise that, now he has gone, I am in command of the battery. But where is it and how can I find it now?

As the column has halted, I get down from the vehicle and run forward. When the column moves off once more, I climb quickly onto the running board of another vehicle and jump off again at the next stop in order to continue my search. Several times I have go into the roadside ditch in order to deal with the dysentery which is sapping my strength. It is getting worse, and I still can't find any trace of my unit. No one I ask can help me.

Perhaps in the confusion the battery with the anti-tank gun has found another way of getting through or is hanging around somewhere at the back of the column? So, I turn around and hurry back to search at the rear.

There is a shout from a vehicle of the 5th Battery. Waving is Senior Corporal Polack who was with me in the winter of 1942–3 near Staraja Russa on Lake Ilmen. He had belonged to the same gun team, and it is hard to believe that he has recognised me here. Fleetingly I wave back without stopping. I have to find my battery, I say to myself again and again, but no one I ask knows where it is and my search is unsuccessful.

As the column sets off again I have to give up my quest because I am exhausted. A vehicle from the signals staff of our regiment takes me on, and the troops in the crowded wagon find a place for me to sit. 'You look awful,' one of them says, 'come and sit down here.' I am infinitely grateful. Once I am sitting there and leaning back a little, all our troubles become more bearable.

After only a few minutes a leaden fatigue overtakes me, the reaction to the great physical and psychological burdens of the day. Before my eyes close, I see fighter aircraft attacking our column, the twitching flames of the machine guns in their wings, and soldiers jumping out of their vehicles like grey phantoms. As if the sound is a long distance away, I hear the rolling bellows of the wing cannon, then listen completely unconcernedly to the machine-gun bullets hitting my vehicle. Common sense, willpower and even the survival instinct are overcome by total exhaustion. I only want to sleep, sleep, sleep, and would at that moment have accepted a quick and painless end completely without resistance and even with a feeling of relief.

When I awake again after some hours, during which nothing in particular appears to have happened, I feel myself wonderfully strengthened. Somewhere nearby there must have been a storm, as for the first time in many days the air is distinctly cooler and I can breathe more easily.

A comrade brings me some denims because, since the loss of my field blouse, I only have a shirt and thin pullover left. Yesterday when my luggage was destroyed I had put them on, despite the great heat, so I wouldn't lose them. The denims have no badges of rank which in this situation is of no importance, and I can't predict how relevant badges of rank will be in the future.

As we drive on I watch the sinking sun and wonder whether I'll ever find my battery. Then the night takes us into its protective darkness and grants us at last a few hours of rest. We all know that tomorrow will be very difficult for us, but despite everything that has happened, we still have hope. Our mood contrasts with that of our commander-in-chief, General of Infantry von Tippelskirch, who knows the situation better than we do and already has taken his leave of the 4th Army. At 11 p.m. the following radio message from him reaches us: 'Deeply moved in my heart and shattered by the feeling of not being able to help. I salute the army of battle-hardened veteran soldiers.' Soon, of course, none of us would be in a position to receive any messages at all. And so this terrible day came to an end and an even worse one started.

6 July

In the early morning hours, as the sun was rising, we drive through a completely destroyed village, still about 20km from Minsk. A nearby patch of woodland now consists of miserably splintered tree stumps, and everywhere there are craters, some of enormous dimensions – the plainest moonscape many of us could imagine. Numerous wrecked vehicles, vast amounts of apparatus of all kinds and many corpses lie strewn around the area. 'It looks as if an ammunition dump has gone up . . .', says one of the soldiers in our vehicle, but he doesn't finish his sentence because at that very moment we are hit by furious fire from infantry weapons, mortars, artillery and anti-tank guns. Immediately everyone plunges out of the vehicle to seek cover in the many craters. From there we can only watch as our vehicle, the first in the column, is destroyed, followed by those further on. The Soviets are firing precisely at this spot and the violence of the blasts leaves us in no doubt that we have arrived at the edge of the enclosing ring.

Bewildered we look at the burning wrecks along the road and cannot believe that this is the end. We think that, if we can break through the ring here, we can achieve our goal even without the vehicles. So, we climb out of our holes and charge with wild determination towards the invisible enemy. The Soviets let us advance a little, then all hell breaks loose and in a few minutes the unplanned and disorganised attack collapses with severe losses. The survivors take flight and no one stays to tend to the badly wounded who are left lying around anticipating being shot like rabbits. To avoid the murderous fire we have to retreat some distance and are completely scattered. I work my way carefully behind a small mound, thick with gorse bushes, to get out of enemy sight. The firing gradually dies down, then stops. I hide myself in one of the bushes on my hillock and consider the situation.

Individuals and small groups are moving about the landscape without any purpose. No one appears to know what is going to happen, and neither do I. So, I decide to stay put and let the situation play out, particularly as the Soviets don't seem to be interested in advancing towards us. But why should they? They can wait and let us come to them, and they can attack us from the air. Their aircraft are continuously circling, always in groups of six, like birds looking for prey. If they see something, they dive with flames coming from the machine guns in their wings and fuselage – such is their passion for hunting. There are no German fighters to oppose them, and most of our light anti-aircraft guns have been destroyed with their vehicles.

The sun is burning hot as usual, but I can bear it for a while in the shade of the gorse bushes. Yet, I know I must do something because I can't lie here alone for much longer. I notice that near a crossroads a few hundred metres beyond the edge of a patch of woodland soldiers are assembling and one by one various vehicles are taking cover there. Although they are a good target for the enemy fighters, I make my way to join them. I don't want to stay on my own and hope my chances will improve if I am with a group.

When I reach the wood I see the men there belong to the Feldherrnhalle Division which has arrived at last. There is no sign of a commander and most of them are gathering at the side of the wood or a little further in so they are concealed from aerial view. While I look around for a suitable place to go, I see how somebody has started in a great hurry to unpack several cartons from one of the catering trucks and is distributing front-line-fighter rations among the troops standing nearby. Since I have not eaten for two days because of my illness and I had lost my last rations in the destroyed artillery tractor yesterday – my God, that frightful event was already 24 hours ago – I stand in line and finally get a package thrown at me. At the time I didn't realise that my basic good health has enabled me to get through the last few days.

I shake my head in delight at the fine things these packets contain: chocolate, biscuits and fruit drops, all in modest quantities. They amount to only a small reward for the men fighting hard in the front line, but they are happy to receive them as they will give them renewed strength. I am thankful that the dysentery symptoms have disappeared for a while and I look up to the heavens to establish what the enemy airmen there are up to. They are not in the immediate vicinity – if they had been we would not have been able to enjoy our rations in peace – but are not far off so I decide to lie under one of the heavy trucks that are standing under the trees at the edge of the woodland. It is already in a battered condition, but I can't find a better shelter.

To increase my safety, I crawl under the huge engine block, ignoring the oil dripping from it, and open the small round can of Scho-ka-kola, the energy-giving drink. I also have a few biscuits and all too soon these tasty items are consumed. I am accustomed to eating hastily at the front, not because of hunger – until now our supplies were always plentiful and good and even during the big battles they were usually regularly delivered – but because I didn't want to risk being killed while doing so.

Just as I am tasting a fruit stick, I hear the rapidly increasing roar of engines and then the feared Ilyushin-Il-2s are on top of us, diving down on the vehicles standing on the edge of the wood and plastering them with their cannon.

But I feel comparatively safe under the engine block, though the flavour of the fruit stick is spoiled.

The attack doesn't stop with one pass and soon the slaughterers are back again. Cautiously I look out from my shelter and see that one of the planes appears to have picked my truck as a target. He comes down in at a low level and I duck back underneath – just in time. Seconds later a belt of machine-gun fire sweeps over the ground only a few centimetres from the left-hand front wheel and a tree standing immediately in front of the vehicle is cut down by the burst. With a howling engine the pilot of the machine passes a few metres above the tops of the trees and vanishes behind the wood. My appetite has now completely disappeared and I ask myself if I am really doing the right thing by lying under a vehicle, but once more an inner voice tells me that it is better for me to stay where I am.

The fighter aircraft give us no peace and they can come and go as they please. There is nothing we can do to stop them – we are fully exposed and can only hope to survive their constant attacks with a lot of luck. Never before had I experienced anything like this!

Now and then I look out cautiously from under the truck to see what is happening. The pilots clearly see themselves as the lords of the air. Between their attacks they put their planes through high-spirited loops and other capers as if they are performing in some kind of air display. Machines of a type I don't recognise are involved, probably American. As I watch them make their turns I wonder if they are flown by enthusiastic American pilots who regard the whole thing as a kind of sport.

Often their elegant loops turn into diving attacks with bursts of cannon and machine-gun fire. The awful booming sound makes me crouch even further down in my hiding place. In hopeless rage I can only clench my fists and hope that at last a few of our fighters will appear and prevent further strafing. But, as before, this remains a wistful dream. Instead, the number of enemy aircraft remains constant and then a squadron of about thirty bombers appears out of the predominantly blue sky. They have come to finish us off. Innumerable black spots are dropping from their fuselages, whistling louder and louder as they fall down on us and then exploding with a single violent thunder as if the world was coming to an end. Less than a hundred metres from me lies the edge of the bombing area and I am glad I haven't moved because in a few seconds the whole wood is simply swept away as trees, men and vehicles whirl through the air. A monstrous cloud of densely burning smoke and dust begins slowly climbing up into the heavens, darkening the sun so it looks as if night fall had come.

Hardly has the din of the explosion died down than a terrible drawn-out moaning and crying begins, and then I hear what sounds like a herd of wild horses galloping over fields. Out of the wall of dust and smoke come the survivors, unstoppable like an avalanche, many wounded among them that can still walk, visibly driven by only one thought: to get away from this Hell!

As if bewitched I stare at this depressing sight – I have never seen anything like it before. I set myself against the stream, trying to remain calm, but I realise very quickly that the situation is completely hopeless. Then I join the latecomers, those who are wounded or so exhausted that they can only make slow, painful progress. Aimlessly we move through the dust-covered area, 2, 3km, perhaps even more, as I have lost sense of space and time.

Finally, along with some comrades who are also worn out with fatigue, I lie down on the edge of a wood near a track, collapsed, dejected and once more devoid of strength.

Without paying close attention we see how at various places small and sometimes large groups of stragglers dash for cover as individual Soviet tanks appear and fire wildly on all sides and then vanish again as they seek further targets.

During a pause in the attacks – no enemy tanks or infantry are visible – I go off alone in order to find a spot where some sort of order can be re-established. Then perhaps another attempt can be made to break out at night as this is no longer an option in daylight hours.

Carefully, keeping a look-out in every direction, I make my way towards the road because I hope to find the spot I'm looking for there. The scene is frightful.

Lying all around are vehicles that have been destroyed by the bombing and shot up by the tanks. Some have been mangled beyond recognition, and the bodies of the dead are caught up in the wreckage – it is a horrifying conglomeration. Here and there are badly injured men who cannot possibly be helped – I can only wish them a speedy end.

In front of the cab of a loudly burning truck I see the corpses of two of the occupants who had escaped before the flames caught them but were then engulfed by the ensuing fire. I feel compelled to pull them out of the flames, perhaps because of a desire to do something good in the midst of this pandemonium of evil things, but the heat is so intense that I have to give up the attempt. It occurs to me that it may be better to burn up than slowly decompose, and I run on without looking back.

Several times I stumble on bits of bodies, pale yellow, with bloody clumps where they had been torn off. My senses have been so dulled that I am not particularly affected by such awful sights any more.

For a while renewed air attack is not a threat as the smoke from the burning woods and vehicles all around us has thickened into a black-grey cloud of fumes and the sun only appears now and then as a pale, weak matt-silver disc, as if it wanted to hide itself from all that man has done in this place.

The hot air is filled with the caustic smell of the charcoaled wood of the trees and incinerated vehicles, along with the penetrating stench of smouldering vehicle tyres, burnt oil and the frightful sweet stench of corpses which are quickly putrefying in the intense summer heat – an infernal mixture of truly strange scents. This is another example of what a cynic had once dared to describe as 'the refreshing bath in steel'. Like so many other things that once appeared valid and inviolable – which we learnt to take in good faith and with warm hearts and which guided our thoughts and dealings – these sentiments come into question as disillusionment and bitterness set in. Such phrases are now degraded – they ring hollow.

In a corner of the wood stands an abandoned artillery tractor. I wonder which battery could it have belonged to and take a closer to look at one the mudguards. Here I read: 1./Art.Rgt.(mot) 18. This was the only sign I ever found of my battery, and I didn't see any of its members.

Even more stragglers have now appeared, and they join the large group of soldiers already in the wood. Several vehicles are parked there, including – this is hard to believe – three assault guns and seven armoured vehicles, and they are ready for action. It looks like some sort of organised resistance might still be possible so I decide to wait with the others to see what happens.

Scattered remnants of several divisions are assembling at this spot, most of them from the Feldherrnhalle Corps, including our 18th Panzergrenadier Division. In a vain attempt to find some of my men in the confusion, I come across an empty artillery tractor from the 2nd Battery, but I didn't know at the time that the remains of my 1st Battery had been attached to it. Many years later their commander, Captain Grunwald, told me: 'I took over a shambles,' he said, 'and it only lasted a day.' Then in the chaos he too lost touch with his battery and like me had an awfully long journey ahead of him.

Late in the afternoon the dark screen of smoke and dust breaks up and the sun reappears. Now too the enemy fighters can return to their work. We hear the droning in the distance and then they arrive. We are expecting an attack and watch their approach, and suddenly we see lots of package-shaped objects drop from their fuselages. At first we think they are bombs and want to throw ourselves under cover, but then, after falling a short way, these packages, still high in the sky, release thousands of individual objects that slowly float down swaying in the wind. Leaflets!

Until now we had laughed at the loudspeaker propaganda, but now after about two weeks without any news and with only rumours to go on, we eagerly grasp the leaflets, wanting to know at last what is happening and what the enemy has to say about it. This time he doesn't need to use any propaganda tricks – he doesn't have to make up stories and tell clumsy lies because the bare facts put the craziest lies in the shade.

We discover that the whole of Army Group Centre has been smashed to pieces, not only the 4th Army, to which we had formerly belonged, but the 3rd Panzer Army, the 9th Army and the 2nd Army, though only a part of the left wing had been involved. It is a catastrophe far greater than Stalingrad where the 6th Army went under. In the leaflet the talk is of colossal losses in dead and prisoners, and after what we have experienced, there is no reason to doubt it. Many generals have been killed or been taken prisoner. In order to prove this, the commander of the 12th Infantry Division, Lieutenant General Bamler, who defended the strongpoint of Mogilev, is shown in a photograph sitting at a table with Russian officers. We are surrounded and there is no hope of help – we have been abandoned.

Under these circumstances, we read, there is only one way to save our lives – surrender, then captivity. Passes will be provided and good treatment and all kinds of other promises are made.

But we don't want to surrender because we don't believe what the leaflets say about how we would be treated – in the past the opposite has happened.

Many have not survived capture, especially the wounded. On the way to a prisoner collecting point or to a transit camp they are shot because they are injured, sick or exhausted. An NKVD (formerly GPU) officer was asked about this by a Russian-speaking fellow prisoner and he got the cynical reply that the very long distance to the transportation point was not unreasonable.

If this big cauldron between here, Minsk and the Beresina was mopped up by partisan units in the next few days, then thousands of wounded would lose their lives. Similar action would be taken by the enemy pilots who had earned their reputation as 'butchers' by diving down and firing their machine guns at overfilled dressing stations and collection points for the wounded. Quite rightly the commander of the 25th Panzergrenadier Division, Lieutenant General Schurmann, had given the doctor who had been left behind with the many wounded who were incapable of marching a letter in which he had appealed to the soldiery sympathy of the Soviet commander. But the Red Army had other priorities and left the field to the partisans who completed the task, for there is no information about the wounded surviving in the Minsk kettle.

No, we will not voluntarily submit to imprisonment – that is what almost all of us think. We have not fought our way through for weeks with the greatest difficulties and heavy casualties only to throw down our weapons. No, never!

In a few hours' time, in the evening, we will break out, and we believe we will soon get to our own lines which must be somewhere nearby.

While I still have the chance I make my way through the wood, hoping to come across members of my battery or at least to find some sign of them, but all I see are strange faces and units, and naturally they are mainly concerned with their own problems. In these circumstances – and because I am wearing a basic uniform without badges of rank – no one pays me much attention, and I can't repeatedly explain my rank and appearance. Although I feel isolated and confused about what will happen next, I keep going.

In a clearing near an airstrip I see a large number of guns, light and heavy field howitzers, two 10cm guns and a 21cm mortar. The breech-locks of most of the guns have been removed and the barrels have been blown out so they stick up into the sky in all directions. Although I've seen so much destroyed equipment over the last few days, this sight really upsets me.

Clouds of smoke are drawing across the sky and that is probably why enemy aircraft appear only now and then. Perhaps the pilots think they have done their job here and are seeking new targets elsewhere.

I use the lull to look for pieces of kit because in the artillery tractor I lost everything apart from my machine pistol. First, I find a field cap – it is at least a size too small so it looks quite comical – then, most important, a field flask without a cup which has been dented but seems to be intact, and finally another rifle grenade which I stick in the pocket of my overalls intending to use it like an egg grenade if I have to.

Then I go to the edge of a wood where I get a good view of the terrain and the many troops from the Feldherrnhalle Division who have gathered there.

Slowly it begins to get dark. We have been told that at about 10 p.m. a breakout attempt will be made in a south-westerly direction in order not to get too close to Minsk and its environs where strong enemy forces are to be found. Everyone is happy that at last we are going to do something positive. The agonising suspense gives way to a sense of relief.

Our morale is not broken, despite the unusually heavy air attacks that have caused so many casualties over the last few days and devastating bombardment which has just hit us. Since then things have improved, and when I look into the faces of the men, I see that the strong-minded ones are looking ahead with quiet determination although they understand how stressful the next few hours will be. Many of them will not survive the night, but each individual hopes he will be spared and realises that there is no choice but to risk everything.

Even while we are preparing to break out there is an incident that claims a victim. Suddenly in a nearby wood smoke rockets, which must have been set off by the burning trees, explode with a deafening noise and climb in a zigzag pattern, then fall like comets from the sky. Some of them explode in our assembly area, but we have experienced much worse and don't worry too much about what has happened.

Late in the evening the assault group, faintly illuminated by the smoke-covered full moon, begins to form up slowly. Approximately 1,000 men have been drawn together from the remains of several of the divisions I've already mentioned and they are joined by men from other units that have found their way here during the day. They get ready for what will probably be the final decisive attack.

We all know that in a breakout attempt like this casualties can't be cared for, so anyone who is wounded will be left where they are – they won't be taken along.

While we are absolutely determined to fight with all our strength to get out of the trap, to survive and see our homeland again, we also realise the full extent of the catastrophe we have been caught up in. As the front is driven further back and the Eastern Territory becomes the first line of defence, we are more than ever prepared to defend our homeland in any circumstances. As we get ready for action, thoughts like these go through our minds.

Yesterday in another part of the cauldron survivors of the shattered 78th Assault Division sang the *Deutschlandlied* as they made their break-out attempt and nine days ago, on 28 June, many thousands sang *O Deutschland hoch in Ehren* as they tried to breakout from Bobruysk. I am also reminded of the battle at Langemark on 10 November 1914, during the First World War, in which young volunteers ran unquestioningly and with brave hearts into enemy fire. The line '*Dulce et decorum est, Pro patria mori*' describes their conduct so well.

There is nothing '*dulce*' or 'sweet' about the course of the war against the Soviet Union in the summer of 1944 and the singing of these songs about love for the fatherland fails to distract us from gnawing doubts and bleak forebodings.

We are now ready to march and slowly this mixed 'battle group' – as it is still called – moves off. The assault guns go in front and the remaining trucks, packed with the wounded who can't walk, in the middle, and the tanks drive on either side to give support. Once again I feel part of an organised, battle-worthy unit.

The full moon, darkened now and then by passing clouds of smoke, enables us to see where we are going, but it also helps the enemy to see us while remaining under cover. He can hear the engine noise of our vehicles at a great distance and has plenty of time to get ready for us, and we don't know when and where he will open fire.

For about half an hour we advance unhindered, bypassing patches of woodland, and soon many of us believe with relief that we have found a hole in the enclosing ring. But then the first shots fall near us and seconds afterwards, without waiting for any orders, from our slowly moving column an absolute storm of shouting breaks out, a wild, elemental 'hurrah' from a thousand throats – something indescribable, which I've never experienced before. Everyone shouts out what he felt – the will to survive, the destruction of the enemy, the determination not to be taken prisoner, and hatred, rage and despair. All of these feelings burst out in this frightful 'Hurrah!' The attack was driven forward by this intense anger and it swept us along so we forgot every danger and focused on a single aim. It is unbelievable what one is capable of if one is driven into a corner and forced to fight for existence!

The Soviets defend themselves bitterly, not yielding a metre. They are confident they will win following their recent string of successes, and they do everything they can to prevent our breakthrough. The overwhelming fire from machine guns, mortars and anti-tank guns causes us heavy losses. There are dreadful scenes when a truck overfilled with wounded gets a direct hit and breaks apart. The survivors cry out to us – they want us to carry them, although they know that it is impossible. One of them swears at his comrades as they storm past: 'You dogs, I want to come with you!', and the sound of the screams and shouts is even worse than the enemy fire. No one can help the wounded and we know that anyone who is left here will die.

Burning with the anger and hatred that has been bottled up inside us, we throw ourselves wildly at every enemy we can identify in the moonlight, and then, suddenly, we are through – we've done it, but with enormous casualties.

In order to be sure of getting away I run on for quite a distance with a small group, then we stop, breathless and exhausted, and lie down for a time in a field. Totally shattered and still under the spell of this mad dash, I drop head first onto the furrows, pressing my hot forehead onto the wonderfully cool and moist earth, and slowly I begin to grasp that I have got through this macabre scenario unhurt. I can't quite believe it.

However, we cannot allow ourselves a longer pause for rest, as we find ourselves in no man's land, and reckon the Soviets will search the area.

'Come on lads,' urges one of the comrades, 'up towards the homeland!'

Although it was a bright, moonlit night, nothing can be seen of our battle group – none of the assault guns, armoured vehicles and trucks carrying the many wounded. Where are they? Have they all been shot up? We don't know and suspect that, as a result of the fighting, the column has broken up and the scattered elements have been pushed further apart. Nor can anything be seen of the enemy. Could his losses have been so high that he is incapable of taking action against us? Have we hit him really hard? Or is he holding off until daylight? Midnight has still not passed and so there are several hours to wait.

'There should be signs of the main front line,' someone says, 'flares, shots or something else.'

But we don't see anything that indicates we are close to it.

'Surely we will reach it tomorrow – it can't be far away', I reply, firmly convinced that I've worked out our position correctly. So, tomorrow will be the big day!

We go on slowly, in a silent and thoughtful mood, without suspecting that we are right at the beginning of an ordeal just as merciless anything we have experienced so far.

7 July

In the hours between midnight and dawn we have used all the available cover as we have moved further west. As soon as it is daylight men from the battle group that had split up during the breakout come back together and, when we reach the Minsk–Bobruysk road towards noon, we are about 250-men strong. Suddenly two Soviet tanks roar past us at nearly top speed going in a westerly direction, without the least indication of attacking. Presumably they have used up their ammunition, as otherwise many of us would have ended our march there. Yet, it is also possible that German soldiers have captured the tanks – which does not happen very often – and now are driving west in the hope that they can get back quickly and safely to our own lines, provided, of course, they have enough fuel on board.

As we march on we suddenly come under strong fire from a village on high ground. Immediately we attack it and take it, but we don't stay there – we only have one overriding aim which is to reach our front line.

During the course of the day other groups break through the cauldron in different places and join us so our number grows to about 500 men, and we even have several armoured personnel carriers and trucks. We start to move quickly again, as on the previous days in the intense heat. Exhausted, I sit on the running board of one of the crowded vehicles. After a few kilometres we stumble on the enemy again – this time three trucks of a supply unit. The Soviets are completely surprised, having mistaken us in the dust for one of their own units, and they are shot up by our armoured personnel carriers. This small, successful action renews our confidence, but of course in the long run it is totally irrelevant.

A little later we come into hill country and the Swislotsch River which flows on to Minsk about 20km to the north of our position. We approach a destroyed bridge and then, as anticipated, the first shots ring out. The enemy is occupying a high ridge not far from the east bank and everyone thinks this is their main line of defence, as was the case with the Dnepr and the Beresina. Almost immediately, without anyone having given the order, the 500 men in our group make a decisive attack, racing with wild cries of 'Hurrah!' towards the high ridge. I have never witnessed an attack as fierce as this and nor have the Soviets who were clearly in a weaker position than we imagined – they were very quickly overcome. But the main front line we were expecting to find is nowhere to be seen.

Just as this attack has finished anti-tank and artillery fire from behind our position starts to hit us. The bridge, which is already too badly damaged to be used by vehicles, is a target and we can't cross it. Suddenly there's a shout: 'Russian tanks!' From behind one of the hills the sound of tracks can be heard, and then the firing begins. The very first shot explodes at a spot where a large group had gathered, with devastating effect. The tank – fortunately there was only one – fires a few times, then vanishes, but the shelling of the bridge continues undiminished. Some soldiers get over the river on exposed pebbles, but on the other bank they are forced to lie prone on ground because there is no cover.

Hours pass and we make no progress. The only hope is to cross elsewhere, and we find a stretch of the river where we can wade through, though we are up to our chests in the water. We try to bring the vehicles across to the other bank, but this is only possible with the smaller ones. The armoured personnel carriers and trucks get stuck in the river. Desperate attempts are made to pull them up onto the land, but they fail as the ropes break, and they have to be abandoned. Again we come under fire and again we have to leave several comrades lying there. I pass a spot where someone has buried a man in great haste so his boots are sticking out of the sand heap. It is seldom possible to bury the dead properly during this period – most must stay where they fell and, in the great heat, they quickly start to decompose.

Leaving a giant cloud of dust behind us, we drag ourselves over the dried-up fields and after a few kilometres reach the Minsk–Bobruysk railway line, which we cross without any enemy interference. The heat and dust parch our throats and when we come to a swamp of brown, bitter moor water, everyone drinks mug after mug of it without thinking what the results could be.

We assemble before a road leading to the west and are joined by more stragglers, mainly from the 9th Army which had held the front line in this area. With them they have various vehicles including a few tanks which is amazing given the scale of the disaster. They represent the remains of the 20th Panzer Division, our 'fire brigade', which had confronted the enemy around Bobruysk and Paritshi and had been forced back from there. They have now landed up with us and can be a great help, at least as long as the fuel lasts.

Since we dare not show ourselves during daylight, our enlarged group conceals itself in woodland, planning to move on at night. We come across fallen German soldiers who in view of their condition have been lying there for several days, and we conclude that the font line must be further to the west. We take the dead men's identity discs and bury them in rough and ready fashion. To be safe from surprises, sentries are put in position everywhere as many hours must pass before the march can be resumed.

During the afternoon the commander-in-chief of the 4th Army, General of Infantry von Tippelskirch, puts out a last radio message conveying his 'undying thanks for our bravery and heroism'. But we don't have any radio reception so his expression of gratitude is left unheard in the ether.

Slowly the day draws to an end. We divide ourselves into 3 groups of about 150 men which will be more difficult for the Soviets to find. They are looking everywhere for the remains of the battered divisions of Army Group Centre trying to fight their way out to the west. The group I belong to has an armoured truck with a 2cm four-barrelled anti-aircraft gun and a VW amphibious car. The tanks have gone – apparently they have had to be abandoned. Before we break off the last of the food is distributed. All I have left from yesterday are a few biscuits from a pack of front-line rations. Now, along with a comrade, I'm given a tin of sardines in brine and a small piece of bread. Then we march off.

The night is cool and damp, which is pleasant after the intense heat of the day. After leaving the wood the route goes through a marsh. The two vehicles keep getting stuck and repeatedly we have to push and pull them out again. A thick haze means our column is difficult to spot. We are marching as quickly as our strength and the terrain allow. Despite the coolness of the night, the sweat is soon running from all my pores and as the kilometres pass I feel more and more unwell. The bowel infection, which I had been suffering from for four days and which had appeared to improve, suddenly makes itself felt again. Probably it was made worse by the marsh water I'd drunk and by the cold, damp air. At last we reach a village and lie down for a short rest. We find a well which contains water that appears to be wonderfully clean so far as we can tell in the moonlight and, at first, after this refreshment, I feel much better again.

Ahead of us flares are climbing high, but there is no indication of a front line approaching. The flares are signals for the Russian aircraft that constantly criss-cross the area, some of them flying so low that one can clearly make out the silhouettes of the pilots. Our march has speeded up and we have already covered around 10km. My strength is failing and I am so exhausted that I would like to throw myself down on the spot, but anyone who gets left behind can just as well write his will, so I gather all my energy and keep going. Soon this stage of the march will be over, and fortunately we do not know what lies ahead of us.

8 July

In the morning we reach another river, the Ptitsch. Nearby there is a bridge which to our great relief is completely intact, so we cross quickly to the other side. As the daylight is coming, as soon as possible we must find a large wood where we can hide. A short time after crossing the river we come to a small village and, as we get closer, we are fired at. Since we think this might be the last obstacle before the main front line – and it might be part of it – we immediately go into the attack. To reach the houses around 300m of open ground have to be crossed, but with a loud 'Hurrah' we rush forward and the first casualties fall. The hurrahs get weaker and more sporadic and die out just as the edge of the village is reached. Then, as we enter it, the game really gets going. A raging fire hits us from all the houses. An anti-tank gun is firing at short range in the village street with devastating effect.

Our attempt to overrun the village without letting it become a house-to-house fight has proved impossible, and now everyone is desperately seeking a way out of this cauldron. With a small group I rush in wild flight to take shelter under a bank covered with numerous fruit trees, then run as quickly as I can, zigzagging through the trees in order to make myself a difficult target for the enemy and to elude the anti-tank gunfire. A soldier near me cries out: 'I think they have shot the sack off me!' 'Keep running, man!' I call out to him and push him forward. After a few hundred metres, completely out of breath, we get to a small river, apparently a tributary of the Ptitsch. At first thick bushes that extend along the whole river bank provide sufficient cover, but bit by bit more stragglers find their way here and there isn't enough cover for them all.

For a good half hour I lie still, not knowing what will happen next. There is no sign of the front line we are still hoping to reach. Suddenly, while I am mulling over our situation, frightful screaming comes from the village. The Soviets – actually the partisans – have begun shooting our wounded. It is deeply shattering having to listen to their desperate calls for help and the dry sound of the shots without knowing what to do to save them. This confirms yet again that anyone who is taken prisoner, especially by the partisans, has a minimal chance of survival and anyone who can't walk has no chance at all.

We want to get away from here as soon as possible, but in daylight that is very difficult. To at least put some distance between us and the partisan village, we creep with the greatest care through the cover of the bushes along the bank of the river, which is about 5m wide and fast flowing. Then, close by, a hoarse voice calls out: 'German soldiers, come out, you will be well treated!' I jump into the river with a single movement, standing up to my neck in the water, holding the machine pistol high with an outstretched arm. Then the strong current catches me, dragging me downstream, and the machine pistol goes under the water, but seconds later I reach the other bank and find cover under thick brushwood. I crawl on as quickly as possible and I am very relieved to come across a group of comrades – I don't want to be left on my own here. My soaking wet clothing is absolutely of no consequence.

A short while later the hoarse voice shouts again: 'German soldiers, come out, you will be well treated!' Naturally none of us would even dream of responding to the invitation, particularly after having just seen what 'good treatment' looks like. But the fellow is slowly getting impatient, firing at random into the bushes and calling out increasingly unpleasantly, 'Come on, come out!'

Apparently a small unit is searching the brushwood, expecting to find just a few stragglers. As we are lying behind the bushes that line either side of the river, we feel fairly safe and can watch the partisans moving about through the twigs. Then some of them come threateningly close to our hiding place and we are scared of being discovered. Although in the circumstances we should have kept quiet and avoided fighting, we react by knocking some of them down with a few well-aimed shots, whereupon the remainder dash away in wild flight.

Carefully we withdraw for a few hundred metres along the river bank, expecting that stronger forces will be brought in to look for us. More stragglers join us so that finally our group grows to about 100 men.

In order to counter an eventual attack, we organise ourselves roughly for defence and keep permanent watch on the partisan village a kilometre away with the few pairs of binoculars we have. We have about 10 hours to hold out until nightfall and during that time we are likely to be attacked. But the time passes and nothing happens. We conclude that there are no regular troops in the area. Instead there are well-organised partisans who, as usual, will only attack when they can see no alternative, and that is not the case here.

A main road runs near the village and considerable traffic passes in both directions. Many of the trucks on the road are of American origin.

Their engines produce, especially at high speeds, a singing sound quite different to that of the Russian ones. Since so many vehicles are rolling past in such an unmolested way we get the impression we are deep in the enemy's hinterland, and it is just as well that we don't realise how far. We also don't know that on this day – 8 July – the Soviets captured the railway junction of Baranowicze – that is about 130km south-west of the clump of bushes in which we had hidden ourselves – and their tanks had already left the town behind them. We still hoped to reach the front in a few hours – here or a few kilometres further on.

For a while everything's quiet, so we have a chance to talk. The soldiers around me come from various units and I get the impression that hardly any of them know each other. Lying near me is a group of four officers, Lieutenant Niedermeier, Second Lieutenants Janasiak and Bauer and Senior Veterinary Officer Richert. We discuss our critical situation and what we should do next, and we agree that we are deeper in the enemy rear than we supposed and will have to continue marching for a few more days. We know that it will soon be impossible for us to continue unnoticed and undisturbed unless we move under the cover of darkness. First we need to decide what we should do in the next few hours. Even if the partisans do not attack us, there is still a chance a Soviet search team will finds us and if it does our dream of escaping will be over because none of us have anti-tank weapons. We decide to get moving once it is dark enough and hope to be left in peace until then.

Second Lieutenant Bauer hands me a small chit with his home address and asks me to inform his parents should anything happen to him. He also passes to me a small map of Russia, as he suspects that he won't require it for much longer. I put the note inside the folded map to protect it from moisture, and then give him my parents' address.

I use the silence to get my wet compass working and clean the mechanism of my machine pistol. It strikes me as strange, but at this moment I regard it as my best friend. Slowly it becomes dark and we prepare ourselves to march off. One of the soldiers gives me his binoculars without my having asked, and they turn out to be very useful.

Then it is time to go, and from all sides men emerge and start to move. First the main road has to be crossed. As the traffic has diminished considerably with dusk falling, we manage this without any great difficulty. A sentry spots us and immediately opens fire with his machine pistol. Although he was quickly dealt with, some of our men are lightly wounded.

After we had put several kilometres behind us without further incident, a small, friendly looking village comes into sight in the moonlight. However, experience has made us wary and so at first we stay some distance away in a field with our weapons ready to fire. For a long time we observe the village, tensely taking note of every sound, but don't see anything suspicious.

We could bypass the village, but we decide not to because we have a new problem to deal with – we need to find food for a hundred men who have hardly anything to eat. Most of the supplies carried during the retreat were lost during the fighting and almost everything that was left over has been consumed, including the last 'iron rations'. During the last few days, in the intense heat and dust, we haven't eaten much – we have been more concerned to quench our burning thirst. The experience of the retreat, in particular the battle in the cauldron and the penetrating smell of putrefaction, has been so traumatic that we lost our appetites. Now though it is clear that food is essential if we are to retain our strength and so we decide to go into the village despite the risk involved. Second Lieutenant Janasiak assembles a few men and I join them as I am now extremely hungry.

We creep up to some houses with great care. Everything is dead quiet, no movement, absolutely no sound. The first house is empty and abandoned, and contains nothing that we are looking for, but the next one is occupied. We knock at the door gently. It opens with a grating sound and in front of us stands a woman. To our surprise she invites us to come in and take a seat. We are simply speechless, having reckoned on being greeted by rifle fire. Hesitantly and still distrustful, we sit around the table that takes up almost half of the room. Soon, however, all doubts vanish as the farmer's wife bring us bread and honey and, for each of us, a container of fresh milk. Greedily we consume these delicious items and are immediately in the best of moods. A comrade who can speak a bit of Russian starts a conversation and immediately there is mutual understanding. Unfortunately, we do not have much time, so we quickly eat the bread, fill our field flasks with milk and leave the welcoming house with profound thanks.

As we wanted to bring something back for the comrades waiting in front of the village, we go into the next farmstead and discover a few sheep, and we take one of them. A soldier hoists it onto his shoulders and reminds me of the famous marble statue from Ancient Greece of a man carrying a sheep. The sheep doesn't appreciate this learned comparison and bleats loudly and continuously, threatening to arouse the whole village. As the soldier takes the sheep off his shoulders, apparently intending to kill it with a bayonet, it tears itself free and rushes off. Although this worthwhile piece of booty has got away, I am actually pleased the poor sheep has escaped, perhaps because I have already been in a similar situation.

As we reach the middle of the village, a completely unexpected short and harsh 'Stop!' startles us, immediately followed by a shot. As quick as lightening we turn on our heels, race down the village street, go over a fence and lie down in the darkness of the night just like the sheep. As soon as we can after this incident, we rejoin the waiting battle group in front of the village. Luckily no one has been hurt and we resume our march. The episode reminds us how careful we have to be even when at first we are received in a friendly way.

Shortly afterwards we reach a small river, apparently the same one that we had stopped beside during the day. It runs in the direction of our march and there are many small and large meanders in its course, but we must try to avoid having to cross it repeatedly. We look out for a bridge but can't find one. Then we discover by moonlight a wide plank over a narrow stretch and, walking with great care, in single file, we move over it.

Soon afterwards on the other bank of the river we have to go over a high ridge and we are not quite over it when suddenly we are hit by fire from machine pistols. Immediately everyone lies flat or hurries back down the slope. Quickly I get together a handful of nearby men in order to attack the enemy from the flank. Under the cover of small bushes we can get close to the summit of the hill, but after that there is open ground. Just then we were spotted. Several hand grenades explode in front of us, the last one right by my feet. I feel my head has been torn off, and have stabbing pains in my throat, on the left shoulder, the left lower arm and the right hand. I reel back a few steps, but dare not lie down because I fear not being able to get up again. For a moment I believe what has happened is only a dream, but then I say to myself: you are still standing, don't weaken now, carry on – iron determination!

Carefully I feel my neck which is bleeding heavily. The binoculars on my chest look like a big lump of blood. Hold on, I tell myself – it can't be long before I get medical attention. Slowly I go up to the top of the hill past the two dead Russians who had thrown the hand grenades. Now they lie next to their telephone apparatus, dealt with by my comrades in close-quarter combat. Clearly they were manning an observation post with the task of reporting groups of stragglers who are doubtless being sought everywhere near the front line.

Where are the rest of our men? I find them a bit further on where they are forming up again to continue the march. The route is now apparently open and, walking faster than before, we try to escape from this dangerous area. My strength is flagging and I need all my will power to keep up. I can't ask anyone to look after me as that would put the whole group at risk, and the others probably can't see my condition in the darkness. Many wounded, sick or exhausted soldiers in such circumstances choose to remain behind, and sooner or later in all probability that is the end of them.

A burning thirst torments me and very carefully I take a drink of milk from my water bottle. Swallowing is extremely painful and I break out in much sweat, and I wonder if my gullet has been injured. Later the pain of swallowing gets worse and I can't take in any solid food. My voice also fails me – I'm reduced to a harsh croaking. Keep going, I tell myself, just don't fall behind – soon it will be over,

Had I known about the ordeal that lay ahead of me, I would have given up all hope, but luckily I didn't know and none of us knew because it was unimaginable.

As we can't find a road that goes roughly in a westerly direction, we are obliged to go across country through meadows and cornfields. I long for a short rest, but we have to keep going as quickly as possible as we have no time to lose – the night will soon be over and there is nowhere nearby to hide in daylight. Finally, we reach a small patch of woodland in which we immediately conceal ourselves. We are just in time because dawn is beginning to break.

9 July

This rest in the shady wood is wonderful and, if the situation allows, we won't leave until dark. I have time to look at my wounds properly and to treat them in so far as I can without my first-aid kit, which was lost with my uniform jacket. In my throat above the larynx I can feel near the soft gums a pea-sized hole and close to it another smaller one. A splinter is sticking into my right cheek – I hadn't noticed before. Luckily it has gone into the skin without hitting the teeth. The other wounds, in the shoulder and right forearm, seem to be harmless, although they hurt a lot. In any case I can move my right arm without too much difficulty and the bones don't seem to be damaged. Finally, my right index finger has been hit and is difficult to move.

From a comrade I get a small gauze bandage. It is not large enough to cover all the wounds so I bandage only my throat, lower arm and finger. Sceptically he watches me and appears to ask himself how long I will be able to march along like this – until I fall over, old chap, I think to myself.

Once I've tended to my wounds as best I can, I lie down under a pine tree and try to sleep a bit. The pain from the wound in my throat is so acute that I can hardly close my eyes. Eventually I find a position to lie in that reduces the pain and I get a few hours of troubled sleep. All of us – but me especially – have only one wish – that is, to be left in peace there.

Fortunately, the day goes by without incident. When it is dark enough – at this time of year, depending on the weather and the phase of the moon, between 10 and 11 p.m. – we can form up into long columns and move off towards the west.

During the course of the day in the cool wood I've recovered to some extent and can again keep up with the march. Yet, I still have to make a considerable effort not to fall behind when we cross challenging terrain – over low hills, for instance, and through marshland where the track rarely goes in the right direction.

With great relief I realise the wound in my neck is not too serious since I can swallow better and speak more clearly with every hour, and also the pain has noticeably decreased. Apparently, the difficulties I've had have been caused by a large swelling that is slowly beginning to reduce. Now what I have to do is keep the wounds as clean as possible in order to avoid infection, which under the current circumstances is not easy. For a time I am elated as I seem to have overcome the worst effects of my injuries and I begin to fully understand how fortunate I have been. Anyone who has survived a hand-grenade explosion at such a short a distance can hold his head high if they are still capable of marching. I had been incredibly lucky to get away with it.

10 July

In the early morning while it is still dark we reach the Minsk–Baranowicze railway line and, although we are completely worn out, climb to the top of the very steep railway embankment. Immediately afterwards we enter an extensive swamp through which a wide and apparently deep river makes its way.

About a kilometre away we see a large patch of woodland which we need to get to in time to conceal ourselves for the day. After we had searched in vain for a bridge over the river or a footpath that would lead us to the wood, and as it was becoming dangerously light, we are obliged to wade across the stream where it is just about passable, with the water up to our thighs. Some of our comrades are really hampered because they can't decide where to make the crossing.

Second Lieutenant Janasiak, an infantryman par excellence, and unmistakably the leading man in our battle group, orders that everyone on that side of the stream should remain hidden there all day in the thick but wet bushes. Only after dark should they join the rest of us in the wood. But predictably none of them want to remain there for fear of losing contact with us so, one after the other, they come across the open ground towards the wood in the growing daylight. In the wood they are greeted in a most unfriendly manner because now our chances of spending a quiet restful day are much reduced.

Immediately sentries are posted to keep watch from the edges of the wood, while the rest of us stretch out on the damp moss further in among the trees. We are soaked through, freezing and exhausted from the exertion of marching through such difficult terrain. Most of us sink quickly into a deep sleep.

But after a few hours we are woken by shots and shouts, and immediately everyone is on their feet. The sentries storm past and report that a troop of Red Army soldiers is approaching the wood. As we feared, we had been spotted the day before, and the brown uniforms of the Soviet soldiers are already closing in on us. Soon they open fire with roars and yells. But fortunately there aren't many of them. They have underestimated our strength and, as we are on the edge of the wood, we are in a much better position than they are. They don't seem to have a plan for the attack or care about casualties, and they are completely annihilated after a short battle.

A few of us are lightly wounded, but Second Lieutenant Bauer's wound is serious. He has been hit in the lower leg, his shinbone and fibula are smashed and he can't walk. This unfortunate chap is suffering fearful pain and is carried off by four comrades deeper into the wood. In normal circumstances he would have been taken to a field hospital and, at worst, his leg might have been amputated, but he would survive. In this situation, though, treatment is impossible.

For the moment we have nothing to fear, but no doubt the Soviets will come back later with stronger forces. Some of the comrades lie down at once to sleep, but many start collecting the large blueberries which are readily available in the wood in order to satisfy their gnawing hunger. We all know that food is going to be very difficult to find especially if we come up against partisans and regular Red Army soldiers as we have just done.

I feel I must go to see to Second Lieutenant Bauer because I know what it is like to be wounded. I am horrified to think of what would have become of me if the hand grenade had smashed my legs – it is amazing that didn't happen.

On the way I come across a badly wounded Red Army soldier. He lies fully stretched out on his stomach. He has been shot in the chest and his breath is rattling in short bursts. His back, under a foamy blood-soaked uniform shirt, rises and falls weakly with his breathing. I would help this defenceless enemy if I only could, but there is really nothing I can do. Perhaps he will be found in time, I think, and I go on towards the moaning sound which indicates where Second Lieutenant Bauer is lying.

He is tossing from one side to another with the pain. I try to console him and give him hope, although I don't believe in what I am saying. He asks me not to forget to write to his parents should I get through in one piece. He knows he cannot take another step and, if we take him with us and get caught up in another battle, he would have to be left behind. He does not want to be a burden to us, he says, and assures me he is not afraid of death, but the thought of ending up like a piece of meat or being massacred by the partisans is unbearable. And for me it is unbearable that we cannot do anything to save this wounded comrade. At such moments so many of my beliefs seem to go down the drain and I doubt the all values I have been taught.

In the late afternoon the sentries report suspicious noises in the vicinity. We grab our weapons and take cover. I lie well camouflaged in one of the bushes with Second Lieutenant Janasiak. We are determined to get through this whatever happens – we understand each other well – and now I simply address him as 'Jonny', which is what he is usually called by the soldiers in his company.

As expected, this time the Soviets come in greater numbers. They attack from the side through the wood, approaching our camp using the cover of the trees and undergrowth. As we have to be extremely economical with our ammunition, we let them get very close before we open fire. Suddenly a Red Army soldier appears standing in front of our bush. Like lightning Jonny raises his machine pistol, but it jams and makes a clicking sound. Then the Ivan notices us. He stares at us wide-eyed and horrified for a moment, then vanishes with a loud cry and an Olympic-like jump into the undergrowth. Probably only then did he realise how close he had come to death. My bandaged trigger finger prevented me from shooting at him, and it would have been pointless anyway to fire and waste ammunition.

In order to avoid being surrounded, we retreat further into the wood. As we go past Second Lieutenant Bauer, he makes a last desperate attempt to get up and come with us, but collapses after only a few paces. Acknowledging the hopelessness of his situation, he asks us to leave him with a pistol. Silently he looks at us and then Senior Veterinary Officer Richert gives him his weapon. We move off without speaking and immediately afterwards hear the crack of a shot. The noise stuns me, almost as if I'd been shot myself. During the day several other wounded soldiers took the same decision as Bauer.

The enemy are so close and the darkness is coming on so we have to leave the wood in a hurry and have no time to bury our dead comrade in peace. Luckily, without being seen, we manage to conceal ourselves in a large cornfield nearby, and we hope no one will suspect we are there. Until nightfall we are really tense, but nothing happens, and at that point we can say we've had the good fortune to extricate ourselves from an extremely awkward situation.

Our experience over the last few days makes us realise how difficult it will be for a combat group of this size to get through enemy occupied territory. It is easy to spot us and, in a crisis, so many men are difficult to manage.

The main problem, though, is finding food for almost a hundred men, and we decide to divide up into groups of about twenty. We stop briefly in a large dip in the ground where we can't be seen so we can organise this. There were disagreements during the process. Some soldiers couldn't decide which group to join, others wanted to join a group that was already full. Since the situation was so serious, a few men, who had not shown the best side of their characters, had to accept an outcome they weren't happy with. All of us had come together by chance, hardly any of us know each other, and many can't come to terms with the circumstances they find themselves in. Also, we recognise that a man who isn't fully committed to keeping going could easily become a problem for all of us.

Finally, however, the men sort themselves out and then the individual groups set off in different directions, towards the north-west, west and south-west, in order to put some distance between them. Soon the advantage of being in a smaller groups becomes apparent. The marching tempo is clearly faster, although, because of the rough terrain, only a moderate pace can be maintained. In my group we stick together so we can take action quickly and effectively if necessary, and since there are only thirty of us we feel more closely attached to each other.

The night of 10/11 July is clear and moonlit, and we have the luck to come across a field path that runs exactly in a westerly direction so for a long time we make quick progress.

Since our group is so small we must avoid getting into a fight. This is a new situation for us because, until now – and especially in the first days of the breakout from the cauldron – we have confronted the enemy and tried to overrun him. On each occasion we believed we had only one final obstacle to overcome before we reached our own lines and, despite our limitations, we were also confident about our fighting ability. But now we can only make use of our weapons if there is no alternative, and we have to remember that we are running short of ammunition after the encounters of the last 24 hours.

I still have a full magazine for my machine pistol and a few loose cartridges in my backpack as well as the rifle grenade which, in an emergency, could be used as a hand grenade, though it remains to be seen whether it will still work after its bath in the tributary of the Ptitsch.

Our role as soldiers has changed. None of the army manuals and nothing in our experience has prepared us for a retreat through enemy territory. We have to avoid combat situations that we've been trained for and develop completely new skills in order to survive. A soldier's rank is less important now, and this would have been unthinkable in the past. The most important thing is how an individual conducts himself, what qualities he brings with him and how effectively he can make use of them for the good of the group. So, a padre, a doctor and an administrator lead a group in turn, and all three fortunately survive.

Shortly before midnight we come near a village and decide we have no choice but to look for food there. Then some shots ring out, apparently close by. Immediately we throw ourselves down in the furrows of a field, listening and watching. The houses are easy to discern in the moonlight. When everything is quiet again, we decide to continue the quest for food despite the danger involved, and cautiously approach the village.

While some of us keep watch from a distance, the others start to search the houses. If we encounter resistance and are scattered, we plan to assemble at a distant clump of bushes.

I go to the first house with Second Lieutenant Janasiak. Inside we hear agitated whispering and then an old farmer opens the door for us. We are relieved to discover that the only other person there with him in the living room is his wife, and Janasiak and I, in our limited Russian, try to make clear what we want. We get a couple of bits of hard black bread and some potatoes.

Unasked, the farmer's wife brings us a jug of delicious milk and with little gulps we refresh ourselves, quickly eat the bread and then, our strength renewed, leave the farm with hearty words of thanks.

Outside we rejoin our comrades, all of whom have found something to eat. Everyone is in a better mood. Two of them report they have spotted three trucks behind the last houses. 'You have got a nerve!' I say. I'm angry with them because farmers couldn't own one truck, let alone three, so they could only be only be Soviet military vehicles – which explains the shots we heard before we entered the village. But why had the Soviets let us eat our food in peace? Perhaps there are so few of them they didn't dare to attack us? Whatever the case, we leave the village very quickly, picking up on the way the soldiers from our group who had stayed on guard outside the village. Then, after making a detour to mislead possible pursuers, we march off towards the west.

In order to get hold of more food, we decide to search in the next village we come across. When we see it lying before us in the moonlight, it is still just dark enough to take the risk of approaching it. Carefully we creep up to it, crossing a wooden bridge over a little stream on tiptoe, and then we lie down on the edge of the village under the cover of a big bush. Then the soldiers who had acted as sentries at the previous village very cautiously go up to the first house and return soon afterwards with a sack of potatoes that they had found in a shed. Since dawn is breaking, we have to break off the search at this point. We turn away from the village and quickly find a wood to hide in. Before full daylight, we light a fire making use of dry wood that gives off very little smoke, and we cook the potatoes in it. Each of us gets four of them. This is the first hot food we have had in a long time so we are really happy about it, and I am particularly pleased because, despite my injuries, I now know I can keep up with the others.

After setting sentries for the night we lie down on the soft but damp ground in the wood to rest. We reckon we have made better progress than expected towards the west even though the many detours we've had to make lead us to overestimate the number of kilometres we've covered in that direction.

11 July

The whole day passes without the slightest incident. The wood where we are lying is a large one and we have a good view of the surrounding countryside so we shouldn't be taken by surprise. We have time to think about what we should do next and learn lessons from the experience of the last few days. In future, in order to be more efficient and waste less time obtaining food, we split into four groups of seven to eight men. These small groups can fend for themselves in the villages and they should have a better chance of getting what they need. No one would be left out. Food would be shared with any group that had run out or didn't have enough to keep going.

It was also decided that we would do our searches at least an hour before dawn – at about 2 a.m. – so that there is enough time for us to get way before daylight. So that we could throw off pursuers as quickly as possible, we would choose villages with woods nearby and would only go into houses on the outskirts.

Throughout the course of this quiet day we keep a careful watch, and we take the opportunity to work out exactly where we are. Second Lieutenant Bauer had given me a map which is very helpful even though, because of its small scale, certain inaccuracies have to be assumed.

We reckon we are about 10km south of the Minsk–Rakuv–Volozyn highway, which runs in a north-westerly direction to Vilna, and Minsk is about 30km to the north-east. It is absolutely essential that we don't get too close to this road which is such an important route for the Soviets. On the other side, the vast Nalibocka forest lies not far to the south of our route, but we can't use it as a place to hide because the area is dominated by the partisans.

They are led by the commander-in-chief of the Minsk partisans and 'Hero of the Soviet Union' Alexeivitch Vaupshassov. During the Russian-Polish War of 1920–1 and thereafter he operated under the cover name 'Voloshinov' and he so distinguished himself that he was then sent to Spain to take part in the Spanish Civil War of 1936–9, where he was known as 'Comrade Alfred'. Afterwards he was promoted to major in the Red Army and was active under the name of 'Major Gradov'. What an adventurous career!

Between the woods and highway, both of which we have to avoid, there is a gap of 10 to 20km through which we can move. We are relieved that we have been left alone all day and that we have had a chance to reorganise ourselves and plan ahead, and we wait for the darkness to come so we can set off. We start the march without any trouble, and don't come across any villages. In order to avoid having to constantly check the compass, and since we don't have an obvious landmark in the west to aim for, we work out our direction by following the 'Great Bear' which is clearly visible in the night sky, and we make good progress.

12 July

As usual we are on the look-out for supplies and when we discover an apparently friendly village at the right time in the day we decide to go into it. We pick an assembly point and then, as agreed, we enter the village in groups. We aren't concerned about any of the individual houses since it is clear that no military are to be found there. No vehicles can be seen and the inhabitants don't look like partisans.

My group is not very successful because, apart from some potatoes, there is nothing to take. The small piece of bread that is offered to us we decline to take as the villagers seem to be very poor and not very well fed. There isn't even any of the milk that is usually available, and so we fill our field flasks with wonderful fresh water from the village well and then go back to join the other groups. These had had more luck, their booty being five hens, a quantity of potatoes and plenty of bread.

We are all delighted at the prospect of the forthcoming feast and, after much thought, someone decides we should cook 'Hen in the Pot'. For the pot we are going to use an old metal can that was been found lying around. But before that we must find a wood to hide in as quickly as possible, as daylight is coming.

If we can't reach a wood in time we will have to conceal ourselves in a cornfield which would be much more dangerous. Also in a cornfield we won't be able to light a fire and so our lovely chicken dinner will be out of the question. We are lucky, though, as a few kilometres ahead of us there is a large patch of woodland, and we head for it as fast as we can. At the edge of the wood runs a small stream with delightfully clear water – perfect for chicken soup. A suitable site for our camp is chosen, one that seems just as good as those we've stayed in before. Everyone is in high spirits because of the coming feast, forgetting for a moment how precarious our situation is.

Our morale would have collapsed if we had known that, far to the north-west, Vilna, the capital of Lithuania which had been declared a 'stronghold', has been surrounded for three days and is about to fall, and Lida, where General Field Marshal Model had his headquarters for a few days, has been in Russian hands since 8 July – and Lida is exactly 100km ahead of us. But that is not all, for Soviet tanks have rolled on without meeting appreciable resistance and have taken Memel with their spearheads, so they are now around 200km from where we are cooking our 'Hen in the Pot'!

Of course we hadn't heard about any of this as we are cut off from the news. We depend on the inaccurate and out-of-date information given to us by the villagers who don't get newspapers. They sit silently and report what they have been told by military units that occasionally pass by.

But I must return to what we were doing at our excellent camp. While our expert cooks are preparing the meal, everyone else tries to do something useful. Razors, soap, handkerchiefs, combs and pocket games – which somehow soldiers have managed to keep with them – are produced and distributed. A complete wash is not possible because we must be ready to break off at any time, and that is why we don't remove our boots. As I lost all my kit a week ago when the artillery tractor was destroyed, Lieutenant Niedermeier lends me his razor. A saucepan lid serves as a washbasin and water I take from the stream at the edge of the wood. Then I set about my thick beard, shaving carefully as I don't want the razor to go near the wound in my throat. It feels great to be clean shaven again, and proudly I examine the result in my little borrowed pocket mirror. Afterwards I hand the razor back to Jonny who also has to get rid of a full beard. We can't change the razor blade because we don't have any spares.

Meanwhile, some of the comrades have collected dry wood from the forest for a fire and in a tin can we boil some of the wonderfully clear water from the stream. Our cooks have plucked the chickens, gutted then, cut them up and thrown them into the can of boiling water with plenty of potatoes. One of them even produces some salt which he surrenders in order to give the feast the right flavour. We have only one wish, which is that we be left in peace for the next few hours. As the preparation of the meal is taking some time, I fill my mess tin with blueberries. They grow in abundance in the wood and I think they will make a fine dessert.

Finally, the meal is ready and expectantly we look at the wonderful contents of the can. Everyone gets a mess tin full of broth and a tidy amount of meat and potatoes. What a delight! Seldom has a meal tasted so good.

We have had a good day – we've been lucky enough to find a place where we aren't disturbed by the Russian military or the partisans. After the meal we need rest, so we lie down in our groups in the soft moss, but the sentries stay alert because one never knows what will happen.

Everything remains quiet. A comrade in my group still has a few cigarettes which he offers us and so, after the substantial meal, we get a cigarette too – what more could one want! Then a soldier brings out the playing cards he has been carrying. Soon, with two members of my group, a game of Skat is being thrashed out. In these circumstances, playing a game is a considerable challenge, I think, but probably he is eager to demonstrate he hasn't been defeated and wants to return to normality – and in the bunkers and other crude accommodation we've been used to, a game of cards is as close as he can get to it. Also, who knows what will happen tomorrow, so he's right to enjoy himself while he has the chance.

We chose the site of the camp, which is near the edge of a wood, so we could get to the brook easily, but we now decide to move further back into the trees as it will be some time before we can continue our march. Quickly we find a suitable place thickly surrounded by pines. In order to check the new position is safe, Jonny and I go a few hundred yards further on to the other side of the wood. About half a kilometre away are two small villages just like the ones we have searched before which look friendly in so far as we can tell from a distance.

On the way back as we near our camping place we hear a crackling in the undergrowth, then some subdued voices, and we see through the branches six civilians, men and women, standing stock-still because they have seen us. Immediately we surround them as we have to find out who they are. A comrade who speaks a little Russian asks them what they are doing and they say a cow has run away and they are searching for it.

We believe their story because none of them look like partisans and they are not carrying weapons. They come from one of the two villages that Jonny and I had seen. Eventually, to our great surprise, they ask us to join them for supper with the other villagers. We are not sure how to respond to this unexpected invitation and look at each other quizzically, but we do not want to offend them, so we say yes. Also, we hope this meal in a friendly village means we won't have to take the risk of looking for another meal in a hostile village later on.

In order to reach the village we have to cross around 500m of open ground in daylight, and I was worried that we were being lured into a trap. I kept looking suspiciously at our escorts but couldn't see any sign of hostility.

When we reach the village, as usual we select a meeting place should anything happen, then we split up to visit individual houses. I go with Jonny and Lieutenant Niedermeier and we are greeted at the door of one of the houses by a farmer's wife. We make a show of laying down our weapons and then sit down at the table in the living room. As in most of the houses in the villages, this room serves as both a bedroom and a kitchen, and is poorly furnished but pleasantly clean, which gives us some confidence. In this unusual situation we watch everything that happens around us very carefully indeed. Danger can threaten us at any moment so we are mistrustful and cautious. Here, however, there seems to be no reason for concern. The good woman brings us a jug of fresh milk and some black bread. In return our lieutenant gives her a handful of tobacco, which she receives with the greatest pleasure and makes herself a cigarette with a piece of paper. She rolls the cigarette with remarkable skill.

The conversation soon comes to an awkward halt because neither side understands each other's language, but we manage to communicate without many words. We are impressed by their excellent tobacco – which has a different taste to the local *machorka* – but the high point is the fried eggs which they serve us with some meat. After the meal we are as satisfied as we were after our chicken lunch. We are even given another two eggs and a piece of delicious black bread. We can hardly believe in all this hospitality and we feel at peace and full of good will since we are being treated as normal people rather than enemies who have to be detected and destroyed.

As time is pressing, we start to leave and thank the good-hearted woman many times. She wishes us all the best and then takes us to our meeting point, a meadow at the end of the village. Everyone in our group has eaten well so we are all in the best of spirits. Since a few of our comrades are missing, we lie down on the grass for a while. The ample food has made us lethargic and we would like to sleep but we know that would be reckless even on a day like this which has gone so well – we need to stay alert. When the last of our people turn up they tell us something that confirms the good impression we have had about the village – in a barn they have found an injured soldier who is being hidden there and cared for until he can walk again.

This behaviour only makes sense if the local people had a good relationship with the Wehrmacht during the occupation and a bad one with the Red Army and the partisans. Perhaps also some of the older inhabitants remembered the activities in the nearby Nalibocka forest of Comrade Vaupshassov whose partisans had not exactly made themselves popular during the Russian-Polish War of 1920–1.

Since everyone in our group has returned, we walk back to our woodland camp to wait for darkness. After a few minutes I feel a burning pain in both my feet that makes walking a torment. I hadn't felt anything wrong before. Once we reach the site of the camp, I pull off my boots and look at the damage. Both the heels are badly swollen and inflamed. There are so many holes in my socks that they are practically worthless and I angrily throw them into the bushes, something I would soon bitterly regret.

It is still too light to set off on the march, so we lie down for an hour. While we are waiting three soldiers arrive who, like us, are trying to make their way home. They ask to join us and naturally we agree.

Once it is almost dark, we move on. My feet are so painful that I try at first to walk barefoot, and I tie the laces of the boots together with slip knots and hang them over my shoulder. At first I make better progress than I was expecting because we come to a sandy path and I can pick out every stone. But then the path turns in the wrong direction and we have to leave it and march across the fields. Unfortunately, dark storm clouds gather ahead of us and visibility is much reduced. Sharp grass pricks me painfully between the toes and pointed stones as well as other rough patches make walking a torment. I tell myself I shouldn't have thrown away the socks because, although they were full of holes, I would have been better off wearing them.

The storm clouds rapidly get closer, lightning flickers, the first drops fall, and then there is a massive cloudburst. In the flashes of light we see a haystack and we hurry over to it, but by the time we reach it we are soaked to the skin. We are happy, though, to have some shelter. Freezing, we crawl into the piles of hay and straw.

A little later a terrified young lad arrives who must have seen us. He bursts in and breathlessly tells us that the Soviets are on our tracks. Immediately everyone gets up and we march on as quickly as we can. It is still raining hard, but for the moment that is of no concern – what matters is putting sufficient distance between us and our pursuers. Even without boots, and despite the dampness, my feet burn like fire. It is pitch black now and I keep stepping on stones and banging into things. We stop in a small wood for a short rest. There a comrade bumps into me, and then the march continues. Soon a village appears where I hope I might get a pair of rags to bandage my feet – then I should be able to pull my boots on again.

13 July

Midnight has already passed when we eventually reach a village. We go into it without any precautionary measures, as we are completely soaked through, freezing and desperate to get warm. We are so wet we don't think about food. The pain in my feet has eased off – the mud is cooling and apparently works as a salve. Once again, a setback has turned out to be for the best. I realise that if I hadn't been suffering from dysentery at the time, I would have jumped into the artillery tractor and taken the seat in which Captain Trost was killed.

We knock on the door of the first house and nothing stirs. Then we knock more energetically on a window, but also without success. 'They are sound asleep', says a soldier near me, but I feel something is wrong. We try shouting and hammering, but again at first there is no response. Then at last a woman's anxious face appears behind the paper curtains. She waves us away, indicating that she can't or won't let us in. We gesture threateningly with our weapons and finally she opens the door. Inside it is pleasantly warm, but the room is seriously crowded once all thirty-three members of our group have squeezed in. Without being asked, the farmer's wife, who still looks nervous, brings us bread and milk.

Then one of our men, who has been taking a look around, hurries up to me and mutters excitedly: 'I believe there is somebody concealed behind the stove!' Immediately we investigate and find two men hidden there. We tell them to come out and, when they don't move, we threaten them with our guns. They emerge from their hiding place, throw their weapons aside and raise their hands, crying out: 'Don't shoot, not Russian, not partisan!' We have to decide what to do with them. Since they hadn't attacked us we let them go unscathed, but we take their weapons so they can't be used against us. We realise we must get away as quickly and inconspicuously as we can because we are obviously in a partisan village. We give the two rifles – German K98 ks which were doubtless captured in some skirmish or other – to two comrades who no longer have weapons, and then we start to clear off.

Not a moment too soon – as soon as we leave the village, wild shouting is heard behind us. The commotion blasts out of windows and from behind hedges and bushes. Dawn is already breaking and we run as fast as can in order to get as far away as possible and reach a protective wood. The partisans begin firing and throwing grenades, but they don't hit any of us.

Using all available cover, we reach a clump of small trees which takes us out of the sight of the enemy. Here we assemble and check that we are all present and find that only a few comrades have received light wounds. Once more a foray into a village has had a good outcome!

We leave the wood, which is not suitable for a long stay in daylight, and make our way to a nearby coniferous forest in which we believe we can conceal ourselves successfully. When we get there and stop at what looks like a suitable site to set up camp, we come across an abandoned partisan camp with numerous small brushwood huts, presumably set up by the inhabitants of the village we have just left. If the partisans search the area, there is a risk they will look here, knowing that this is a good place to hide. Nevertheless, we decide to stay there as the huts offer some protection from the rain and wind, and we are wet through. Since the situation is so uncertain, we post sentries on all sides and keep a careful watch.

The rain has eased off a little and a foggy mist lies over the landscape. Although it is risky, we start a fire in order to dry our wet clothes. Only damp wood is available for the fire so it doesn't burn properly and it creates lots of smoke.

One of our group got hold of a bag of ersatz coffee yesterday from a friendly village, and as a stream with clean water runs nearby, we can make hot coffee in our cooking pots or drinking cups, and we really enjoy this. The damp bread dries out like toast in the heat and tastes especially good.

Then suddenly there is a familiar roaring sound in the air and immediately afterwards an explosion. Apparently the smoke of our campfire has been spotted and now grenades are being fired at us. Tensely we listen, and another shot rings out, falling only about 100m from the site of the camp, but on the other side. If the enemy gunners have been able to observe the impacts, the next round would land precisely on our position, but fortunately no more shots are fired. Although we realise we may have been spotted, we can't decide whether to leave the camp or not. We don't want to move in broad daylight without knowing that we can find a suitable hiding place, and there is a chance the partisans will leave us alone anyway as they avoid fighting in the open. In any case, we assume a Red Army search team has been alerted and soon it may become extremely uncomfortable where we are. We will have to wait for 12 hours before we can march on, so our nerves are on edge.

Once we have had something to eat and drink, most of us lie down to rest, but I sit down next to Second Lieutenant Janasiak by the embers of the dying fire and discuss our situation with him. Clearly we are on the edge of the Nalibocka forest which is full of partisans, and we made this mistake because we don't have the equipment that would have allowed us to find a better route.

'When we march tonight we simply have to go in a more north-westerly direction to get out of this dangerous location', Jonny says.

'If so, we will get close to the Minsk–Volozyn road', I add.

'But that would be better than this partisan woodland', he replies and goes on, 'When I think how well everything went yesterday, and today, a few kilometres further on, the exact opposite happens. In one village everything is fine, in the next we get shot at. If we can get to Lithuania everything will be much easier.'

'But that is still round about another 100km according to my map', I say.

'If it's 100km it is going to take another two weeks, and even then the front line may not be in sight. But another two weeks to get to the front line seems nonsense when one thinks that it has already been a week since we broke out from the cauldron.'

Of course, we haven't a clue about how long the march will actually go on, with no end in sight.

Jonny goes into one of the big huts and I give my machine pistol a thorough examination and clean it as best I can. The barrel looks fine inside but the other parts are covered with rust. With a shudder I see that the mechanism that feeds the bullets into the barrel is so rusty that I couldn't fire a single shot! One of the comrades still has some weapon-cleaning kit with him, and above all some oil, which he lets me use, and so I am able to return the weapon back to working condition, and I am delighted I've discovered the damage in time.

Since I know we will have to continue our march in a few hours, I turn my attention to bandaging my feet. The inflammation of both feet has been reduced by the moisture, and the burning pains have subsided, so that I can try to get my boots on again. Although I can walk relatively well in bare feet, I can't do this for long and certainly not in the dark. After cleaning my feet with damp moss and grass, I wrap one foot in my handkerchief as a footcloth then wrap my other foot as well using a handkerchief lent me by a comrade. My boots have dried out and become bone hard since I last wore them, but they begin to soften when I put them on. The pain in my feet is not too bad, but I worry about what it will be like when I'm walking. It is no exaggeration to say that, in these circumstances, one's fate could depend on the state of one's feet.

Once I've dealt with my feet, I decide to get some rest so I slip into one of the huts where there is still some room. These huts are extremely primitive in their construction. They are about 2m high. They have slatted, sloping roofs covered with pine needles to keep off the rain. At the front two poles support the corners and there is space inside for only two people. Although the air is damp and cold and my clothing is still not dry, I soon fall asleep.

Slowly the time for us to leave draws near. We start earlier than usual so we can see our way through the extensive woodland. As we go forward we discover more rifle ranges and trenches, and well-built partisan camps. When we come to the edge of the wood it still isn't dark and we wait there for a while.

There's a village not far away in a hollow and, through binoculars, we carefully scrutinise it and its surroundings. As we can't see anything suspicious, we decide not to wait for complete darkness before we march past it. A few cows are grazing peacefully in the meadows but there is no sign of the villagers. The quiet feels somehow unreal. Then we see a woman with a sack on her back vanishing behind the bushes on the edge of the village. What does that signify? Until now the inhabitants of the villages have never hidden from us, and we suspect that something is not right here. As we get closer, we see a man with a gun in his hand hurrying along the street.

So, partisans! One of our men fires hastily and pointlessly at him, without hitting him, and we know we must get away from there as quickly as we can. Then a white rocket goes up, followed by a green one – the partisans' signal to attack. Immediately we turn back and conceal ourselves on the edge of a nearby grain field, and then we see the first figures coming out of the bushes and hedges towards us.

We open fire at a distance of 50m and knock some of them down, but more and more of them emerge and come towards us. They seem to be so confident about their superior numbers that they are prepared to ignore their usual practice of not attacking us in the open. Without doubt they had been waiting for us for some time and there is no way out for us other than to run.

In the semi-darkness we race over meadows and fields which are completely without cover. The green tracers of the rockets fly past and the earth sprays up as bullets hit the ground. In this situation we can't return fire. We can only run, run, run and hope to get away again.

No one dares to fall behind even though they are at the very limit of their strength, because they won't survive if they do. Everyone knows this and remembers perhaps the despairing cries for help in the partisan village that we tried to pass through a few days ago.

Near us Sergeant Ademeit gets a shot in his left shoulder, cries out briefly, then runs on. Once the gap between us and the partisans has increased a little, we try to counter their fire. Soon I am too exhausted to keep up. My feet are burning like before, but I ignore them. A bit of woodland appears before us that we have to reach at all costs. I struggle to run a few metres, but I am exhausted and can only go slowly, and reluctantly I turn to look back. I am so weary I don't care what happens. The dream of escape may be over, I tell myself. That is how one feels when one is at the very end of one's strength. But as has already happened so often, I am lucky and reach the woodland intact. The partisans hurled a few grenades into the wood, using grenade launchers, and then opened up with rifle fire.

We joined up in the wood. Several men are wounded, and one is missing. Sergeant Liicke, one of our best men, is no longer with us. We can only hope that he has found a quick end and has not fallen wounded into the hands of the partisans – everyone knows what will happen to him if he has.

Once we have left the wood behind us, we lie down for a short break in a meadow, something we all need, especially our wounded. Sweat is running in rivulets down my face. I drink my field flask empty and then feel a bit better. At a swampy spot nearby I refill it with brownish moor water that tastes bitter and stale, but is beautifully cold. I didn't think of the possible consequences!

Second Lieutenant Janasiak presses us to move on, as we must get out of this dangerous area on the edge of the Nalibocka forest and leave our pursuers behind. Under cover of darkness we walk on, taking the more north-westerly direction we decided on, and fortunately for once there are no incidents.

14 July

It is midnight. We have passed through a stretch of really difficult hilly terrain but, although we are exhausted. we keep going strictly in the same direction, avoiding all big detours and slipping through the landscape. Some comrades, especially the wounded, are near to collapse and can only continue with great effort. Fortunately, they appear to be lightly wounded, but they are not as strong as usual and, given the circumstances, they are at the limit of their ability to carry on. I had had the same experience a few days ago, and I am really happy that despite everything I can keep up well.

In the cover of a patch of bushes we stop for another rest. We sink to the ground and literally within a few seconds I am fast asleep – previously this would have been absolutely impossible for me. After some time, a comrade wakes me and right away I find I can go on with renewed strength, and I'm astounded by how quickly the power returns to my legs.

Our exhaustion is partly caused by hunger and everyone has been affected by it. The last small meal we had was at the camp fire in the partisans' wood, and we need to get hold of some more rations.

At dawn we spot the outline of a house near where we are hiding, and we quickly approach it. Since we have come a good distance from the partisan area, we feel confident enough to take the risk of looking for provisions. The house belongs to an isolated farm which is set aside from a small village, so it is well suited for our purpose. We knock and, despite the early hour, the farmers receive us in a thoroughly friendly manner. The attitude of the local people can vary so much between places that are only a short distance apart. The farmers even offer to put us up for the night, and as we all would like to have a roof over our heads again and we are all very tired, we accept this completely unexpected offer with thanks.

As there is not enough room for all of us in the living room, some of us go into the adjoining barn. As is generally the case in Russia, the living room serves as both kitchen and bedroom, and so the farmer's wife lays out a few blankets and cushions for us on the wooden floor. Then we eat the bread we have been given and lie down, and we are asleep in an instant. When I wake up in the morning the comrades are already at breakfast.

The farmer's wife has set out a basin with peeled potatoes together with plenty of bread and milk. After my meal I feel wonderfully strengthened and once again I'm full of energy and confidence.

Jonny tells me he slept very badly as he was afraid we would be caught in a trap. This hadn't occurred to me, but during a long conversation with the famers we discover the Russian military had been in the neighbouring village yesterday and had left a few hours before we arrived. None of us had known about this until now. Perhaps they hadn't told us because they didn't want to disturb us and they also know that Russian troops don't often pass through here.

As always we decide to get away immediately in order to find another wood before daybreak where we can conceal ourselves. We say farewell to the famers, thank them again for their friendly reception, and search for a nearby bit of woodland where we can set up our camp.

Soon the early morning the sun is shining, turning the sky a delightful blue, so that I can almost forget the war and our dangerous situation. I pull off my boots and lay the two pocket handkerchiefs I use as footcloths on a tree trunk to dry. From the farmer's wife I had obtained a length of old linen which I divide into two pieces that I can use instead of the less suitable handkerchiefs. The boots I put in the shade under a small pine tree, as they harden in the sun which makes them difficult to put on, especially when I'm in a hurry.

After I have yet again checked my machine pistol, I lie down in the soft moss and sunbathe. Then I pull out the map I received from Second Lieutenant Bauer who left us so tragically three days ago. I study this valuable piece of paper for a long time and reckon we must be in the area south of Rakuv, which lies midway between Minsk and Volozyn. As we had marched for a long time in a north-westerly direction, we could be near the highway I've already mentioned, and this would explain the appearance of the Russian military the farmers had seen. I keep wondering where the front line could be. We've seen no sign of it so the situation must be even worse than we had thought.

The craziest ideas occur to me. I imagine a Ju 52 could land in a nearby field and take us off so that we would be home again in no time, or a panzer division will mount a counterattack and set us free. These are all lovely dreams which are understandable in such a situation. But suddenly a loud engine noise brings me back to reality, A low-flying biplane cruises over us. It is not unlike the German aircraft I dream about, but it is a Russian 'Sewing Machine' or 'Coffee Mill'. Although I've already mentioned these planes, this is the first time we've seen them during our march.

The machine comes down so low that I can clearly see the pilot, and I cannot get rid of the feeling that he has also seen us, although everyone immediately takes cover. Then he comes over again, at the most 30m above the tree tops, and crosses over our camp, the pilot leaning far out of his seat to look down. We can clearly see the Red Star on the wings, and the aircraft is so low we could easily fire at it. But then the pilot turns away, doubtless convinced he's seen enough, and the plane vanishes.

We are certain we were spotted when we left the farm in the daylight and know that the search for us has begun. We prepare ourselves for any eventuality but cannot risk leaving the protection of the wood. Many agonising hours pass before nightfall, but nothing happens. Then at last it is time to set off. We have just reached the edge of the wood when we hear some distant shots and we stop at once. Apparently Russian soldiers are in the village near the farm we had stayed in. We can hear loud voices and the bawling of men who sound as if they are drunk. We wait where we are until it is a bit darker, then we go into the cornfields and patches of undergrowth, trying to get away from this dangerous place.

We are still vulnerable for a little later we come under isolated rifle fire from a nearby cornfield and, even after night fall, we can hear the noises of an invisible enemy, presumably the partisans. We are fed up because of the day's encounters – we have neither rested nor covered much ground. The tracers show that the shots are going far too high, so we lower our heads and change our direction of march, going to the north for a while in order to put some distance between us and the Nalibocka forest. Afterwards we turn back west towards home.

15 July

Gradually the morning begins to dawn, so we look for a village where we can obtain some fresh food. We come across two isolated farms. Since we are exhausted and worried about what is going to happen to us, we are in an impatient and aggressive mood. As a result, we split into two large groups and barge our way into the houses without knocking. The inhabitants cower in their beds and we quickly take everything we need.

On the table of the house that I enter with my group is a big jug of milk that immediately vanishes into our field flasks. In addition to this we provide ourselves with bread, salt and some eggs, and then quickly leave as the daylight is coming. Just in time we reach the protective darkness of a thick pine wood near the houses. This appeared to be a really good hiding place, but people kept passing close by so we went further on.

Looking back on our behaviour today it seems rude and insensitive, and I try to justify it by arguing that the villagers were better off than us and weren't having to struggle just to survive, but nonetheless I am embarrassed when I remember how welcoming and helpful they were.

We found a passable camping site once more in a clearing and lay down exhausted on unfortunately very wet moss. It is very cool and damp in the early morning in the wood and so we cautiously kindle a small fire. We queue to cook the milk and flour we had taken from one of the two houses in order to make a soup which we dilute with plenty of water from a muddy stream near the camp. The flour does not look good – it is dark grey and tastes very coarse, with a lot of husk and bran – so we have to force ourselves to eat it. But what I would have given for a few spoons of it a few days later!

Rashly I lie down in the cool, damp moss and immediately fall asleep. I soon wake up again, plagued by frightful cramping body pains accompanied by diarrhoea which force me to go and look for a suitable place some distance away from the camp. Only after some considerable time am I in a fit state to go back, and I am so worn out that I can hardly stand up. During the course of the day – which fortunately passes without incident – I recover a little and can continue the march. Dubious food had evidently caused the diarrhoea, but I seem to have overcome it.

We set off again as we want to get through this apparently extensive wood by daybreak. As we come to the edge of the trees, we see before us a small 5m-wide stream winding its way through swampy meadows. There is no bridge in sight, but we are lucky to discover a place where someone has laid two long tree trunks next to each other across the stream. The trunks are thickly covered with moss which is damp and slippery, so that we have to take special care not to slide off into the water. Since I am feeling so weak I am not sure I can get over, but I go slowly, carefully putting one foot in front of the other, and manage to reach the far bank like the others. The night is so clear that we can march using the Great Bear to find our route – we don't need the compass.

In order to give some respite to our wounded, we take a short rest in a small area of woodland at about midnight. At daybreak we discover that the three comrades who joined us a few days ago have left us without being noticed. Certainly this was not a casual decision as a small group is more independent, can move more quickly and is not so likely to be discovered, and will find it easier to get hold of enough food. Yet, a larger group feels more secure and within it a strong feeling of comradeship develops.

16 July

There is still about 3 hours until dawn. In the pale light of a waning half moon we get a good view of the terrain and so we march as quickly as we can along a road that runs for a long distance in the right direction. One behind the other we walk along the verge. This is risky, but we want to make rapid progress.

Suddenly a cyclist appears, hazily in the distance, and like lightning all of us take cover in the roadside ditch. As he gets nearer, we can see he is wearing a Russian uniform, and as he clearly slackens his pace, we assume he has noticed something. Immediately we jump up, blocking the road and forcing him to dismount. Only now does he realise who he is dealing with. He lifts his bicycle with both hands and smashes it down with all his might on the nearest soldier's foot, then makes a swift turn and runs, shouting loudly for help, running in giant strides in the dark over the field next to the road. But after he had covered just a few yards a well-aimed burst of fire from a machine pistol brings him down. Under the given circumstances there was nothing else we could do, as we would be in the great danger if he had reached his unit and then aroused the whole area.

We are at war against an enemy from whom we can expect no consideration should we fall into his hands. During these days and weeks a merciless hunt is in progress for us and other stragglers. It is being conducted with great bitterness and energy and not without appreciable losses when there is confrontation. The hunt is going on in the previously undisturbed hinterland of the Red Army. Because of the extreme danger and uncertainty of our situation, we react more cruelly than we did when we faced the partisans in the areas we had occupied. This is not really surprising since we had only a negligible chance of survival.

We search for the dead Russian and see from the number of stars on his wide epaulettes that he must have been a senior officer or commissar. We hide him and his bicycle behind a small bush beside the road and hope he will not be discovered too soon.

Despite this unpleasant incident, we continued the march along the road – we want to cover as much ground as possible – but we go more cautiously now, keeping to the roadside ditch. We know too that we must get hold of some food while it is still dark, and we increase our pace when we see an unusually large farm surrounded by a solid wall. While the rest of the group takes up positions around the wall, I go through the gate with Lieutenant Niedermeier and Jonny. We set our machine pistols ready to fire because for some reason we feel we must take special care. As we go one after the other into the yard we see in the right-hand back corner the outlines of three trucks. Immediately we stop as if rooted to the spot, and then we try slowly, without letting the vehicles out of our sight, to back out of the yard. Then three figures come towards us out the darkness. They are carrying machine pistols on their shoulders so they can't be ready to fire. As we only want to use our weapons as a last resort, we wait tensely, with our fingers on the triggers, to see what will happen next. Slowly the three come nearer, still not showing signs of caution or mistrust. At first they assume we are Red Army soldiers, but then they realise who we are. They jerk their machine pistols off from their shoulders and one of them blows a shrill whistle as a warning signal. But we are quicker than they are and we have to be if we are to survive. My machine pistol and Jonny's only make a metallic 'klack', but the others fire normally and rescue us from this otherwise hopeless situation.

Probably there are many more Red Army soldiers in the farm so we quickly take to our heels. When we get to the road we race along it, heading back in an easterly direction in the hope that they wouldn't search for us there. On the edge of a large cornfield we take cover. We don't go into the field itself because we don't want to leave tracks. Shortly afterwards wild firing breaks out behind us, accompanied by piercing shouts, and we have to work out what is happening. It seems that the angry Soviet soldiers had rushed off towards the west, assuming that is where we would be, and as a result only a few isolated shots come in our direction – we see the tracer flying harmlessly high over us. We use every bush, every ditch, every crease in the soil as cover. Then, out of breath, we climb a slope to a big wood where we lie down for a short rest. From there we can see shining in the distance the blazing headlights of many vehicles on the road. They are driving to and fro, no doubt looking for us. But with cunning and much luck we have survived and are safe. We don't like to think about what would have happened if we had been caught.

Cautiously we go further into the wood and finally find a suitable place to set up camp. Immediately we put sentries in position, and we change them every hour. Then we fall into exhausted sleep knowing that somehow we have come through another day unscathed.

17 July

The morning is cool and grey. The sun has hidden itself behind the clouds and only now and again sends some warming rays onto us through the trees. Our mood is as subdued as the sunlight. We will have plenty of time to think about our predicament during the day's march. We ask ourselves how long can we survive in this crazy situation and wonder where the front line is since we have seen no sign of it so far. Even if we reach it, how will we get through the Russian lines? We will need an enormous amount of luck, and we know we may be killed at the last moment, when our goal is in sight.

The truth is there isn't a continuous front line anymore because the fighting is constantly moving westwards. The Soviets have already crossed the Memel at several points and are about 100km from the East Prussian border. We still have a distance of over 200km to cover even without any diversions.

Fortunately, we have not the least idea how bad our situation is. If we had done, our determination to get through would have weakened, especially as in the eleven days since the breakout from the Minsk cauldron, we have covered barely 80 or 90km of ground. So, it is understandable that our spirits are so low. We are irritable, anxious and pessimistic, and some of us no longer believe we will escape.

Each of us concentrates on his own condition. My wound doesn't give me much concern, but there is another problem and that is my feet. In order to prepare myself for the day's march, I pull off my boots, unwind the cloths I've wrapped around my feet and look at the mess. Puss is trickling out of pea-sized holes in both heels and the toes are in an awful state, and I wonder if I can continue. But I have no choice. Strangely the pain in the feet is bearable and it is nothing in comparison to the pain of others who are in an even worse condition. I wish I could get hold of new foot wrappings, but I will have to go on with the ones I've have. Jonny too has his worries – he has a large boil on his right foot which makes it very difficult for him to walk. Even the lightly wounded are suffering badly now and there is absolutely no chance of getting professional medical attention so we can only hope to complete the march soon. Of course, we don't know how quickly the end will come and it may not be the end we wish for.

18 July

During the march late yesterday, after the encounter with the Red Army soldiers and our flight, we failed to find anything to eat. Now, though, we succeed – we find a lonely farmhouse which has provisions that can be spared. Unfortunately, this is followed by a fierce squabble between some of our soldiers. They rip the food out of each other's hands, knock over a milk jar and crush some eggs. This incident is the result of overstretched nerves and acute impatience, but in our situation a breach of discipline cannot be tolerated in any circumstances because sooner or later it will lead to the disintegration of the group. Those responsible are told that, if such a ruckus occurs again, they would have to leave the group.

Shortly afterwards the march resumes and we see in the moonlight not far away a group of about twenty men coming rapidly towards us. We presume they are German soldiers who, like us, are looking for the front line, yet we don't dare give up our cover and go over to them because it is possible they are Red Army soldiers who are on their way to search the area. It is also strange that they are not heading westwards, although they may be making a detour in order to avoid obstacles in the terrain. We have to worry about such things – wherever possible, risk has to be avoided.

We are now between Volozyn, about 75km west of Minsk, and the 20km-wide partisan-infested Nalibocka forest. We have reached a wide area of moor and swamp which will be a nightmare to get through. The boggy ground is carpeted with thick grass into which one sinks 20 to 30cm with every step. There is always the possibility that one will break through the surface and sink even further into the mire, and the very thought of this makes me break out in a cold sweat from every pore. Progress involves an enormous amount of physical effort. By the time we get to firm ground we are absolutely exhausted, but we can take only a short break because there is no wood nearby where we can find cover. Unfortunately, a heavy storm breaks over us and soon the first drops of rain begin to fall. In the flashing light of the storm we spot the silhouette of a barn and we make our way quickly towards it. As we reach it there is a cloudburst and the rain falls just as heavily as it does in the tropics, and we can't decide whether to keep going or not. Finally the rain begins to die down and we go back into the open. Dawn is already breaking. We march on as fast as we can in the hope of reaching a wood where we can shelter. The group becomes strung out and the wounded in particular fall behind.

It becomes even lighter and minute by minute we become more uneasy. We reach a small hillock in this this almost completely flat landscape and linger there for a short time in order to get a view of the surroundings and allow the stragglers to catch up. There isn't a wood in sight but not too far away there is a small village. Impatient and increasingly concerned, we wait for the arrival of the last of the group, then we set off again. In our efforts to put some distance between us and the partisan-occupied Nalibocka forest, we may have come close to the big town of Volozyn where Soviet soldiers are probably based, and now we need to make a wide detour around the village in front of us. The result is that all day long we have hardly any chance of getting under cover. In the full daylight we don't dare to go any further and decide to hide in one of the big cornfields nearby, with all the danger and uncertainty that that involves.

In this exposed position in the bright sunlight we have to restrict our movements to those that are strictly necessary, and eating and drinking can only be done lying down and with great care. There is a pressing need to keep still because the slightest movement of even a blade of grass might betray our presence, and we post sentries covering the terrain on all sides.

Before we reach the cornfield we glimpse near bushes about 300m away some figures we can't identify – they run off immediately when they see us. We calm ourselves by thinking they were German soldiers that had taken us for Russians, but that is probably wishful thinking.

Although we realise what a precarious situation we are in, most of us, exhausted by the acute stress of the last few hours, are soon overcome with sleep. About 3 hours later we are suddenly awakened by a loud noise and several shots. We jump up shocked and look into the muzzles of Soviet machine pistols. The Soviets have surrounded us on all sides and order us to raise our hands. Any resistance or attempt to flee is completely futile – it would be suicidal. Had any of us grabbed a weapon, they would have finished us off. Thankfully no one lost his nerve or recklessly fired. Instead, we stand up, one after the other, with our hands in the air and submit to our fate.

The dream of a happy return home is broken. The extreme stress and deprivation we have endured with such strength of will during the march and the preparations we had made to put up a fight are behind us now – they count for nothing. We have been captured and have an uncertain future. I can't believe it – it is unimaginable. But the Soviets are standing there, earth-brown figures with their machine pistols and carbines. It is fact – a reality.

The Soviets come forward cautiously and take our weapons, but they are surprisingly casual. My pockets are not searched and in them are rifle grenades and loose rounds for the machine pistol which given the pressure of recent events I have completely forgotten about.

Then the officers have to step forward. Lieutenant Niedermeier, Second Lieutenant Janasiak (Jonny), Senior Veterinary Officer Richert and myself are put at the head of a sad procession and we set off in the direction of the village I referred to. This is called Makarovka and is 3km south-west of Volozyn. From here we were spotted by four villagers who reported us.

On the way our guards play with the captured weapons, firing them across the countryside. A lieutenant has acquired two pistols and is firing with one in each hand like a Wild West cowboy, one magazine after another, fortunately into the air. Understandably they are in high spirits so we have nothing to fear at the moment.

Slowly I recover from the shock and start to think clearly and methodically. How unbearable the loss of freedom is, especially after we had struggled so hard to hold on to it, and I resolve whatever the circumstances to escape at the first opportunity. I am absolutely determined about this and I feel better once I've reached the decision – and I'm confident I'll succeed. I look around for ways to escape, wondering whether, when the guards aren't watching, I can dip into the cornfield beside the road, but that won't work. Don't make a mess of it, I say to myself, no thoughtless acts, keep calm, don't rush things and wait for an opportune moment.

Soon we reach the village and are told to sit down in a meadow beside the houses, the officers somewhat apart. The villagers – men, women and children – come to look at us with curiosity. For a moment I think of throwing the rifle grenade and trying to get away in the confusion that would cause, but I immediately reject this absurd idea because of the likely consequences for my comrades. Instead, I carefully dispose of the rifle grenade and pistol ammunition by pushing them into the saturated ground of the meadow. I do this just at the right time as the Soviets begin to search us more thoroughly, looking for plunder and starting with the men and NCOs. Boots and other equipment as well as private possessions – especially watches and rings – change owners.

One Red Army soldier tinkers with a pistol and fires a shot that hits another soldier in the foot. His fellow soldiers grin or watch him with complete indifference while he rolls around on the ground, groaning with pain. I get the impression that here behind the front line the Soviets are intoxicated by their victory and feel they can do what they like. Civilians, especially half-grown lads, who have got hold of guns fire them gleefully at jam jars, bottles and other targets.

The journey starts to a transit camp near the large town of Volozyn. We've heard some talk about this, but know nothing more at this point. First the NCOs and men set off, escorted by sentries with fixed bayonets. The officers have to wait a bit longer, apparently to prevent any contact with our men. As soon as they are out of sight we are searched and robbed. Watches, rings, pocket knives, fountain pens and whatever is of interest vanishes never to be seen again. Also taken is my map of Russia together with the home address of Second Lieutenant Bauer which I had folded into the map to protect it from damp. I try to grab it back from the two Russians who don't seem to know quite what to do with all their booty – I was hoping they would see it was of no value – but I'm rapped across the knuckles and have to give up the attempt. At the same time I lose my compass which I would need if I was to make a successful escape. Finally, all four of us are told to lie down on our backs and, with a short tug, our boots are removed. The Russians are evidently disgusted by the pus and blood they see in my filthy footcloths and it is only with greatest self-control that I am able to suppress an angry outburst.

Now I've lost my boots a successful escape attempt appears to be impossible but knowing this doesn't weaken my resolve. I remember the line from the 1812 'Song of Flight' which goes 'Fleet without shoes, nowhere rest and peace'. This doesn't help much as for the moment I can't see how I can proceed without boots.

The day is glowing with heat, as it has been for days and weeks. After the plundering, the only kit I have left is my badly dented field flask and the drinking cup that goes with it. Shortly before we were taken prisoner, I had filled it with water, but I had stopped myself from drinking from it even though I had a burning thirst because I didn't know when I would get more water.

We started walking barefoot, with sunken shoulders, one behind the other along the village street, separated at short intervals by four Red Army soldiers with cocked machine pistols. To me it was a hardly comprehensible, unspeakably depressing scene. Now and then we throw each other enquiring glances, but we don't dare speak. All of us have the same thought – our struggle to get back to the safety of our own lines has come to nothing. Although, as I've said, there is no chance of escape at the moment, I continue to look for opportunities. I calculate the distance to every bush, ditch and cornfield, and work out how good the cover would be, and I wonder how far I could run before being shot down.

Tired and moving without thinking we trotted along the sandy road which is easy going in bare feet – less painful than wearing boots – but of course this soft surface wouldn't last. Ahead of us we see our men who are marching more slowly than we are. In order to increase the gap, the guards tell us to wait, so we sit down under the roadside bushes, thankful for the short break.

Then one of the guards spots a wedding ring on the hand of Lieutenant Niedermeier which he had managed somehow to conceal during the plundering. When the guard comes over to take it, the lieutenant refuses and the guard threatens him with his gun. The confrontation looks really dangerous so we ask the lieutenant to give up the ring. Aflame with anger he throws it at the feet of the guard who quickly bends down, picks it up and puts it into his pocket. After this incident the march continued.

We pass a meadow where there is the burnt-out remains of a fighter, a Bf 109. It is such a depressing sight. This is first fighter we've seen for weeks and it's a wreck. The fuselage has been destroyed by the fire but the tail, with its swastika symbol, is intact. In these circumstances this is a far from inspiring sight. The wreckage of the aircraft symbolises the catastrophe of which we have become victims.

Between us and the aircraft lies a body dressed in black and I assume it is the pilot in his leather kit, but as we pass close by a thick cloud of black flies rises from the body and I see it belongs to a soldier in a field grey uniform. Perhaps he had been shot because he could not keep up or while trying to escape. He too has been deprived of his boots.

The march goes on. The crews of a couple of T-34 tanks, who are working on their machines in a field, turn to watch us go by, and one of the men there points unmistakably at my water bottle. Immediately I realise he wants it and I try to save it by making a friendly gesture, smiling, and offering him a cup of water. In response he laughs loudly and rudely and grabs the water bottle without its cup from my hand, and then he tells us to hurry on. If only I had drunk the water in the bottle while I had the chance because the heat is intense and I'm burning with thirst.

So now I have lost my last piece of kit – all I have left is a linen rag I use instead of a handkerchief. Like the survivors of Sir Winston Churchill's bombing of our cities, you could say I have only a handkerchief left to cry in.

Finally, we reach Volozyn which we understood was our destination. We stand among the buildings at a crossroads where many local people have gathered – soon there are hundreds of civilians and soldiers. They form a thick circle and they do not look well disposed towards us. Then the shouting starts up: 'Hitler bandits! – Nazi swine! – dammed officers!', and all sorts of other kind words rain down on us. It is remarkable how many of the civilians have a good knowledge of German.

We hope the insults will be limited to words, but then someone points to the eagle on Lieutenant Niedermeier's uniform and shouts out loudly: 'Gestapo!' That acts like a signal! Immediately four brutal-looking men attack him, including a colonel who, with a truncheon he pulled out of his pocket, hits him rapidly again and again on his head. Then he is dragged to a house and the vicious colonel seizes him by the hair and hits his head several times against the stone wall. We watch this attack with an overwhelming sense of outrage and alarm, and then someone maliciously asks whether we are from the SS. Struggling to keep calm and with great effort we prove to them that we are Wehrmacht soldiers by pointing to our uniforms and insignia. If we hadn't convinced them, I doubt we would have survived for more than a few minutes. Now it was Senior Veterinary Officer Richert's turn.

'Officer?' they ask.

'Doctor, surgeon', he replies.

'Ah, doctor, good, good', they say.

The tone is respectful, somehow conciliatory, so there were no blows, but one of the German-speaking civilians cannot let the moment go without ripping off his shoulder straps with some nasty abuse.

An ugly, aggressive woman in the crowd is not satisfied with this. In order to inflame a situation that was calming down, she thrusts towards us with quick steps and stops, stretching out her arms in a most theatrical way and pushing her 2-year-old child in front of her.

'Why have you served the damn Führer', she shouts at him. 'What have you done with the Yiddish children? Why have you chopped off their hands?'

Since the Red Army soldiers standing around clearly didn't understand what she said, she didn't get the reaction she expected. So she strides forward to act herself, spits angrily at our vet and hits him with a hate-filled cry several times right in his face. Consciously I have to calm myself down in order not to react to her attack, for that would have certainly had dire consequences for all of us.

I wonder why this woman was raging about the children's hands – a piece of shameless propaganda put out by the Allied press during the First World War – and not the terrible extermination camps and the crimes committed there. It would have been more appropriate to mention those. But apparently she didn't know much about them so she attacked us for serving Hitler and didn't give us the chance to respond by telling her about the humiliation of the Versailles treaty and the awful economic and social situation that we had had to deal with.

But too much was happening in Volzyn for me to think about such things then. Lieutenant Niedermeier has been badly hurt during the assault and now can only stand upright with difficulty. In comparison I get off lightly, perhaps because I am in dressed in simple overalls with no badges of rank and don't look like an officer. I'm punched in the neck and someone treads on my injured feet, but it seems that, with my makeshift bandages and the blood-spattered clothing, I am less of a target. Jonny, who is clearly identifiable as an officer, is even luckier. Just as they start to close in on him something completely unexpected happens.

The brutal-looking Soviet colonel and a major who had previously stood inconspicuously among the other spectators start suddenly without any apparent reason to scream and gesticulate at one another. Their faces are bright red with anger. Possibly a disagreement about how prisoners of war should be treated has led to this commotion. They decide on a boxing match to resolve the issue, and it is riveting to see how bitterly the two comrades get stuck into each other. The spectators' attention is drawn to the fight and luckily we become completely unimportant. The crowd is so enthusiastic about the contest that the two fighting cockerels are spurred on to give an even bigger performance. Red Army soldiers – all of them apparently from the lower ranks – are standing around grinning with pleasure and applauding first one side, then the other in a provocative way.

It is wonderful how abruptly the situation has changed, and our escorts – who turn out to be reasonable men – use the distraction of the fight to usher us unobtrusively out of the arena. Before we have gone a hundred metres an elegant car comes towards us, an open-topped Mercedes like those Hitler has, without doubt a captured vehicle. It stops jerkily in front of us. Out of it climbs an immaculately dressed commissar, and I ask myself what does he want? With quick steps he comes up to us and searches our pockets without a word, pulling them out as far as he can. Then he turns about, climbs back into the Mercedes and roars off as if it was the most natural thing in the world. The whole episode went like lightning, like a stage performance, and I'm astonished to discover that he has taken my tattered ersatz handkerchief.

Other passing Soviet soldiers search us too, but find nothing. We shake our heads when this happens, thinking that they can't possibly win the war if they behave like this. But of course we don't know how hopeless our situation is, and we are still dreaming of final victory ourselves.

Volozyn is full of troops. Apart from lots of Red Army soldiers there are many *Girls in Uniform* (the title of a film of that time). They are smartly dressed. Their uniforms appear to be brand new and their chests are covered with decorations and medals, and the large pistols they carry in leather belts look distinctly out of place. They act like an elite, and they hardly glance at the ordinary soldiers.

As part of my plan to escape I very carefully observe what is going on around me just in case it will be useful in the future. I feel much more confident now because I am so focused on my task – I'm determined and I firmly believe I'll succeed. But as well as watching everything closely I must get hold of items I'll need during the escape. At the moment all I have is the uniform I'm wearing, and I don't have any footwear. How I'll acquire some, I don't know – I'll have to wait and see. Without sufficient preparation I haven't a hope of getting away.

The march goes on. Tractors with wide tracks approach us from behind. As the road is narrow, we quickly move over to the right-hand side and they rattle past, but they drive deliberately close to us so that I'm afraid of being run over for fun. I remember the frightful fate of the 200 flak soldiers whose heads were crushed by tank tracks, an atrocity that isn't widely known. I don't want to exaggerate but I am beginning to appreciate that the life of a prisoner is regarded as not much better than that of a mangy dog. Sadly, I also know that Russian prisoners are treated in a similar way in our camps, even if awful crimes like the one I've just mentioned don't happen there.

At last we reach the transit camp. The soldiers we had been separated from are already there – they had been brought by another route and we hadn't seen them during the march. We sit on the ground with them in a small square in front of a massive camouflaged building that reminds me of a manor house on a nobleman's estate – without doubt the most striking building in the whole place.

Stone steps lead up to the entrance door which is flanked by walls decorated with two Doric columns. I can see they are not made of marble because the paint is flaking off. This building has been set up as a transit camp, apparently the only one in the district. I'm relieved to see it and feel much calmer. Many rooms are available, but a relatively small room has been allocated for prisoners and we are led into it. Around fifty soldiers are already there, including a few wounded. Like us, they have been rounded up near Volzyn and are waiting to be transported east. So in all there are about eighty men in the room which is very crowded. The wooden floor is thickly strewn with dirty straw.

The situation in the Minsk cauldron was so chaotic, and so many attempts were made each night to break out, that I can hardly expect to find anyone else from my regiment. As new arrivals we immediately ask how things function here, and discover that today at 5 p.m. an interrogation by the city commandant, a colonel, is going to take place. We can only hope he is not the same colonel whose highly unfriendly acquaintance we have already made. This fear unfortunately turns out to be true, and some of the soldiers who have already experienced such interrogations prepare us for them. They tell us that anyone who isn't cooperative is beaten with cudgels and clubs and is left lying in a bloody mess in the interrogation room. Here is another reason to escape as soon as possible.

We are told we will stay here are until a sufficient number of prisoners have been assembled and then we will be taken to a larger camp in Minsk, a distance of about 80km. As that is too far walk in a day, we will go first to a transit camp at Rakuv, about halfway there. This news has a big impact on my plan to escape. We had just completed an exhausting and dangerous march from near Minsk and I couldn't bear the thought of having to go back in the opposite direction as a prisoner. I'm also worried that my feet are in such a desperate state that I wouldn't be able to complete the journey. My wounds are partly healed and are not a serious problem anymore, and for the last few days I haven't been troubled by dysentery. But I still don't know if I am fit enough to try to escape and of course I can only dream about proper medical care. So, I decide I should wait before making the attempt, and in the meantime I should try to get the necessary equipment together.

Before I can start on this though Red Army soldiers come into our room to search us again but more thoroughly this time. They are not looking for weapons – that is no longer necessary – but for more interesting personal items. Some of my comrades have been lucky enough to get through previous plundering sessions without giving up some of their belongings, but they can't get away with this now. I'm not worried about the search because I have nothing left to lose – the makeshift pocket handkerchief was the last piece of my property to be taken.

One of our soldiers has a beautiful silver tobacco tin which he tries to keep, but when the 'liberator' reaches for his weapon we persuade the soldier to give up the tin to avoid anything worse happening. Carelessly our wallets – if we still have them – are opened and emptied. Field-post letters, photographs, pay books and German banknotes (which the Soviets show no interest in) flutter across the room and soon the floor is covered with them, but hardly any of the owners is concerned about what is happening. The paper money no longer has any value, and the letters, family pictures and other keepsakes which lie in a heap on the straw show how deeply shocked we all are and how crippling hopelessness and resignation have overcome us.

Once the Russians have left, I look for anything useful among the things that had been thrown away and immediately find a plastic container of the Losantin tablets we carry to decontaminate wounds. The container is the size of petrol lighter and an adhesive band makes it airtight and waterproof. This is a really important find because it will allow me to keep matches – if I can get hold of some – protected from damp and, when I have to swim across rivers, they should stay dry. The next thing I come across is a mess tin that belongs to a soldier who had hidden it in the straw. I plead with him to let me at least have the lid and he agrees. I am deeply thankful for this as I can eat and drink from it and, should the occasion arise, I could use it in a wood as a small cooking pot over a fire. I also have the tremendous luck to discover a pair of torn socks which have been thrown away by their owner because they seemed to him to be so worn out that they are not worth keeping. For me, however, they will be really valuable during my escape which would be unthinkable if I'm barefoot. Finally, I find a badly rusted razor blade which I plan to use as a knife.

I am so satisfied with the success of my search that I have already gone back to my place in the room when a guard comes to the door, goes over to where my neighbour is sitting and begins to search through the straw. I assume he is looking for the usual things, but then he pulls out a pistol! Without showing any emotion, he picks it up and leaves the room. But he returns at once with three of his fellow guards in order to take away the presumed owner of the weapon. Stunned, we sit there waiting to see what will happen next. The suspect tries to convince the Soviets that the pistol does not belong to him, but since he can't speak their language, they don't understand him. In desperation he shouts, 'Who speaks Russian?' Fortunately one of our soldiers who knows a bit of Russian comes forward and speaks for him. With great effort he persuades the four sentries that the weapon has been lying there for days and that it must have belonged to a previous prisoner who had left it when he was transported. The soldier who had been suspected of hiding the weapon was deeply shocked.

Immediately afterwards we are all turfed out of the room and forced into a small pitch-black room where we are packed in like sardines for half an hour. A thorough search of the large room is carried out, then we are let back in. We are relieved that this dangerous incident hasn't led to any reprisals and realise this is due to the soldier who spoke some Russian – his knowledge of the language and the persuasive argument he put forward have saved the situation.

While some of the Red Army soldiers we've encountered have shown themselves to be decent men, the same can't be said of the civilians who now enter our room. At first they make a good impression. They sit down beside us as if they know us well and begin – in almost perfect German – to talk to us in a friendly manner, asking about our homes and what our wives and children are doing. Once they have discovered who the married ones are, they rudely demand their wedding rings which they assume they have hidden. A few of the civilians who don't know German simply point to the patches of pale skin on fingers, from which the wedding rings have been removed, and they get what they want in that way. But neither of the methods these rascals use is successful as our 'jeweller's shop' has already been completely cleaned out.

As soon as they realise there is nothing more of this sort to take from us they become visibly irritated and threatening. Those of our men who still have uniform jackets and trousers which are in good condition – and which might have sale value – are told to strip off. With unmistakable gestures the Russians indicate which items they've selected, and then the men stand there barefoot in their underwear. These are degrading scenes which I would never have expected to witness, and I am outraged by them, but there is nothing we can do – we can't defend ourselves. Although my clothing is hardly desirable, I quickly cover myself with some straw and pretend to be sleeping. I don't want to lose any of my kit as I will need it when I escape.

One of our men rips a big hole in his uniform so that it will no longer be considered an object of value, and I follow his example, using the razor blade I found to enlarge a small tear in my trousers. I don't have to worry about my overalls because they are flecked with blood from the wound in my throat ten days ago, and the same goes for the pullover and shirt I picked up in the wood on the west bank of the Beresina.

Finally, the thieves walk out carrying a heap of jackets and trousers and, having seen how they behave, my determination to get away from this camp as quickly as possible is even stronger than before.

I search through the straw again, but find nothing else that I need. As I do so I glance at discarded letters and photographs and even read a few sentences in which leave and happy homecomings are the main themes – which can no longer be fulfilled. Carefree and pretty young girls look out from the photographs as if the world is in order and nothing can go wrong, and for a moment I forget my misfortune, though immediately afterwards I find my situation even more threatening. In some of the photos proud and self-conscious soldiers appear in lovely clean uniforms. Now, of course, they are lying here, scruffy, dirty and disheartened. Some of them are completely apathetic and despondent, and for many of them a hopeless future lies ahead. These impressions make me even firmer in my resolve to escape however difficult and dangerous the attempt may be.

Every half hour or so a sentry comes into the room, checks that everything is all right, then vanishes. I would have expected to be under constant guard, but really there is no need for it. Perhaps, too, the sentry doesn't want to stay for long because of the smelly stale air in the room. The stench is not surprising since we have had to endure extreme conditions for weeks without being able to change our sweaty clothing or wash.

Just then one of the sentries comes in again. I notice he is wearing a German military belt which he's taken as a souvenir and I see he has fastened it wrongly so that the motto '*Gott mit uns*' on the buckle is unreadable, and I can't supress a malicious laugh.

As soon as the sentry leaves, three 'maidens in uniform' enter the room and stand at the door, observing us in a superior and self-conscious way. They are wearing exceptionally clean, well-fitting uniforms, and are really pretty too. Two of them can undoubtedly be described as beauties, but their glance is cold and hard, and I guess they belong to one of the veteran female battalions of the Red Army in which there are so many exceptional snipers. Supposedly they aim at the left eye when an enemy soldier looks briefly over the edge of the trench.

I recall an episode that occurred on 20 June, two days before the beginning of the Russian offensive, as a tank unit drove up to the front line. Before setting off the radio operator, Vera Proschina, standing on her tank, gave an inflammatory speech, in which among other things she said: 'Today the dream is fulfilled as my tank mows down the Hitlerites. My father and mother have been killed by the fascists, I will therefore destroy them without mercy. I will show what a Russian girl is capable of. Death to the damned conquerors!'

The three heroines by the door of our room appear to have the same fervour and determination. The tired, demoralised soldiers on the floor show little interest in their visit, many of them turning away and dozing in front of them.

Now the curtain lifts on the next act. A sentry, a small fellow, proudly makes an announcement. A 3-year-old youngster is brought in. Like the women, he is dressed in a brand-new, immaculately fitting uniform – the shirt and short trousers have knife-sharp creases, and undoubtedly the outfit is of the highest quality. The most impressive thing about him, however, is a machine pistol – not a toy, but a genuine machine pistol – which he aims at us with a fixed expression like a professional trench-fighter. He swivels from side to side and fiddles with the gun as if preparing to fire. Immediately I take cover as it is perfectly possible that the gun is loaded and not secured, and the lad has a nervous trigger finger. After all I've gone through it now looks possible that I'll run out of luck and be promoted to kingdom come by this young whippersnapper. But nothing happens and one of the three ladies – probably the mother of the little boy – belatedly ensures that no nonsense occurs. As the four of them leave, they get a round of courteous applause from me and my comrades which keeps up our spirits. The 'Three Graces' look delighted, as are the sentry and the little Hero of the Soviet Union.

One of our soldiers asks the sentry, who can understand a little of what we say, for permission to use a latrine which is located behind the building. I join him, using the opportunity to take a close look at the surroundings. We go through the entrance past two sentries to the latrine. I am pleasantly surprised to see there is no barbed wire anywhere, and reckon that, with proper preparation, it should be possible to get past the sentries and escape.

Right next to the building there is a large fruit-and-vegetable garden with numerous redcurrant bushes. They extend for about 50m and are densely packed together so they would provide good cover. So now all I have to do is wait while I work out a way of getting out at night from the room where we are being held. But I am relieved to know that at least I won't have to contend with any barbed wire. On the way back from the latrine I find in the grass a long length of Wehrmacht telephone cable which I roll up and stuff into my jacket pocket. I'm delighted with this find – it should come in useful.

The cable clearly indicates that German troops were accommodated in our building, and I later discover that two weeks ago it was the headquarters of the VIth Corps which was attached to our army after it had been separated from 3rd Panzer Army during the fighting around Vitebsk. General Model even came here on 3 July from his headquarters in Lida in order to prepare a defensive line between the Small Beresina – not to be mixed up with the Beresina that we crossed on 2 July – south of Molodecano and the swamp south of Volozyn (the swampy area we crossed with so much effort yesterday shortly before being taken prisoner). But the Soviet advance was not to be held up by this line, and Volozyn was captured by the Red Army two days later on 5 July, thirteen days ago today. Of course, we didn't know about this because at that time we were still about 100km east of here in the Minsk cauldron where the 5th Army was destroyed.

We can't tell the time any longer because our watches have been taken, but I reckon it must be around 5 p.m. when the interrogations are supposed to start. There is a long delay – no one appears and I assume the colonel must have more important things to do. I doubt there is anything of value we can disclose anyway because we have been cut off from communications and have been moving through country to the rear of the rapidly advancing Red Army.

So many things had happened during the day that I feel I need a long rest. In order to distract myself, I look closely at the only picture in the otherwise empty room. I had noticed it as soon as I'd come in. It shows a historic scene in which the Prussian General Yorck von Wartenburg on 30 December 1812 acted independently to agree the Convention of Tauroggen with the Russian General Ivan Diebitsch. He had failed to obtain the approval of the Prussian King Friedrich Wilhelm III and was dismissed for exceeding his authority and breaking his soldier's oath of obedience. This is certainly a thought-provoking episode, but I ask myself why this picture is hanging there and what is its significance. Perhaps someone wants to send a signal?

While I was considering this I spotted a second door to our room that I hadn't noticed until now. It looks really interesting and I'm determined to discover what is hidden behind it, providing it is not locked. To reduce the risk I wait until the next sentry has completed his check and has left our room. Now I should have enough time to look around without being disturbed. Carefully I press the door handle down and the door opens. Through a narrow gap I see the floor of the new room is, like our room, lined straw, so it can't be quarters for the guards which I had thought was a possibility. I go in and discover that it is a long room, considerably larger than ours and is obviously intended for holding further prisoners. In one corner lies a pile of junk and I immediately search through it. I find another length of cable end and then, much to my surprise, an old peaked cap. This is a really valuable item because it can be adapted and used as a shoe.

I am so pleased with this valuable find that I completely overlook the balcony outside the room. Fortunately, the door leading to it is not locked. So as not to be seen from outside, I only take a small step on to the balcony and find to my surprise that it is open on its left side. Even more importantly, a wooden staircase leads down from it to the garden I had seen before. Immediately it is obvious to me that I have discovered the least-dangerous escape route because it will allow me to get into the open without using the door to the room we are being held in and the door of the house which is probably guarded. Tonight when it is dark enough, towards midnight, I decide I will make the attempt, and I am carried away by an indescribable feeling of optimism – at last the great moment has arrived and longed-for freedom seems so near. Quickly I leave the room so that I won't be spotted by accident by a passing guard. I don't want to stir up trouble which would result in the guards watching us more closely.

Having got back unnoticed, I tend to my left foot which is in particularly bad shape. I put the cap on it, pack it with straw and wrap the whole thing tight with the length of cable. I feel so much better now that I will be able to walk again, even though the makeshift shoe won't last long. I hope it will fulfil its immediate purpose and then I'll see what happens.

Slowly it is getting dark and most of my comrades are already asleep, including Jonny who has a place not far from me. I hoped he would come with me because his strong character and experience would make the escape easier – going on my own would be an enormous strain. I wake him up, describe as persuasively as I can the escape plan and ask him if he would be prepared to risk the flight with me. To my great disappointment he says no. I was most surprised since he had shown extraordinary willpower, endurance and leadership during the march, cold-bloodedly dealing with problems and contributing so much. Without him we would never have got as far as we did, and we were unlucky to be captured – no one was to blame. But Jonny, like many others, has had enough. He says he can't foresee a successful outcome anymore, particularly as the boil on his foot is much worse and is making things so difficult for him.

An inner voice tells me not to hesitate – that I should act firmly, with determination – but I dread the idea of escaping alone and after much agonising thought I decide to stay put. Then, before I have a chance to change my mind again, a paralysing fatigue overcomes me and in a few seconds I fall asleep and the tensions of that eventful day come to an end.

19 July

I have not slept so well for a long time, but when I wake up I'm very hungry. Unfortunately, in this transit camp – and presumably in other camps like it – no plans had been made to feed the prisoners. We had learned this from comrades who had arrived some days ago. All they had to eat was the remnants of food they had brought along with them, and we had to leave our meagre supplies behind in the grain fields after being taken prisoner. I ask a sentry who has just come on duty if there is anything to eat – I am so hungry that I put the question to him even though there seemed to be no chance of success. The man understands German well and to my surprise gives me a comforting reply: 'You don't eat here, but in the big camps you have bread, soup and everything!' At the same time he spreads his arms out wide to show I could expect paradise on earth. This Ivan appears to be sympathetic – regretfully he has explained the reality of our situation and, to keep us calm, has indicated that things will get better. I must say that some of these guards conduct themselves in a friendly and correct manner in contrast to the dishonourable behaviour of the others. This man gives the right response even if he may have no idea what conditions are like in the 'big camp'. Also he won't be able to conclude from our conversation that I'm intending to escape.

Some time later several guards come in to get prisoners for a work detail. I volunteer at once, intending to use this opportunity to find out more about the building which may be useful when I escape.

Under the supervision of two guards we leave the camp and then move stools and tables from an empty building to a larger building on a hill on the edge of the town which is going to be turned into a soldiers' home or club.

We are soon out of breath and streaming with sweat as we climb uphill in the heat, and to our hunger is added a burning thirst. I start to regret having volunteered for this strenuous job, especially as I ought to be conserving all my strength for the more urgent task ahead. Yet, now I've chosen to do this I'm determined to make the most of the opportunity.

From the hill there is an outstanding view over the whole area and I spot an extensive woodland to the west which I am especially interested in. If only we had been able to reach it yesterday, we might have avoided capture, but there is nothing we can do about that now. The wood, though, would give me somewhere to hide if I am followed after my escape, so volunteering for the work detail has been worthwhile after all.

The house on the hill was obviously turned into a strongpoint during the German occupation, as a protective wall of crudely cut, thick tree trunks has been built around it. Judging by the strands of cable lying around a wrecked radio truck, it was a communications centre.

Junk is scattered across the area and I look out for things I can salvage, but only find a small piece of metal that might be useful. We have to clear all the junk and throw it into a ditch behind the building not far from a vegetable garden. Every time we go past the garden we glance at it to see what we can eat. Carrots are ripped out and consumed at once without removing the earth sticking to them, peas in their husks are eaten too, and unripe redcurrants are considered delicacies.

I see a small mouldy bit of bread. I hesitate for a few seconds, then take it. While I am looking around for more bread, I notice lying there between the bushes is a single rubber boot. I can hardly believe it. Someone has thrown it away because it is worn out – among other defects, the upper has been torn down to the sole – but it is still better than walking in a sock full of holes. My chances of getting away have much improved because I now have something to wear on my right foot.

After several hours we are allowed a short break and I find I am so exhausted I can only stand with difficulty. Some of my comrades have found a big roll of roof paper and make ridiculous-looking boots fastened with the bits of cable which are similar to those I have made myself, but in contrast mine are quite elegant. I wonder how long their makeshift items will last!

Our guards are visibly pleased with the clearing we've done and are in a good mood. One of them proudly shows me a case with a pocket mirror, comb and nail file, perhaps because he thinks I look so unkempt. I appreciate his friendly gesture, look in the mirror and see a man with a strange face standing behind me. Only then do I realise who I am looking at – I am so dishevelled I don't recognise myself.

We start on the job again and I hope that, if we can complete it quickly enough, we will go through the town on the way back and perhaps get something to eat from the people there. The thought of fresh bread, cool milk or soup distracts from our fatigue and we set to work like boy scouts. As the veterinary surgeon and I are sweeping up the straw on the ground I have the good fortune to spot a Sulima cigarette, like those we often used to get with our supplies, which has been dropped. We divide it into two, get a light from one of the more sympathetic guards and smoke it with indescribable bliss. This small episode shows that the guards are prepared to treat us correctly, especially now that they have become accustomed to us. Perhaps the Soviets had recruited men from Volozyn as guards and their experience of German occupation hadn't been too bad.

Just as we have finished and are expecting to get away, several officers and commissars appear with long whips and they let fly with them, making a terrifying whistling noise in the air. Immediately the moderate attitude of our guards changes – perhaps they were acting the part. Harshly they order us to keep working, although there is practically nothing left to be done. We have to pick up every blade of straw and splinter of wood and we do so very carefully so that the whirling whips won't land on our backs. Perhaps the officers only want to frighten us and demonstrate the power they have won over a once-feared enemy.

In the presence of the senior officers our guards didn't dare to take us through the town, so we didn't get the food and drink that we had so hoped for. We were deeply depressed by this – our hunger, thirst and exhaustion felt much worse because our expectations had been raised.

As we wind our way through the streets in ranks of four we pass a small pond and a meadow where Red Army soldiers are cheerfully and loudly larking about. How peaceful and normal everything seems. Nobody here is interested in us and I realise my objective, the new front line, must be a very long way off. It is fortunate I don't know how far!

If only it had been possible to have slaked our thirst with the dirty water from the pond. During the march we have often drunk water from swamps, streams and shell holes without knowing what they contained.

Four weeks have passed since the beginning of the Soviet offensive, and as of tomorrow it will have been two weeks since we broke out of the Minsk cauldron and marched towards an uncertain future. I try to take stock of what has happened during those weeks and wonder what lies ahead. But I'm distracted from these thoughts by the sight that greets me as we reach the camp and approach the stone steps before the main entrance. Standing there on the top step flanked by the two Doric pillars is a man with an imposing figure. If he had worn a toga he would have looked like the Roman Cicero about to begin his famous speech with the words '*Quousque tandem*'. Unfortunately, he has no toga. Instead, he is wearing an earth-brown uniform, is clearly overweight and has an unpleasant countenance with a red nose from drinking too much vodka and malicious eyes which show no sign of intelligence.

I might have been amused by the comparison to Cicero if the man hadn't climbed down the steps and started to tear the spectacles off the men wearing them. We stand there dumbfounded, waiting to see what would happen next.

He stages a performance for us, putting on the spectacles one after then other, propping his hands on his hips, turning to all sides and laughing at us. While wearing spectacles can make some people appear more intelligent, in this case they have the opposite effect whichever pair of spectacles he tries on. Despite my hunger and thirst this comical performance makes me want to laugh, but I restrain myself because laughter would be provocative. However, some of us aren't able to restrain ourselves and suddenly the fat man, now in a raging temper and with a bright-red face, mashes all the spectacles on the flagstones. None of them are undamaged. This incident, as with many others, reinforces my determination to escape because I don't want to be a victim of the brutal, unpredictable nature of such individuals.

When we get back to our room, we throw ourselves down hungry and tired on our straw and are assailed by the soldiers who had been left behind – they beg us for something to eat. But we have brought nothing with us, and the few carrots and unripe redcurrants we found were eaten on the spot and they weren't very nourishing anyway. Finally our hunger drives us to remind our guards of their offer and, after much discussion, they say they will take some of us into town – only those who worked today. So in the light of the sinking sun we make our way through Volozyn, though this time understandably in a far better mood. First, we come to a spring and immediately we throw ourselves at the wonderfully clear and cool water which is an indescribable pleasure since we have been plagued by maddening thirst all day.

From one of the first houses a young, very friendly farmer's wife brings us some milk and bread, but it is only sufficient for three or four men and I don't get anything. But when she sees I've gone without she fetches a couple of onions from her small front garden and, judging by the way that she holds them out to me, I get the impression she sincerely regrets having to leave things at that.

After I have accepted the onions with deep thanks, we go on to the next house in the street, and I see the front door is open. Quickly I glance at both our guards and when I see that they are both looking in another direction I dart through the doorway and almost trip over a fully grown black pig. The pig is as surprised as I am and retreats to the back of the room, grunting angrily and knocking over a metal bucket of food which spreads out in a mushy mess on the wooden floor.

The presence of a pig in this otherwise absolutely clean, very orderly and unoccupied room is totally unexpected. In normal circumstances after such an embarrassing and indeed painful entry I would have left the house immediately. But my hunger is even stronger than my fear and it leads me to the kitchen cupboard at the back of the room in the left-hand corner. In great haste I pull open various drawers in the hope of finding something edible, but without success. Finally, I reach the two doors at the top. There is nothing behind the door on the left while the door on the right is locked so something valuable might be stored there.

While I am considering how I can break it open – how impatient one becomes when one is hungry – the door of the room suddenly opens and a young man appears dressed in brown trousers which might be part of a uniform and a snow-white shirt of the sort that civilians wear. I stare at him expecting the worst, but he remains quite calm, glances as a matter of course at his bristling animal, and astonishingly ignores the mess on the floor. Then he goes up to the cupboard without a word and opens the locked door. Surely, he is going to take out a pistol, I think, and I watch him paralysed with fear. But instead of a weapon he produces a loaf, and he breaks off a bit as big as a fist and hands it to me with a friendly gesture.

This is one of those times when one simply wants to break in tears. I am unable to say a word. Dumbly I clap him on the shoulders like I once did to our motorcyclist who had saved me at Drut from a completely hopeless situation, and hugged him. At that moment – and this is not an exaggeration – I regarded myself as one of the luckiest persons in the world because I had been given some bread and because I hadn't been treated as an enemy, but as someone in distress. I was reminded of the words from the Lord's Prayer 'give us this day our daily bread' which, under normal circumstances, is taken much too lightly and thoughtlessly. How differently I would regard the world if truths like this one determined my thoughts and actions. It also strikes me how important it is to see things clearly without getting carried away by sweeping generalisations. If one avoids telling the truth and facing up to the problems of the past, then, as the writer J.G. Burg warned, in the future we would all drown in a sea of hatred and revenge. As I leave the house I give the young man a last grateful look, then I rejoin our group which has stopped nearby. The episode I have just recounted only lasted a few minutes.

A farmer's wife then comes out with some crusts of bread which she holds up in her pinafore. In a moment the starving soldiers tear the bread from her and consume it, leaving only crumbs. As I've already had something to eat, I didn't join them. I was saving my bread as iron rations for the first hours after my escape, but even so I hope to get something more to eat now. And I am lucky. At the next farm the farmer puts a small basin of soup out on the dusty street, and even provides six spoons. This time I don't hold back and six of us kneel down around the basin and spoon the contents down so quickly that I can see the level in the soup going down.

I am relieved that in my garb I am not identified as an officer as in full uniform the local people would certainly have regarded me with mixed feelings, and I am determined to do everything I can to build up my strength in preparation for my escape.

The inhabitant of the last house that we visit appears with a bucketful of cold bread soup. We grab whatever implements we can, mainly empty tin cans, and scoop up the mixture that has been so kindly offered to us. It is thick and sour and, despite our great hunger, we have to force ourselves to drink it. In no time the bucket is empty, and impetuously the farmer goes off to get another.

We wait expectantly at the fence until he returns with a second load. We go for the bread soup straight away, with a clash of containers and loud swearing, so it is difficult to pour, but finally everyone gets his portion and has something in his stomach – for once the worst hunger has been stilled.

When I reflect on this, and on the behaviour of the guards, I conclude that most of the local people and the German troops that were stationed here must have got on fairly well.

When we return to the camp we are immediately surrounded by comrades who beg us for something to eat. I break off a small piece of bread and hand it to those standing close to me and I'm shaken by the look of gratitude with which it is received. Then I go off to find Jonny who, because of the boils, couldn't work and hadn't been on the march through the town.

He gives me such a hungry look that I share the remains of my bread with him. Then I eat what remains of my iron rations because it makes no sense to save them up for an escape that may never happen.

It is dark outside and I ought to concentrate on planning my escape for tonight but – as on previous days – I am overcome by a crippling fatigue. This is a result of hard work in intense heat and a reaction to the food which has renewed my strength but made me tired too. This time Jonny is prepared to go with me, but I cannot make up my mind to go through with it, and within a few seconds I am fast asleep.

In the middle of the night I am awoken by a terrible cry, and immediately the sentries crash in through the door. Soon there is an explanation. One of our men has had a bad dream, which is not surprising after everything we have lived through, and probably it will happen again in the future.

20 July

When I wake up in the morning the sun is already shining through the windows, and there is a lot of hustle and bustle on the street in front of the house. My eyes alight on my comrades lying apathetically on the dirty straw. Outside it is such a lovely day while in here it is gloomy and miserable.

Really it is high time for me to escape and I fix my eyes on the door which is my way to freedom – and I make a startling discovery that gets the blood flowing rapidly in my veins. The handle has been bound up with wire and this promising escape route is blocked! Without doubt while I was out one of the prisoners had inspected the neighbouring room as I had done and he had been seen by a guard who had decided to stop further visits. When we returned from working in the town the room had been so dark that I hadn't spotted the change.

For a moment I am very close to giving up my plan, and I reproach myself for failing to seize the chance as soon as it presented itself. Then all of a sudden, incredibly, without prompting, I was suddenly filled with an inexplicable, overwhelming urge to live in freedom. All my depressing thoughts were swept away and I was filled with the firm conviction that an attempt to escape would be successful, although at the time I had no idea how I would do it. Of course, this sudden burst of confidence may have stemmed from my overstretched nerves, but perhaps it also came from some more mysterious cause – there are so many things in heaven and on earth that we can't possibly explain.

Now my mind is made up again to try to escape I take the risk of asking some of the other soldiers if they would be prepared to go with me. I only approached those who looked like they might be willing, but none of them accepted. Most of them regarded the proposal as completely pointless, and some of them even regarded me as being slightly crazy, commenting that the Soviets had advanced a long way already and were still advancing so probably we would be on the run for weeks and most likely we would be caught and liquidated. And even if we got to the front lines, we would still have to find a way through them which would require lots of luck. This is the right line to take if one is prepared to put up with captivity in the hope of surviving all the suffering and seeing the homeland again. The determination to reach our own lines and avoid becoming a prisoner seems to have faded away.

Finally, I ask Lieutenant Niedermeier but, because of the maltreatment he had been subjected to, he is in no state to join me and the veterinary surgeon fears he will not get through the ordeal to come. Although Jonny has already turned me down twice, I ask him again, as I don't want to undertake the venture alone. He declines because of his boil, but he also gives me the same argument against going that I'd heard from some of the other soldiers.

The fact that we survived our capture uninjured stems from Stalin's order that prisoners of war should be put on parade to demonstrate the scale of our defeat. On 17 July 1944 55,000 prisoners taken in the Minsk cauldron and before at Vitebsk, Orsha, Mogilev and Bobruysk were marched through the streets of Moscow past thousands of emotional spectators in a similar fashion to a Roman triumph. The column was 3km long and many of the men were barefoot.

A further reason for our survival was, as I've said, because we had offered no resistance nor attempted to escape, especially when we were in the transit camp near Volozyn. Also, of course, our captors were soldiers of the Red Army rather than partisans who probably hadn't heard about Stalin's order.

I had just finished talking to my comrades when our guards came in and told us that at 6 p.m. we would be transported to Raku and then to the big camp at Minsk. Before then I will have to have put my escape plans into effect, but how I am going to do that I have no idea and it is even more difficult now because of the shortage of time.

Somehow I have to get out of this room into the fresh air, into the garden behind the building, where freedom seems so attainable. While we have been kept here no one has tried to break out so the guards have overcome their initial mistrust and are no longer suspicious. We can now go to the latrine without a guard and even into the vegetable garden to look for something to eat. All I have to do is to say 'Salad' and point in the direction concerned. In response I get a muffled affirmative from the guard who gestures towards the door and soon I am quite alone in the garden. I pull up a couple of red turnips, then sit down on a heap of straw next to a door that apparently leads down into a cellar which I hadn't noticed before. It turns out that it will play an important role in my plan. I put the turnips down beside me so that if a suspicious sentry should go past, I can say they are supplies for our forthcoming journey.

As I have already said, it is a lovely morning, with a blue sky and radiant sunshine, and I'm inclined to stay where I am for a bit longer. My eye wanders over the many redcurrant bushes and the immediate area where, as for as I can see, there are no fences to keep me in. I could simply walk off in the broad daylight for a long way, but across almost coverless country – which would be pointless. So, it would be best to wait.

Suddenly I hear footsteps approaching and I carefully grasp my turnips, expecting a guard. But instead four of my comrades appear. Hunger has driven them into the garden and they sit down beside me. As I had not met them before I assume that they have just arrived, and tell them I have decided to escape at the first opportunity. Three of them clearly regard me as a bit stupid. They tap their foreheads and get up and go, leaving me with the fourth one. Naturally I ask him whether he is prepared to come with me and, to my great delight, he says he is.

My future companion is called Georg Maag, is 18 years old and comes from Ravensburg. He is a signals corporal from the de-motorised 25th Würtemburger Panzer Division. On 23 June – four weeks ago, on the second day of the Soviet offensive when a massive attack was made towards Orsha – he was recovering in a centre for convalescent soldiers. From there he had tried to make his way back through the heavy defensive fighting to his artillery regiment. With a lot of luck he succeeded in doing this, but there is a snag – Georg hasn't got any shoes. He had been forced to give away his boots and uniform. Nevertheless, he is prepared to march with me in his socks, and he tells me he's willing to put up with the lack of kit without complaining so long as he can get away. With a strong handshake we seal our fateful association. There are no big words or heroic gestures, just unspoken assurance that in every situation we will stay with one another. We both know exactly what we are letting ourselves in for. There is nothing heroic about it.

We decide we must carefully find out what is hidden behind the nearby door. We guess it is not locked, and we are right. As no one is to be seen far and wide, we open it quickly and close it immediately behind us. Unexpectedly we find ourselves in a cellar. Through two small windows we can see out into the area around the building's entrance where the sentries are going to and fro, so we have to move around as silently as possible. There is enough light for us to orientate ourselves and, and as we become accustomed to the gloom, we discover some wonderful things. The experience is not quite as exciting as Howard Carter's when he looked through a hole into Tutankhamun's burial chamber, but with great delight we find – which is for us more valuable than the Pharoah's gold – two mineral water bottles to replace our lost field flasks. In the middle of the cellar stands a great paper sack which we open at once. It is full of tea leaves and lying around it are a lot of bags that are apparently going to be filled. We fill two of the bags, intending to use this surprising find as ersatz tobacco if we get the chance. Next to the big sack are five old, shrunken, small potatoes which we also put in our bags. As before, we come across more lengths of telephone cable and, in a corner, some rags. Georg takes two rags, wraps them around his socks and secures them with the cable, just as I had done with my cap, in order to fashion some emergency footware. I select some scraps of material to cover my feet in when my wrappings disintegrate.

Further inspection of the cellar reveals a dark extension which is half full of fine wood shavings which would be a wonderful place to hide, and immediately the thought occurs to me that we could simply conceal ourselves here when it is dark outside and then make our way to freedom. When I propose this to Georg he agrees at once. We are happy that this completely unexpected opportunity to get away without taking big risks has presented itself.

It is now around midday so there are about 6 hours before the start of the march to Minsk, and we decide to interrupt our stressful search of the dark and musty cellar and then find our way back when the time comes. This shouldn't be difficult because we only have to ask for vegetables and we will be let out into the garden and our hiding place. We shouldn't be missed, especially as we haven't been counted or registered and this is merely a transit camp.

We start to feel hungry again, but we have our five potatoes and a few red turnips and we are in such a good mood we decide to eat them now. So that we can see out and not to arouse any suspicion, we make our way to the doorway of the house and there meet a comrade from whom, with a stroke of luck, we get some matches. Then we find some twigs in the garden and kindle a fire in which we roast our potatoes. Eagerly we blow into the glowing fire – too eagerly in fact and I get covered in ash.

The comrade who gave us the matches blows especially strongly on the fire in the hope of earning himself a potato, which of course he gets. We give him the largest, while we share the smaller ones, and we cannot believe how good the potatoes are – and the red turnips are delicious as well!

Two guards have made themselves comfortable by the walls on either side of the steps, leaning against the pillars and watching our activities, which is apparently a welcome change in the monotony of sentry duty.

Where we are the atmosphere is highly stressed even when we are lighting our fire to cook the potatoes, but far away in the Wolf's Lair, Hitler's headquarters, the atmosphere is even more tense because at

12.42 p.m. Count von Stauffenberg's bomb exploded and Hitler was wounded. Of course, we didn't know about this assassination attempt till sometime later.

Once we had completed our modest meal, we witness a scene that was less dramatic than a bomb going off but still shocking. Four civilians brought a wounded soldier in a box cart into the camp. He had been shot through both heels and could not take a step on his own. His miserable dressings were thoroughly soaked through with blood and numerous flies had settled thickly on them, so that they looked quite black. We immediately jump up to bring him into the room, and when we move him he groans loudly. Hardly had we laid the wounded man down carefully on the flagstones of the entrance than the two Red Army guards fell upon him and quite callously began to rob him. They showed no compunction at all. Everything they don't want they throw away, including a box of matches that one of the four civilians snatches for himself.

We watch this atrocious incident with intense anger, but can't take any action because we can't predict the consequences. One of the villains, apparently unhappy with the results of his search, goes through my pockets and finds the length of cable wire, looks sideways at it, mutters to himself, and then throws it onto the ground with all the other things that are lying there. When he goes off again I quickly recover the wire as I will need it to bind up my foot wrappings. Before the sentry returned to his position, the man with the matchbox, apparently a farmer who has a magnificent full beard, came up to me slowly, looked briefly all around and stuck the box in my pocket, perhaps because he had seen how interested I had been in him. Speechless and full of gratitude, I clap him very quickly on the back, hoping that the guard won't notice and react in an unfriendly manner. Having witnessed so much truly bad behaviour I realised more clearly than ever how important it is to behave correctly and humanely.

We carry the wounded man into our room, but unfortunately we cannot do anything else for him. I wonder what will happen to him if he can't join the march to Minsk. When one is seriously threatened one is liable to think like this, but it is essential not to let such thoughts take hold – one needs to repress them. While the death of close comrades like Captain Trost and Second Lieutenant Bauer can't be forgotten, they have to be accepted, and one has constantly to consider with one's own fate. This is especially important when the situation is extremely difficult as it has been in the last few weeks, in particular when the physical burden reaches the borders of the bearable or even beyond them.

In order to gather sufficient strength for our planned escape, we remain in the room and rest on the straw. I tell Georg that he shouldn't stay close to me as that might arouse the suspicion of the guards. We can't be too careful and try to think of everything.

Judging by the position of the sun it must be about 2 p.m., so there are still about 4 hours to go before the march starts, and we decide to go into the cellar again in about an hour and wait for events there. I take the valuable matches out of my pocket and transfer them to the plastic container I'd found.

As the container is so big, I separate the two sandpaper strips, stick them on to the wooden ones and make it watertight with the adhesive band. This arrangement should allow me to reopen it quickly.

I am now so optimistic about the escape that I'm in an almost euphoric state. The idea of failure doesn't occur to me and mentally I am already far away. I feel full of energy in the same way as I did early this morning after I had found the door to our adjacent room locked.

I am so keen I make another attempt to persuade Jonny to change his mind. I point out Georg to him, who had been immediately prepared to participate, and describe the new plan to him which involves a much simpler means of making an exit. When he responds by lying there silently without giving any sign of encouragement, I pull out all the stops in my art of persuasion:

> Do you want to go to the dogs in Siberia? Look at yourself – you are sick, no one will help you, and you will have to go out in the freezing cold, living on iron rations and with inadequate clothing, and most likely you will be forced to work so hard you'll have an accident. And apart from this, you don't know if, with your boil, can make the 80km to Minsk at all. Almost certainly you have already been reported missing and your family won't know what has happened to you, and you won't be able to contact them. But if you join us in a few hours you will be free and you'll be able to do as you like, get bread and milk for yourself, and perhaps be home again in a couple of weeks! So, are you coming? I will even give you my rubber boot for your bad foot!

And that does it – if I give him the rubber boot, he says then he will come along. Immediately he looks happy, but then there's a catastrophe that threatens the whole plan.

The door of our room flies open and two sentries charge in shouting wildly: 'Get up! Get up!' At first no one knows what is happening, but then it becomes clear that our march is about to start 4 hours ahead of time, presumably so as not to have to go so far in the night. When this news sinks in I see that our plan cannot be carried out and for several seconds I am in a panic, but then despair gets the upper hand. There must be a way out of this somehow, but where and when? Calm down, I say to myself, calm down, and see what can be done.

We leave the room slowly, one after the other, and go along a long, narrow corridor. About halfway along there is a fork. The turning to the right leads towards the main door of the building where two sentries guard the route to the street. After this turning the corridor goes on for a few metres further before it comes to an end. As soon as we reach the fork I realise it offers us perhaps the one and only chance to escape, providing we can find an unlocked door in the stretch before the wall at the end. So we have to chance it, yes or no, as once we have left the column we will be committed – there will be no way back. I throw a questioning glance back at Jonny, but he shakes his head – he's given up. Georg, though, is willing to go through with it, thank God!

'Stop there!' I call out in a subdued tone and, when both sentries look out at the street at that moment, we get out of the line and race along the rest of the corridor hoping to find a door. When we reach one we throw it open at once, although it could be accommodation for the guards or even the office of the camp commandant, and we have terrific luck, for the room is completely empty – nobody, no furniture, no straw as in our room, nothing. Undecided, we remain standing at the door, looking around and not knowing what to do next. I am so tense after the last few minutes that at first I don't realise that we are in the large long room that I saw yesterday through the now-blocked door. At one end is the balcony and we rush over to it in the hope that we can get through the door that opens onto it. Having reached the balcony, we quickly look round and see no one nearby, and then we dash down the wooden steps, slide down some worn steps, and end up in the garden below. We run along the side wall of the building and stop in front of our cellar door.

'Come on man, get in!' I call to Georg, and in a second we have vanished into the cellar. It is hard to believe that we have reached our original escape route through just one door and under completely unexpected conditions. But it is not dark yet so we aren't out of danger, for in broad daylight anyone could have seen us, even from a distance, and at any moment the door could be opened and it would be all over.

Completely out of breath, we crawl at once into the pile of wood shavings and stare as if hypnotised at the door of the poorly illuminated room. The minutes pass slowly in the highest state of tension. Sometime later, when everything seems to be quiet, we come out at last – once more we have been very lucky, at least for the moment.

About 8 hours lie ahead of us before it will be sufficiently dark for us to leave the cellar. 'They have all been marched off', says Georg quietly. 'And the guards too', I whisper. We are both convinced that the camp has been completely cleared and that only a few Red Army soldiers remain behind to deal with more prisoners who will be coming in soon.

Silence reigns in the cellar and, as far as we can tell, in the building above us. Only now and then we hear a gentle rustling caused by the mice that have nested in the wood shavings – otherwise there are no suspicious sounds.

After 2 or 3 hours, suddenly the door opens and hesitantly a Red Army soldier enters the dark room next to ours. We are buried up to our necks in wood shavings so surely no one will see us, but we are very anxious and wonder what we should do. We notice that he is carrying his machine pistol crosswise on his chest, which means it is not ready to fire, and it follows that he is not suspicious and is apparently going about some routine business.

We lie utterly still, as any movement could betray our presence. Even the rustling of the mice could make him distrustful. He is perhaps a metre away from us. Stay still, listen, I tell myself. Why has he stopped right there? I struggle to hold my breath and not make the slightest movement. I am scared that he might decide to probe around in the wood shavings, and I dig my fingernails into my clothes. My heart beats audibly – I can hear it pulsing quickly and so loudly that I think the man must hear it too, but of course he can't. He goes on past the paper sack containing the tea and finally out of the door. We take a deep breath. How lucky we have been to find this small dark room with the heap of wood shavings – if we had remained in the main cellar we would have been discovered at once. As a precaution we remain absolutely still, unable to say a word about this nerve-racking episode.

I tell myself to relax and listen and think the whole thing through. We have plenty of time to do this, and I ask myself whether the escape will continue to go as well as it is now. For the first time I realise that we have already accomplished so much, even though many of our comrades thought we were crazy to make the attempt, including an experienced, prudent and resourceful front-line officer like Second Lieutenant Janasiak who, despite his boil, had the same opinion.

But we have taken our decision, the preparations have been made and the situation has developed in such a way that there can be no going back now. We must dismiss such thoughts which will only discourage us – we must focus on our purpose and carry out our plan even though we know it may fail.

We decide that if we are stopped within the camp, we will both run off immediately and go as fast as possible in two directions, Georg to the right and myself to the left, and meet up again just beyond the garden in the cover of the bushes and shrubs. This way we believe we will confuse the guards and make it difficult for them to reach a quick decision, and we will gain enough time to conceal ourselves in the darkness.

The tension grows with every minute. We don't know if everything will go according to plan, but we are hoping it will go well and our situation will improve, and we are looking forward to being able to act independently.

Then the great moment arrives. Carefully we open the door just a crack at first and look outside where nothing suspicious can be seen. Almost complete darkness reigns, and apparently there is a new moon. The conditions are just right, and we only have to cover a short distance and know which way to go. But it is possible we won't spot a sentry until it is too late, especially if he is concealed by a bush or tree.

But we are on our way. We open the door wider and move out into the open. Slowly, watchfully, and without making a sound we set off step by step towards the enclosed garden. There it is! After just a few seconds and completely unexpectedly from only a few metres away a short, hard 'Stop!' comes out of the darkness. Like lightning we run as we'd agreed in different directions, and we gain the few seconds we'd hoped for. But after about 20m I stumble over the split in my rubber boots and fly in a high curve and land on my stomach, while at the same moment the sentry's machine pistol lets loose. The red tracers fly away just half a metre over me, and if I had not stumbled at the right moment, then everything would have been over. I wait until the firing stops and, as the burst had been a long one, I assumed the guard had fired off a whole magazine. Quickly I creep under one of the redcurrant bushes and immediately afterwards hear approaching footsteps. I grip the ground with my fingers and pull my head in and see the sentry's boots coming straight towards me. The tension is agonising, but he does not discover me and vanishes into the darkness.

For the last few moments I had been wholly taken up with myself, but I now ask myself what could have happened to Georg. Apparently he has not been shot at and has disappeared into the night. But where is he?

Perhaps already behind the garden as we had planned. Suddenly finding myself alone in this situation depresses me, and I'm worried that I might have to go on with the escape without a companion, which I am desperate to avoid. But now I need to concentrate fully on my predicament as the danger is by no means over. Behind me, luckily some distance away, I hear the voices of several guards who are beginning to look for us. Crouching down, I wriggle my way deeper into the protection of the bushes and undergrowth. I have almost crossed the garden when I am suddenly stopped by a palpable scratch on the face, not a sharp branch or thorn, but a prick of wire. This isn't a small garden fence – it is a well-constructed wire entanglement of the kind one encounters on the front line. As I immediately discover, it is only about a metre high, but at least as deep, so if I try to climb over it I run the risk of being caught up in it. Then I'll hang like a fly in a spider's web. As the barbed wire is covered with many shrubs it can't be seen from the building in the camp, and I was glad I hadn't run off through the garden in broad daylight. Now I understand why the guards had allowed us to go to the latrine in the garden behind the house so freely.

I'm disconcerted to find such an unexpected obstacle so close to my goal. Near despair, I creep along the wire looking for a gap I could get through as quickly as possible. Then I realise Georg must have been confronted with the same problem, and just then I hear rustling nearby and see the outline of a German field cap. 'Georg, come here', I whisper though my voice sounds much too loud. In a moment he is alongside me. It is difficult to express the joy of not being alone anymore. 'I thought they had got you – he fired off the whole magazine', Georg says quietly. But we cannot keep talking as we have to get further away as fast as we can.

Now we are together the barrier seems to be only half as difficult to cross as before, and we establish that the lowest length of barbed wire is close to the ground, at least at this position. So we lie down on our backs and push the wire up. Then, stretching out our legs and rotating our shoulders, we wriggle our way through centimetre by centimetre. Since we are completely helpless in this situation and reckon we will be discovered at any moment, every minute stretches to eternity.

Close by we hear the guards talking in an agitated way among themselves as they are puzzled and not sure about what to do next. Obviously their first step should be to systematically check the barbed-wire barrier so we struggle to work our way through it quickly. After about 10 minutes of immense stress, we finally manage it. With a feeling of immense relief we realise we have made it – despite the unforeseen incidents and difficulties we have succeeded. Now freedom is palpably before us, though it is not yet the final freedom we are aiming for.

For the moment we don't have to worry about being pursued as the guards are still having a lively discussion about it, and they are hampered, for a time at least, by their own barbed wire.

As quickly as we can we want to put a comfortable distance between us and the camp and its surroundings so, taking our direction from the Great Bear, which is clear in the starry sky, we set off, keeping a careful watch on all sides. Despite the late hour, there is plenty of activity in the village. In a nearby smithy we hear loud and continuous hammering, lights are still burning in several houses, and we hear animated conversations which are often interrupted by almost triumphant peals of laughter – perhaps the Soviets have already heard about the assassination attempt at the Wolf's Lair. As yet we don't know this has happened and maybe that is a good thing because the news would have distracted us from our purpose.

Very cautiously we move on, thinking it would be unbearable to meet with some misadventure now after we've taken such trouble and been blessed with such luck. At the end of the village we have to cross a main road and we throw ourselves down immediately into the roadside ditch as a truck with bright headlights approaches. Frightening seconds pass before it drives on without stopping and without noticing us.

Sometime later, in open country, we sit down on the edge of a cornfield for a short rest. This is the first break after hours of extreme strain. But instead of relaxing I suffer a form of physical collapse. In the past days and weeks so many stressful things have happened to me that I haven't been able to take them all in. Frequently the boundaries of the tolerable and reasonable have been reached and often crossed. Now that excessive strength isn't required, my body reacts – I find I have no strength left.

A new phase lies before us, and we don't know what will happen. It was predictable that we would be taken prisoner as part of a marching group, but since then all sorts of unpredictable things had occurred, and now we are faced with the most difficult challenge of all – getting safely through the Russian positions to reach the front line.

21 July

Midnight must have passed before I recovered sufficiently for us to continue. Making use of all the available cover, we keep moving in a westerly direction. As we no longer have compasses, we are guided by the Great Bear.

This means that we have to march when the sky is clear or at least not too cloudy so that we don't lose our sense of direction and make no progress. The western, weathered side of trees are of no help to us because we have to move at night when we can't see them, and we have to go through extensive forests where there is a danger of being seen during daylight.

During the last few hours of stress and continuous concentration, our feelings of hunger have receded almost completely, but now suddenly they revive so strongly that the elation from our successful escape fades away. The trouble is, we haven't gone far enough to dare to look for something to eat, and so we keep going and our strength dwindles minute by minute. When we come to some hills I find I am so exhausted that I can hardly stay upright, and on the steeper elevations I can only manage on all fours.

Georg, who is even weaker than I am, agrees when I insist we should go up to the next house to ask the people there for some bread – the risk has to be taken. When we find a field of peas we lie down hungry and exhausted for a break, and tear off one pod after another, eating them unopened as we did yesterday. We don't feel any stronger afterwards – what we really need is some bread.

As there isn't much time until dawn, we have to get going again soon, and we need to cover a bit more ground as we have only put around 3km behind us. In addition to being hungry we are very thirsty, and we can't see a stream or a pond nearby and there aren't any houses where we might obtain some milk. Then, when we are passing through a swampy area, we drink – yet again – some bitter brownish, muddy moor water from a pit and fill our water bottles.

A little later the outlines of some houses appear and we approach them expectantly – in fact we rush towards them as far as our weakened condition allows in the hope of being given bread without running straight into the arms of partisans or Red Army soldiers. I am so excited and careless that I stub my foot against a tree stump and the pain is excruciating – I've seriously injured my big toe, possibly even broken the bone – but I don't mind since there is a chance of at last getting something to eat.

At the first house we bang heavily on the door. We have unscrewed the necks of our flasks, having decided that if the person who opens the door shows the least hostility we will hit them over the head. This is the sort of decision that only someone in our desperate situation can understand. There is a delay, then the door creaks open and an old man leaning on a stick appears. We beg him for bread – '*chleb, pan, chleb!*' – and we are relieved to see that he seems to be friendly. Without a word he looks us up and down, turns around and then with shuffling steps goes slowly back into his house, while we wait and hope that he will return. Then he comes back, holding out to us dumbly, but with a friendly gesture, a large square of black bread. We almost tear it out of his hands, break it into two pieces and eat, eat, eat. After the first bites I feel stronger and in an unbelievably short time I am fully restored. Calmly and with effusive thanks we say goodbye to the kind-hearted old man, whom we have without doubt dragged from a deep sleep. He had helped us in such a friendly and obliging manner and had treated us not as enemies but as people in distress. I had often had similar experiences when I was retreating with the column, even after I had forced my way into the house in Volozyn where I was richly rewarded. I can only keep repeating to myself: look at everything objectively, without prejudice or resentment and above all without generalisations!

Before he has a chance to change his mind and perhaps drag us into an awkward situation we go on quickly to the last house in this friendly village, hoping to get a small supply of bread. Here we are met by a farmer's wife in just as friendly a manner. When her eyes fall on our flasks with their brownish water, she takes them and, shaking her head, goes into the stall next to the house and brings them back full of fresh milk. We drink them immediately, down to the last drop, with indescribable pleasure, where upon she smiles and fills them once more and gives us bread to carry on our way.

Gratefully we take our leave from this helpful woman, and then we search for a wood and we find one at just the right moment. We choose a suitable site for the camp and camouflage it carefully with pine needles which lie profusely on the ground, hiding our flasks, the bread and my mess-tin lid in a hole in the ground which we cover with a few wild flowers. Then we lie down ourselves. Now for the first time we are fully aware of the extraordinary good luck that we have had in the last few hours and we are determined to hang on to the freedom that we have gained.

It is cold in the early morning hours and the floor of the forest is damp so we get hardly any sleep. We have lain down close together and covered ourselves with my denims, as Georg is only wearing his uniform shirt. After short spurts of restless sleep, the first, though not at all warm, rays of the morning sun come through the branches. Wild pigeons coo continuously in the wood and settle on the trees so close to our camp that I could easily shoot them with a pistol, if I only had one. Pigeon would be a welcome supplement to our diet, and we have our cooking pot to roast it in and my waterproof matches for the fire. But we can manage without it thanks to the kind-hearted people in the village, and we hope for similar help in the future.

The behaviour of the wild pigeons worries us a bit because someone in the neighbourhood might choose to investigate the reason for the constant noise and fluttering. How many hours must pass before we can get going again? After all we have experienced we have become extremely cautious and mistrustful, and we are determined to keep the freedom we've regained so arduously.

We eat a small breakfast – a piece of bread and a few sips of milk. We cannot allow ourselves to eat any more as we have to save up our food because we don't know what will happen next.

During the day we are restless – we have to put up with the noise of the pigeons, and we are well aware of how risky our position is on the edge of the small wood. In a nearby meadow children play games, harvest carts drive past and a rider, fortunately a civilian, gallops in front of us along the edge of the wood. All this looks very peaceful, but we decide that next time we will camp deeper in the wood we've chosen, although that means we won't be able to check it so thoroughly.

In the afternoon the situation becomes uncomfortable as we can clearly hear voices and bullets smack into the treetops. We calm ourselves with the thought that shooting is a common activity in the area and the people we hear are probably hunting. We don't have to move to another site because quiet returns and stays until the evening.

Before it is completely dark, we have a good look at our surroundings because, with our makeshift footwear, we need to watch out for fallen branches, tree stumps and other obstacles. My big toe is hurting again, but fortunately is not broken. Carefully, avoiding every twig lying on the ground, we creep silently along a cutting that could lead in the right direction. Again and again we stop briefly, look all around and listen to every suspicious sound. When we reach the edge of the wood we wait under the cover of a tree for darkness and the appearance of the first stars, as we are dependent upon the Great Bear. If we keep going in the same direction, we should reach the area between Vilna and Lida where we hope to come across a newly fortified front line. The distance is 60 to 70km and, if everything goes smoothly, we can cover this well within a week.

Fortunately, we do not know exactly what lies ahead of us and how much we are mistaken!

We painfully miss the map Second Lieutenant Bauer left behind, as with its help we could have chosen a more direct and less dangerous route.

We would have been able to find our way around rivers, lakes or woods, and we could have avoided the big towns and country roads where we might run into the military, especially as we neared the front line. As it is, we go ahead into unknown country and have to rely on sometimes untrustworthy or inaccurate information from the local people at whose houses we ask for food.

We pass a wood and see a single house not far beyond it, and we take the opportunity to ask for food. When we knock on a window it is opened and the head of a young man appears who at first glance does not appeal to us. 'You want food? There isn't much', he says in an unfriendly way, then he brings us two small pieces of bread and gives us an unpleasant grin. I feel he is playing for time. 'There are only two of you? And you don't have rifles or pistols?' he asks, and alarm bells immediately ring.

Keep calm and don't appear anxious, I say to myself, and glance at the wood behind us. 'Oh, our Bolshevik comrades, more than a hundred of them, are over there, all armed with carbines and pistols. We are on our way to Chleb, where others are waiting for us', I say, trying to appear convincing. Apparently it works because, judging by his expression, he seems to believe me.

We don't want to leave a bad impression behind us and are keen to get away as soon as possible, so we give him a somewhat curt thank you and make our way cautiously back to the wood where the 'hundred comrades' should be hidden, then we resume the original direction of our march.

Once more we've seen that the local people react to us in different ways and we need to be careful – just because some people have helped us in the past doesn't mean that others will do so in future. So, before we make our next attempt to obtain bread, we go on for quite a distance, then find another solitary house, and here everything goes well. The farmer's wife not only give us the bread we are yearning for, but also hands us four eggs, one of which Georg, who is so excited, drops and breaks. For the whole of the following day he is excessively angry about this and reproaches himself. She also gives us a few potatoes and plenty of milk with which we can fill our flasks and, in her final act of generosity, she gives us a small linen sack after remarking how difficult transporting food must be. We leave her with a feeling of enormous gratitude, look for the Great Bear and set off again on our march.

As we can't find an easy way of going in the right direction, we frequently have to cross fields. We come to a barbed-wire fence surrounding a large field which we can climb over or go around, but Georg, apparently still frustrated about his misfortune with the egg, simply attacks the fragile wooden uprights of the fence and barges his way through. This is not exactly the best solution because of the noise it makes, and we don't want to leave any traces of our presence behind, certainly not so near where we had camped. But, given our recent experience and the ordeal that lies ahead, I can understand how he feels – sometimes things get on one's nerves, and one becomes irritated, impatient and morose.

22 July

Before dawn, Georg notices a small building behind a house of a kind that we have not come across before and, when we get closer, it proves to be a storage cellar. Although we have already been well provided for, we cannot pass the building without having a look. Carefully Georg climbs down the few steps and appears shortly afterwards with a small earthenware pot in his hands. As it is too dark to identify the contents, he puts a finger in it and stirs the thick mixture. The sample we try tastes like butter and, whatever it is, it contains fat which is of great value to us.

We go on and find an especially well-sited place to camp which is thickly surrounded by pine trees. Early in the morning we decide to light a fire and prepare for ourselves what is in the circumstances an opulent breakfast. The mixture in the pot looks like unrefined watery butter, but it is all right to eat and quite tasty. With great delight we spread the butter thickly onto slices of bread – so thickly that there is almost more butter than bread. If I had indulged myself in the same way at home, my father would certainly have had something to say about it, but in reaction to our difficult situation we have simply gone over the top.

Georg has finally got over his depression and so we prepare baked potatoes with fried egg. It is all there, three eggs, sufficient potatoes and the requisite butter. We take the potatoes out of the sack and, using my rusty razor blades, we slowly peel them. A few hours ago we would have been forced to eat them without peeling, but now we feel we have time, lots of time.

Only 4 or 5 hours are available for our nightly march and so for about 20 hours we have to wait in a hiding place. These long hours are filled with alarming noises and tension, and each day we had to find a new place which brings with it new threats and dangers.

Yet, for the moment we do not appear to have anything to fear, so we quickly collect some dry wood and light a fire with the matches out of the waterproof container. We use a short branch to extend the handle of the lid of the mess tin so we can hold it over the flames without burning our fingers. Soon the potatoes baked with butter are giving off a tempting smell and we then break the eggs over them and stir them in, and we can hardly wait to consume the dish we have produced with such culinary skill.

From the piece of sheet metal that I had picked up during the work at Volozyn, I have made an unwieldy spoon which fulfils its purpose here, firstly for stirring and then eating, We have to share the spoon, each of us taking three mouthfuls then passing it across. Then, wonderfully full, we lie down, ever so pleased with what we have done. In our dire situation such small successes are important, as they reinforce our self-confidence and give us the will to keep going.

Thinking back to the days of captivity, I realise how right the decision was to try and escape, however bad the conditions we have endured. We are at liberty again, we have taken our fate into our own hands, and there is a chance that, with luck, we can get back to our lines. We are sure that all the privations and dangers in front of us are preferable to a miserable existence in a Soviet prisoner-of-war camp for an indefinite period and with little chance of survival. I wonder how many of my comrades have reached the camp at Minsk, and how many failed to get there.

Would Jonny have survived the long march?

At Minsk the prisoners were marched through the town in the same way as they were in Moscow, and emotional spectators spat at them and threw stones and various items. Partly this was to demonstrate their support for the Red Army which they had not cooperated with during the years of the occupation. Now the Red Army was back in control they feared retaliation, especially against the anti-communist supporters of the 'White Russian Self-help Organisation'.

Probably this was the result of the moderate administration run by General Commissar for White Ruthenia, Wilhelm Kube, who opposed the Soviets and also opposed the introduction of SS security organisations and operational units whose radical measures he described as 'unworthy of a Germany of Kant and Goethe'. He was later discredited as being completely unsuitable for the position on the grounds 'that he had reached his hand out to the Jews and had even given sweets to Jewish children'.

Soviet opposition to Kube's policy of conciliation was so strong that, under the direction of P.K. Ponomarenko in Moscow, the Central Staff of the Partisan Movement was tasked with his removal. A plan was made to persuade a Russian woman working in his kitchen to poison him, but this was rejected because other Russian workers were getting the same food. Then, on the September 1943, he was blown up by a mine placed under his pillow by his maid, Ossipova, with the assistance of the partisans Masanik, Drozd and Trojan.

Moscow, in its efforts to set the local population against us and to increase the number of partisans, went so far as to put special commandos in German uniforms. These units brutally liquidated the populations of whole villages, even when they had not been actively collaborating with us, but were carrying out everyday tasks or had been ordered to do so. As a result of these measures even fewer witnesses were left alive to describe 'the misdeeds of the fascists'. The details of Stalin's so-called 'Torch Bearers' Order' of 17 November 1941 were as follows:

1. All housing developments in which German troops are located are to be destroyed in a depth up to 40 to 60 kilometres from the main line of battle and set on fire 20 to 30 kilometres right and left of the road. For the destruction of housing developments in the designated radius, the air force is to be consulted, artillery and mortars are to be used, as well as the commandos of the reconnaissance, ski and partisan divisional groups, which are to be equipped with bottles of inflammatory material. The hunting commandos, disguised in the uniforms of the German Army and the Waffen-SS, will carry out the destruction orders. The fomenting of hatred of the Fascist occupier facilitates the recruiting of partisans in the Fascist hinterland. It is to be ensured that survivors remain who can report 'German cruelties'.

2. In every regiment hunting commandos are to be formed of 20 to 30 men with the task of carrying out demolitions and fire-raising in the settlement areas. Courageous men must be selected for this task of destroying settlements. Those that destroy settlements behind the German lines in German uniforms are especially to be recommended for awards. Among the population the news is to be spread that the Germans have set fire to villages and places to punish the partisans.

This is an example of a scorched-earth policy whereby extensive destruction was attributed to the partisans quite apart from the massive damage that was caused inevitably by both sides during the fighting. During the Soviet retreat in first phase of the war, according to Stalin's explicit instructions, his men spread the destruction as far as possible, including everything that could be of use. Villages were shelled and burnt, and houses that we could have used during the winter months as accommodation were destroyed, without regard for the remaining occupants.

In such circumstances, and with some of their own citizens joining the resistance, it is not surprising that few prisoners survived, especially if they fell into the hands of the partisans. It was later established that, of the 55,000 prisoners who were marched through Moscow and then transported to various camps, less than half returned to their homeland.

Knowing how slim the chances of survival in captivity were, I was determined to escape and to do everything I possibly could to get back to the German lines. The fact that we have come this far already is a gift from heaven, and it would be something of a miracle if we can go the whole way.

Nothing much happens during the day apart from a few wild doves fluttering around our site and disturbing us. My cap is showing signs of wear and tear so I cover it with the remainder of the material that Georg found in the camp cellar and from which he made his own footwear, and I secure the whole thing with a bit of electrical wire. Once again I realise how important it is for us to prepare as best we can for whatever lies ahead and to make the best use of everything we find.

This carefree and restful day comes to an end. It is a month since the big Russian offensive began in nearby Vitebsk.

23 July

At twilight we leave this pleasant camp and make our way through the extensive wood without difficulty. When it is completely dark we move confidently and, fortunately, as quietly as we can along the edge of a grain field until suddenly across the field a small, yellowish light flares up and then remains as a glowing red point. Someone has lit a cigarette! Startled, we stand motionless. We wait a few seconds and then move back slowly step by step, keeping the burning cigarette constantly in sight. Clearly the glowing point is not following us, so we carefully make an about-turn, first towards the east, then after a detour, once more back to the west.

We carry on, reacting to every sound and looking to all sides in the coal-black darkness. We have to be very careful as ahead of us we can clearly hear voices accompanied by the sound of shots. Green tracers rise vertically into the sky and could be signals. Fortunately, the flashes of light reveal the position of the person with the gun so that we can get out of the way in time. He might be a partisan or just a harmless hunter marking his position.

As always, we want to leave the empty, coverless stretch of land as quickly as possible and vanish into the nearest woods.

More quickly than we expected, we find what we are looking for and we conceal ourselves among the trees. It is lucky for us that the stars haven't come out yet, but we can't see where we are going. Then we stumble on a path and see the Great Bear right in front of us, which we follow.

Suddenly we hear the sound of snapping twigs nearby. Immediately we lie flat and crawl under the cover of the nearest tree. In the faint moonlight appear the shadows of two, then four, then even more figures. Eventually twenty-five to thirty men pass us, one behind the other, only a few metres apart. Weapons and steel helmets flash briefly and with every step we hear the metallic clang of bits of equipment. We hardly dare breathe. Are these Red Army soldiers? Or perhaps German soldiers on a night march to the west? The second possibility is most likely, but we dare not show ourselves in order to confirm it – the risk seems too great. If we had guessed wrong, we would not be able to get away from a group of this size, especially not in the vicinity of the front line. So, we wait until the group disappears into the darkness, then continue our march.

Just behind the wood is a small settlement of several widely separated farms which looks like a good place for us to find the food we need. The first house is apparently uninhabited as no one reacts to our repeated knocking. As we approach the second house, when I am trying to open the little gate in the fence, a dog barks loudly and maliciously, and we disappear as quickly as we can. 'Beware of the dog!' Since the dog continues to bark at us we go on to the last farm where we are far enough away from the dog not to bother it. Barking dogs are really dangerous in our situation, but in this peaceful and well-maintained settlement surrounded by woodland we aren't as worried as we would normally be. We decide to approach the house we are standing in front of.

The door opens to our light knocking and we see two gentle old women. Somewhat disconcerted, we don't know what to say to them. We don't want to ask for food immediately, so as not to appear impolite, and we aren't desperately hungry as we have been on similar occasions in the past.

We don't know what to say, but then something totally unexpected happens, as one of the two ladies, recognising our embarrassment, puts a question to us: '*Parlez-vous français?*' '*Oui, oui, un peut*', I reply, surprised at being addressed in French, as I would not have dreamed of this happening here. Immediately the spell is broken and, with friendly gestures, they invite us to come in.

This reception is incredible from our point of view for we feel we are being treated in a normal way although we look untrustworthy, just like vagrants, especially in our makeshift footwear. The hospitality of these ladies is astonishing because they must have identified us as German soldiers and we know what a risk they are taking by asking us into their house. They also look after us by giving us food which of course we were hoping for.

Formally we introduce ourselves as we had been accustomed to do in the past, which seemed somewhat grotesque under the circumstances, then we hesitate before entering their living room where we are confronted by a sight that makes us think we have been transported to another world.

The spotlessly clean room is very attractively set out. Right next to the door stands a stately kitchen dresser holding many beautiful glasses, and next to it is a chest of drawers. There is a brass chandelier and colourful plates are hung on the wall opposite a small bookcase. There is also a wall clock, an old adjustable one that has seen better days. I notice its hands point to 2 hours after midnight and when I ask whether it is really that late, I'm told the time here is always 2 hours ahead of Moscow, something that hadn't occurred to me.

In the middle of the room stands a massive table covered with a cloth, on which a petroleum lamp sheds a tranquil light, which of course makes precautionary measures necessary, so both women proceed to cover the windows carefully with woollen blankets. Then we all sit down and quickly get talking together, during which I happily recall a lot of French vocabulary I knew in the past. Even if the grammar and the phrases are perhaps not always entirely adequate, we can understand each other well. As Georg doesn't speak any French – though he has some knowledge of English – I translate the essential points for him. We discover these two Polish ladies were formerly schoolteachers and are now seeing out their lives in this small place near the Curzon Line.

Naturally the most important subject is the military situation, so I tell them briefly how we had escaped from a prison camp in Volozyn a few days ago and now hoped to reach the Vilna–Lida area which is where we expected to find the front line. When I ask how far away that is, they reply: '*Soixante kilometres, messieurs, environ.*' We are pleased to hear them say '*messieurs*' considering the suspicious glances they had exchanged when we first arrived. But when I go on to ask them about the actual distance to the front line, they give the shattering reply: '*Messieurs, les Russes ont*

*déjà atteint le territoire situé entre Gradna et Kovno, en face du Njemen, et on
dit que Grodno est occupée.'*

As I passed this on to Georg, he exclaimed: 'What, at the Memel, that
can't really be true!' But unfortunately it is, and what that means for us is
that we still have at least 150km to go excluding unavoidable detours, not
just 60km. The march would take us three weeks for certain, and every
day our physical strength would diminish, and the daily distance covered
would become shorter and shorter the closer we get to our goal. So it
is hard to estimate how long we would really need to get to the vicinity
of the Russian front line. Of course we now understand why we haven't
seen any sign of a front line in the remote countryside we have marched
through. It is difficult for us to grasp our situation and to face the physical
challenge it represents. Already, since the break-out from Minsk, we have
walked 100km and now we find we have another 150km ahead of us,
always assuming that the front holds at the Memel until we get there.

Depressed and disillusioned, I ask the ladies for further information,
and we hear some news that is hard to believe at first – which takes our
breath away.

They tell us that for days now England and the USA have been fighting
on the German side against the Soviet Union. I think I have not understood them correctly and ask if this really is the case. '*Oui, oui, c'est vrai*',
they say. They sound convinced, as if they had heard the news on the radio.

They have also heard that weapons and other materiel deliveries from
the USA to the Soviet Union have been going on for some time and, most
astonishing for us, English troops are already on the march in Lithuania
and hold the airfield at Olita (Alytus) which lies precisely on our direction
of march between Grodno and Kovno on the Memel. The first British
aircraft had landed there and were ready for action. So, it seems that all we
have to do is keep on going towards a joyful meeting with the English.

This news is being spread everywhere by the Soviets, and is also
confirmed by resistance groups. The whole thing does not seem completely
unthinkable. But as always in our situation we tend to disbelieve such
rumours, though we hope something good comes out of them.

Georg regards the whole story with scepticism: 'Do you really think
that we can believe all this?' 'Why not? I reply. 'The Americans and above
all the English know what would happen to them if the Soviets win more
ground to the west, and apparently think we are finished. Also the Soviets
have also gone over the top with their secret police and purges and years
of terror. But, whatever is going on, we should continue our march.'

Without being asked our hosts give us a large cheese sandwich along with plenty of milk, which we really enjoy. The way they treat us makes us almost forget the situation we are in. We would have liked to have stayed longer and found out more about what was happening in the area, but it is late and we don't want to outstay our welcome. Their clock indicates it is 3 a.m. which is 1 a.m. our time, 2 hours ahead. When I ask if we can call in on them shortly before we set off the following evening, they say yes in a friendly way. So we thank them wholeheartedly and leave to spend the day in a nearby barn that we've been told about.

24 July

Carefully, looking in all directions, we approach the wooden barn, silently open the door and immediately close it behind us. Inside it is pitch dark and so my matches, which have already given us such good service, have to be brought out again. Georg quickly puts a little pile of straw together and sets light to it, producing sufficient light to allow us to orientate ourselves. About half the barn is filled with hay and straw up to the roof and, with some effort, we climb high up to where we feel safest. There it is pleasantly warm. About 20 hours now lie before us in which we have nothing else to do but wait until darkness breaks. As always, we can only converse quietly, and the long hours are filled with sleep or thoughts about our future.

The first question that concerns us is what to make of the news that our enemies have switched sides. Since the two Polish ladies, who seem to be down-to-earth people, are convinced the report is accurate, there is probably some truth in it. (And later on we discovered that, during the final phase of the war, the possibility that the Western Powers might become allies of the Germans was discussed.) I was more optimistic about this than Georg who said: 'I can't believe that England will give up on trying to maintain the balance of power. Like in 1914–18, they won't want us to become too strong.'

I haven't got to know Georg well. He's introverted, somewhat taciturn and touchy – which is perhaps understandable in our situation.

'And then there was that business of the Polish guarantee,' he continues, 'you can forget it – it was a waste of time. They didn't do anything when we went in – didn't fire a shot or drop a single bomb. Or have you heard of one? And then when the Russians invaded from the other side, they didn't do anything about that either!'

'Not so loud!' I warn him – he had spoken with such anger. Then I go on: 'Yes, I know, but now we aren't really competing with them anymore. Our cities have been completely smashed up, and our industries too, and militarily it does not look so good for us, does it? Think of what is happening here, for god's sake. In another year we will be on our knees. The front hasn't gone as far back as Silesia yet, but you never know.'

For a moment we think about the wider war and forget our immediate problems. If some time ago fighting was going on along the Memel, who knows what has happened there since then. And if the Soviets cross the river in several places, as they did at the Dnepr and the Beresina, they will approach the German border with giant strides.

For us this is a really threatening thought, for the retreat might have gone back at least another 100km. Perhaps, though, the Soviet offensive could still be brought to a standstill if all the available forces were put into the fight, and surely they would be.

We stop talking and mull over the day, and soon we feel so warm and comfortable in the hay, and so secure that we fall asleep.

When we awake next day, the sun is already shining in a cloudless sky, and everything seems quiet and peaceful. But we are careful – we check on all sides looking through the gaps in the planks of the walls of the barn. We don't spot anything worrying outside. The sun is at full strength and with every hour that passes the temperature rises in our hiding place. Eventually it is so unbearably hot that we strip off our clothes and wait impatiently for the coming of darkness. We decide to start earlier than usual because we want to visit the old ladies again and get more information from them.

Finally the time comes. Gently we open the barn door and approach their house with great care. Once more they welcome us in a friendly way as if we were old friends and were visiting their home in peacetime. With a polite '*Bon soir, Mesdames, merci beaucoup, c'est très gentils a vous*', we go in. When the windows have been carefully covered again we sit down around the petroleum lamp and begin chatting. We are especially keen to find out about the adjacent district which we will have to pass through in the next few days. Soon, we are told, we will have to cross the Little Beresina River, which lies only a few kilometres away. The bridges are not at present guarded, but we will have to be cautious when we make the crossing.

Field Marshal Model intended to erect a defensive line here three weeks ago, but the Russians arrived before he could do so. We also learned that a main highway ran just beyond the river and, a few kilometres beyond that, the Lida–Molodeczno railway line. This was very useful information as we would have to take special care if we were to get across these two obstacles. In order to learn more, in particular about the distances involved, I asked the Polish ladies if they had a map, thinking that as former school teachers they might well have such a thing – and indeed they did. From this we gathered that the railway was about 15km behind the Little Beresina, and we couldn't get around it because it ran mainly in a north–south direction. We were more pleased to discover that this was only about 20km from the Lithuanian border. Although Lithuania had been part of the Soviet Union since 1940 and so was in theory enemy territory, we regarded it as an advantage to be able to move around in a country whose inhabitants – just as in Estonia and Latvia – were basically friendly. This in no way applied to the Soviets who had frightened the inhabitants and did not fit in. In Lithuania we wouldn't have to worry so much about partisans, but we would have to watch out for Red Army search teams when we got near to the front line. We assumed they would stop us on sight. We preferred not think about this, trying as always to look on the optimistic side of things.

The obvious place to set up a strong defensive line to stop the Soviet advance towards East Prussia was along the Memel River between Kovno and Grodno, a distance of around 150km with few deviations to the north or south. The Memel would make a better defensive position than the Dnepr and the Beresina, and we could only hope that the line had been organised there. We couldn't ascertain much more from the map because its scale was too small, but what we did learn was useful.

Suddenly we heard shots, and the two ladies made anxious gestures, but we quickly quieten them down, as we reckon – quite rightly – that the shots came from people who were just larking about. We chatted to the ladies for a while, and everything remained quiet. They treated us well. They made us scrambled eggs with buttered bread and the usual milk, followed by a kind of pancake with redcurrant marmalade. Everything they prepared for us tasted good and, since we hadn't had anything like it for so long, we really enjoyed it. As a dessert we had fresh redcurrant berries from the little garden near the house, and again and again they asked if we wanted another helping, and we didn't hesitate to say yes.

It was time for us to move on. The clock showed 11 p.m., and so we prepared for departure. On saying farewell the ladies gave us bread, a few eggs and a bottle full of redcurrants, and Georg even received a spoon though he hadn't asked for one. Looking back on this episode, it is really hard to believe how, as complete strangers, we were so well treated. It was as if we had been at home for two days. This experience during a journey that was making severe physical and psychological demands on us renewed our strength and determination, even though we now knew that it would take us longer than we had anticipated to reach our goal.

After we had thanked them, they wished us '*Bonne chance*' and we left. We were unlucky when we started off because the sky was overcast and the Great Bear was hidden, only showing itself now and then through gaps in the cloud. This was very frustrating and, since we couldn't find the right direction, we decided to look for our barn and spend the day there.

When we try to open the door, we are surprised and shocked to find that someone has locked it during our absence. But we are determined to get into the barn and so we walk around it looking for a place where we can pull a few planks out of the wall without too much difficulty. Quickly we find a suitable place in the planking, just as the moon makes another appearance and illuminates the area. As soundlessly as possible we loosen two planks, slip through the opening and then carefully put them back.

As he had done the day before, Georg lights some straw and we find our way back to our old hiding place high up under the roof. We are happy to spend another comfortable night here, and hopefully another undisturbed day, but we will have delayed our journey by 24 hours.

25 July

We enjoy a refreshing sleep which contrasts markedly with the disturbed nights we've been accustomed to, especially during the early morning hours on damp ground in the woods with the constant fear of being discovered. When we wake the sun is shining out of a bright blue sky and it looks like there is a good chance the night will be starry and clear.

After hours of complete rest we hear voices in front of the barn. Quickly we cover ourselves with hay and watch the door open. Several men, women and children come in carrying scythes and hay rakes. They are leading two horses which they harness to the wagon standing in the middle of the barn, and then drive out to gather the hay harvest.

Cautiously we make no contact with them – we have no reason to – and how right this decision was is proved a little later when several shots are fired close by and then a short burst from a machine pistol. There must be Red Army soldiers in the village. Like lightning we cover ourselves with an even thicker heap of hay and wait tensely for whatever happens next. Outside we hear rough, unfriendly voices – apparently Soviet soldiers are demanding something and, in typical fashion, are reinforcing their demand with a warning shots. We wonder if they are looking for us but decide they would have come into the barn at once if that had been the case.

Soon calm returns, though engine noises can be heard in the distance. Presumably these come from military vehicles, as the local people probably don't have any powered vehicles. But maximum alertness is still called for, especially when the farming people return with their fully laden harvest wagon and begin making a heap of hay near us, and then drive off again to get a new load. However, they show no sign of concern or agitation. The whole afternoon passes like this until the work comes to an end with nightfall and they go home.

At last we have peace and can look through the holes in the planks to see if anything we should be concerned about is happening nearby and to check on the weather. There are no clouds in the sky so this evening we can go on, but we wait until it is sufficiently dark.

When it is dark enough we slip out of the hay with our sack of supplies, taking care not to break our eggs or let the redcurrants roll out of the bottle, separate the two planks and step out into the open with our usual alertness. In the village, as we hoped, everything is quiet and peaceful. As we go past the old ladies' house, we would have liked to thank them again for all the help they had given us, but did not want to disturb them so late and even endanger them. If we had seen them to say farewell we would have said: '*Adieu, Mesdames, merci beaucoup encore unefois, et bonne chance aussi pour vous.*'

'So, Georg, off we go to the Little Beresina!' I say, although of course it may be difficult to get to, and he responds: 'If all goes well, we should be able to cross today – it is only a few kilometres from here.'

We take our direction from the position of the Great Bear, expecting to find a road leading west to the river and, with luck, a bridge across it. We don't know how wide or deep the river is, but think we may be able to wade across if we have to. We want to avoid swimming because then we would lose most of our equipment and utensils. First, however, we go through extensive cornfields, a time-consuming business as Georg's footwear keeps coming loose and he has to stop to retie it each time.

Finally, we reach a big road, almost a highway, that runs in the right direction. Although it is risky, we follow it because it will save time, and we expect it will lead us to a bridge. When we come up to a nearby farm, we decide to ask for bread there, as we may be entering a sparsely settled area where we will only have berries and mushrooms to sustain us.

A woman opens the window when we knock. She has a surly expression, but she is clearly nervous and, with remarkable speed, she hands us two slices of dry bread. At first she won't give us milk or even water from the nearby spring, but eventually she comes out, fills our flasks in great haste, looking around anxiously on all sides, then goes back within her four walls.

'Watch out, there is something wrong here', I whisper to Georg, and then, as we carefully go around the corner of the house, he pulls me back with a firm grip. There's a truck in front of us, a military vehicle, which explains the woman's manner. 'Quickly, over the road!' I say to Georg, and we cross it then run along until we are far enough away not to be seen. Despite this incident, we stay on the road towards the Little Beresina, and we don't see a single vehicle.

A little later we hear not far away the sound of rushing water. We have reached the river, and we can make out the bridge in front of us in the moonlight. Now we have to be especially careful because the bridge is probably guarded. We creep up the bank and conceal ourselves in a bush next to the road. There is absolute quiet and we can't see anything suspicious. Nothing moves, not even after we have thrown a few small stones at the wooden planks of the bridge. 'Seems everything is OK', Georg whispers to me. 'Looks like it', I reply quietly. But we wait cautiously for a while, listening and observing. Then we go up to it, slowly, walking on tiptoe, silently, looking around.

At some point a hurried attempt has been made to stop vehicles crossing so in several places gaps in the roadway have been repaired with loose planks which we avoid because we don't want to make any noise. We got to the far bank without getting our feet wet and without causing any disturbance. I remembered that someone had told me that the bridges over the Little Beresina were unguarded, but to find that this was actually the case was wonderful and unexpected.

Our next goal was the Molodeczeno–Lida–Bialystok railway line, but that was too far away to reach tonight. As we wanted to be sure of crossing it tomorrow, we carried on for as long as possible and concealed ourselves before dawn broke in a nearby wood.

26 July

About 24 hours lie ahead of us before we can get moving again, and we have time to rest and think back over events. A month ago, on 26 June, we left the 'Dnepr Balcony', four days after the beginning of the unbelievably fast advance of the Russian summer offensive against Army Group Centre. By then it was much too late to escape the encirclement and destruction of our 4th Army in the cauldron east of Minsk. During the fighting the commander of my Artillery Regiment 18, Colonel Gunther, and the divisional commander of the 18th Panzergrenadier Division, Major General Zutavern, met their fate, though I didn't hear about this till much later. At the time I didn't know what had happened to my comrades from the observation post and Senior Corporal Schaffrath, our faithful motorcyclist, but I am thankful that he survived to read these lines.

I ought to return, though, to the present. The hours pass without any disturbance. We had had plenty of time in which to find a place to set up camp thickly surrounded with pine trees. As the area seems safe, we decide to light a small fire and scramble the four eggs we had been given by the charming Polish ladies in our cooking pot. We also have some butter and so the meal was – like some of the others we had had over the last few days – a great success. To finish off we have some bread, a cup of milk and, as dessert, half of our exquisite redcurrants. Then, staggering from having eaten so much, we remember the tea from the cellar in Volozyn which we have in our reserve bag. This will serve as ersatz tobacco, so we roll two huge cigar-sized cigarettes out of a piece of paper and take a first expectant draw. When we have finished we quickly cover up all signs of the meal.

The following hours pass undisturbed, and then we set off towards our next goal, the railway line, which shouldn't be too far away. It is lucky that the old ladies had given us so much detailed information about the situation in the area and we hope that, when we stop at houses to look for food, the locals will be just as helpful. This turns out to be the case at an isolated farm where we ask for bread. The farmers are especially obliging, giving us not only bread and milk, but also warning us about the next village on our line of march where there are Russian soldiers. Once more we realise we need to take great care because while one village may be safe for us the next one may not be.

A little later in a wood where we are struggling to find our way we suddenly catch sight of the railway line. The tracks go straight through the middle of the wood. In order to make it easier to defend the line from attacks by partisans, the trees have been cut down on both sides to make a clearing about 100m wide and barbed wire has been laid down. Fortunately, the circumstances are less dramatic than they were a few days ago in Volozyn and we are able to cross the line without difficulty. As we go over we discover that the tracks have been blown up, either by the partisans or our men during the retreat. Since the Soviets have haven't repaired the track, we wonder if their advance hasn't progressed as far as we previously feared. We cling on to the slightest of hopes!

27 July

We crossed the railway line unmolested and left the wood behind, and soon we were able to find our way again using the stars. Without being spotted we pass the village which was occupied by the Soviet soldiers, giving it a wide berth, and we come to another river, apparently a tributary of the Little Beresina. It is considerably narrower and doesn't seem too deep so we could probably wade through it without difficulty, but we want to avoid this and so we look for a footbridge. Eventually we find one and cross over to the other bank without getting wet.

Next we come to patches of woodland in a hilly area where there are collapsed trenches and ramparts dating from either the First World War or the Russian–Polish War of 1920–1. As it slowly begins to get dark, we pass through a thin birch grove which isn't a suitable place to stop, and go on without finding a wood we can shelter in.

Since we don't want to take the risk of visiting one of the isolated farmhouses nearby, we decide reluctantly to go back into the birch wood. We do the best we can to conceal ourselves in the bushes, trying to avoid the many pits that have been dug in the ground. Suddenly I hear furious swearing behind me – Georg has sunk up to his waist in one of the holes. Unfortunately, he is carrying the sack containing all our supplies and other gear, and so now almost everything is damp. He moans like a fishwife, blaming me because I had picked this route.

Still irritated, and without consulting me, he kindles a fire. This is a reckless thing to do in such an exposed position, but I see he is shivering with cold, and in our situation it would be very difficult if he fell ill. While he spreads his clothes out on a branch he's broken in order to dry them over the fire, I toast a couple of slices of bread. When we have eaten them we feel in much better humour.

We agree the situation could be worse, then lie down on the moss which is almost always damp at this time in the morning. A fresh wind springs up and Georg, whose clothing is still damp, freezes and can't sleep. We decide that the only thing we can do is to take the risk of seeking cover in the farm we've spotted in front of us. In the morning, before 6, we break cover and approach the property with great care.

A young man, who is feeding his pigs in the yard, sees us coming and tries to hide, taking us for Russians. This is difficult to understand given our appearance. When we make it clear that we are Germans, he is very friendly and visibly relieved, and he asks us to come into the house. He wakes his mother and his sister, saying they will prepare a big breakfast for us of bread, milk, cheese and even some butter. Our mood improves once we have had enough to eat, and Georg recovers in the warm room. Innumerable flies cover the walls, but that doesn't disturb us because for us 'men of the woods' every room is a little paradise.

The farmer has – like so many people around here – a passable knowledge of German, but he can't give us any information about the military situation. But we hear the Soviets are recruiting able-bodied inhabitants in the areas they have re-conquered, including men from the Polish minority living in White Russia. This policy explains the shock of the young man who had at first taken us for Russians but, knowing the history of the area, I can't say I am sympathetic.

Soon we say goodbye to these friendly people and go off to look for a birch wood in which to pass the day. On our way we come to the trenches I've already mentioned and discover, hidden in a small bush, a well-preserved, half-spherical concrete bunker, similar to the one that we had found in the 'Barenstellung' (Bear Position) on the Dnepr, only a little smaller. As the position of the bunker is surrounded by trees it is difficult to see, so we decide to conceal ourselves in it, protected from wind and weather.

It feels odd to occupy a bunker in which our fathers might have taken shelter. There isn't anything left inside the bunker now and the wind has been blowing through the entrance for years. I get the impression that no one has been here for decades, and that it is just right for us. We turn our attention to our footwear, taking from our supply sack the necessary bits and pieces in order to put together the foot wraps we so badly need. Our feet are damp from Georg's bath in the water hole but at least they are cool – they really were in a desperate state before. Georg has far fewer problems than I do – I could no longer walk in leather boots if I had any.

We leave the bunker for short periods to try to find out what we can see from a half-collapsed trench running in front of it in which a young tree is already growing.

The air in the bunker is musty, cold and damp like a cellar so, to let Georg's things fully dry on his body, we light a small fire with great care. We choose a spot and remove the undergrowth until we reach the sandy ground. Then, since we don't have any dry wood, we pile up green twigs from the young trees around us and add plenty of leaves from the bunker. The bunker originally possessed a second exit that has been sealed with broken loose stones and we remove some of the stones at the top to make an outlet for the smoke. The whole room is then soon filled with acrid smoke that only disperses very slowly.

In order to breathe, we have to lie flat on the floor. As the fire takes hold it produces even more smoke but also spreads a comfortable warmth and, feeling full after our copious breakfast, we doze off. We are in such a relaxed, peaceful and apparently carefree mood that it is difficult to anticipate what the next days or weeks will be like – whether we will be lucky getting through the Russian lines, and the frightful possibility that we might collapse shortly before reaching the longed-for goal.

The knowledge that in our situation it is impossible to maintain contact with our families, and even to let them know that we still exist, is an additional burden. We wrote our last field-post letters to our families over a month ago, and the post takes so long to arrive. Probably any replies will be returned to the senders with an upsetting note, 'Not deliverable at the moment' or 'New address awaited', which will increase the concern of anyone at home who has followed the Wehrmacht reports on events in the East. Probably the gravity of the situation has only been hinted at. The explanation that enormous bits of territory have been lost in 'surprise moves' won't be convincing, especially when the fighting is reported to have reached the Memel.

Slowly we let the fire go out as it is warm enough in the bunker, but we find that the heat has aroused our 'travelling companions' – lice – which now make their presence felt by causing itching in various places on our bodies. A short inspection confirms our worst fears – somewhere and somehow we have definitely come into contact with lice and this will only add to our difficulties. They are highly unpleasant and we know that we won't be able to get rid of them until we reach our destination. We can only keep them at bay by whenever possible searching through our clothing piece by piece and cracking them between our fingernails. Since we have time to spare we begin this unsavoury process straight away, after I have checked the area around the bunker is safe.

This eventful day draws to an end, and we resume our march under a starry sky. Thoughts of Georg's misadventure in the early morning and the lice at midday recede into the background. On this day a week ago we left the camp in Volozyn behind us.

28 July

The night march goes without incident. Several times we hear a dull rumbling in the distance and hope this indicates the front line, although the sound of explosions may have come from air attacks, presumably on the towns of Vilna and Lida, which lie more or less on our route.

At nightfall we reach a large, mixed woodland well suited for camping. Since it will be chilly and damp in the morning, we break off lots of twigs from the fir trees and spread them out on the ground, then add twigs from the deciduous trees. During the strenuous march we've sweated profusely and we must take whatever precautionary measures we can to avoid getting ill. We aren't in good condition anyway, and an injury or infection would be the end of all our dreams, especially as it looks as if there will be no chance of medical assistance for a long time to come.

After we have rested for several hours, I go out in search of blueberries which grow in large quantities nearby. When I get back and we are stretched out at the camp we hear whispers nearby and the cracking of twigs.

There is no time for us to move to a better hiding place and we can only hope not to be discovered. Through the undergrowth we watch two men in civilian clothes approach and stop a few metres from our position where they speak quietly to each other. Apparently, they have seen us, for they suddenly turn around and walk rapidly away.

Although they seem to be unarmed, we quickly pack up our things so that we can conceal ourselves in a denser part of the wood. But almost at once they come back and, as I think they have already spotted us and show no signs of hostile intent, I go towards them and, signalling with my hands, ask them to stop. When I ask what they are doing, they reply in broken German that they have been hiding in the woods to avoid being pressed into military service by the Soviets. '*Polski nix wollen in Krieg gehen*'[*], one of them says.

We believe him at once, though this is the first time we have heard that men from the Polish minority were being conscripted. Despite the fact that they had identified us as stragglers from the German army, they treat us as comrades or good friends, and the two of them sat down with us. One of them pulled out a packet of cigarettes (real ones this time) from

_____

[*] 'We are Poles and don't want to fight in the war.'

his pocket and then we all smoked happily together. I recalled my last cigarette which I'd shared with the vet at Volzyn, and I wonder where he is now.

During a rather mundane conversation we discover that three comrades had camped close by in the same wood a few days ago. We search for the spot and find the remains of their campfire, a pile of ashes with two branches sticking out. The two Poles then say goodbye to us and go on their way. Although we are confident they won't betray us, we clear our camp and walk on through the extensive wood that we had to cross in daylight, orientating ourselves by the position of the sun.

Coming to the far edge of the wood, we see for the first time the land around us. Further on there was another large wood we could hide in for the rest of the day. We are taking a risk by moving in bright daylight, but we reckon that, from a distance, we will look like two farmers' boys, one of them carrying a sack over his shoulder. Also we think the hiding place selected by the two Poles isn't a good one because several Russian soldiers are nearby. So we sauntered through the landscape in an relaxed way, but glancing sharply to all sides and listening out for any threatening sound. We are relieved when we are able to take cover in the wood without being challenged, and we set up a well-camouflaged camp.

It is a delightful summer's day. The sun shines in a clear blue sky – it is still strong even in the late afternoon – and we lie down at peace with God and the world in the soft, dry, warm moss. For a moment I feel as if I'm on leave in a safe place, but then something rustles in the undergrowth. Again, we hear it, clearly, coming closer. We jump up in shock and an animal goes past us unbelievably fast through the trees. 'As fast as a dog!' says Georg. But then it turns back and we see it is a fox. It sniffs at our camp and then trots off and vanishes. During our journey we worried that dogs might be used to search for us and had left them well alone – like escaped criminals we didn't want to leave a scent for them to follow.

As we don't know how deep the wood is and don't want to go round it, we decide to go straight through, starting out early as usual so that we can be sure we are going in the right direction. When, without much difficulty, we reach the other side, we see a small village in front of us which appears to be so peaceful that we decide to get supplies there before nightfall. As hoped, we were received in a friendly manner and given bread and milk. In a short awkward conversation we learn that fighting is taking place on the Memel, but we don't know whether a firm front line has been established. The war didn't seem to have touched this village, but we could never tell which villages would turn out to be friendly when we went into them looking for food.

When we knock on the door at the last house in the village a lovely girl opens the window and smiles at us in a friendly way and, as our appearance doesn't give a good impression, I quickly smooth my hair and smile back. Georg reacts similarly because he is as impressed by her as I am and, much to our surprise, she reciprocates. Perhaps our romantic dishevelled look appeals to her. It is reassuring to be treated in such a kindly fashion and I haven't grown so apathetic that I fail to be touched by it.

Having had our milk flasks filled and been given some bread and a couple of eggs, we say farewell with hearty words of thanks. After a period of thoughtful silence, I couldn't help saying: 'Wasn't that a lovely girl, Georg?' And he answered in excellent Swabian: 'A beauty!'

This is all there is to report of these days and weeks. Once more I realise how senseless the war is – the contrast between it and the reception we received in the village couldn't be more stark.

29 July

The hours to midnight pass without incident, but seeing the clear traces of tracked vehicles on the sandy road brings us back to bleak reality. Far behind us sustained, muffled detonations can be heard which surely come from a German air attack. Judging by the direction of the sound, the railway junction of Molodeczno is being bombed to destroy the supply traffic. The town was retaken by the Soviets on 5 July, at the same time as our 4th Army was being defeated in the Minsk cauldron. Some survivors from the cauldron broke out after suffering huge casualties and began an unimaginably long march on foot.

For a long time we haven't seen any woods and fear that we will have to hide in a cornfield, but just in time we reach a birch wood with just a little undergrowth. This is much less risky than a cornfield like the one we stayed in near Volozyn.

We search for a suitable site to set up camp and find a deep and wide depression, similar to a big bomb or shell hole, and decide to use it, although the ground is damp. We cover ourselves with copious birch twigs. We sleep almost the whole day through and are only startled twice, once when some shots fall in the vicinity – almost certainly some random shooting – and later when a couple of children drive a small herd of cattle immediately past the wood, but without coming near us. I have become used to sleeping very lightly, just like the animals in the wild.

When we get up in the evening the march continues through rough, strength-sapping terrain. Several small hills have to be climbed and there are broad stretches of newly ploughed land which give us considerable difficulties because of our footwear. We have to be careful in order to avoid injuring our feet – they are very sore because of the constant chaffing. Our stamina begins to run out and finally we have to lie down exhausted under a bush. I feel morose and dizzy and I am tempted to stay lying here.

Georg recovers more quickly and is eager to go on, while I need more rest. 'Don't make a fuss,' he says, 'come on now. We can't hang about here any longer!'

Laboriously I get up. It is dark in front of my eyes, darker than the night. As my weak condition is partly due to thirst, I drink copiously from our supply of milk, which has so often kept us going, and soon I'm revived, and so we are able slowly to continue. I wonder what can be wrong with me. My wound has hardly troubled me recently, but my feet are really painful and the symptoms of dysentery are getting worse.

During our daily – or rather nightly – marches we average about 5km, under favourable circumstances even a bit more, although, as I've already said, the distance covered to our destination is less because of unavoidable diversions.

At the end of this untroubled day we camp in a dense, large wood full of bushes.

30 July

The new day begins badly. While the wood offers good cover, early in the morning it is thoroughly damp and we are seriously chilled. As a result we wake up much earlier than usual and are so cold that we are unable to close our eyes again. Our foot wrappings are completely soaked through and our feet are icy. We jump about, trying to warm up, but that doesn't work. Then we unwind our wet foot wrappings and massage our feet, which look as if they are frozen. And this is high summer, the end of July!

Our feet feel as if they are on fire – the cuts are full of pus and some of them are bleeding – but we run around like lunatics between the bushes on the cold, wet ground. Finally, we find ourselves on a small rise, a sandy, dry patch where dance around in a way that a casual spectator would have taken for gaiety. We begin to regain our warmth and, when at last the sun comes out, we are back to normal and soon, because the day is so hot, we find a shady place to rest. Earlier we had thought about lighting a fire but the wood we were in was so small the smoke would have been too conspicuous.

We prepare a proper breakfast, although we don't dare cook anything. We have enough bread and the remains of the butter and the fresh milk. Also there is a large portion of blueberries which grow all over the woods in the area. The site of the camp is well hidden and we spend the next few hours searching our clothing for the lice that have come to life in the warmth. The day is a peaceful one and we recover our strength.

31 July

When we come to a solitary, prosperous looking farm, we knock several times at a window in the hope of obtaining something useful, but nothing stirs inside. We guess the house has been abandoned or the owners do not want to be disturbed, which is quite understandable. But we are not sure.

Near the house is a separate cellar – such cellars are common in the area – and we decide to inspect it. On tiptoe we climb down the wooden steps and then strike a match in the pitch-dark room. We see a couple of barrels and examine them closely. Also, on a table there is an empty jute sack and a large cardboard box. 'Come on, another match', says Georg. When we open the box we see that it is full of Hindenburg lights*, which we had often used in our bunkers and other accommodation. How did they get here and in such quantities? 'They could have been captured by partisans', Georg suggests. 'Come on, we had better take them', he goes on and with that we grab the jute sack and a number of the lights, and then leave as quickly as we can.

We are now in White Russia, very close to the former Lithuanian border. While in the last few days we have had good experiences with the population, we must continue to exercise caution and approach everyone with a level of mistrust. If there are soldiers in the neighbourhood, we must assume that our presence will have been reported because the local people would get into serious trouble if they failed to do so.

In contrast to the last few days, the night sky is clouded over which makes it difficult for us to find our way by the stars. For a while we rest, waiting

---

* A shallow pasteboard bowl of tallow with a short wick which would burn for hours. Named after the First World War German commander Paul von Hindenburg.

until the Great Bear appears again. Since we now have two sacks we split our gear between them in order to make the load easier to carry. We are so well equipped that we should be able to survive if we are separated by some incident – if we run into the enemy in the dark, for instance, and have to run away in different directions.

1 August

In the early morning we have a frustrating search for a suitable hiding place. Finally, we have to make do with a clump of conifers on the edge of a wood which doesn't conceal us as well as we would like. Four trees standing close together become our camp. We are so concerned that, once we have settled there, we do all we can to fill the gaps between the trees with leaves and twigs, hoping that this will give us sufficient cover from the nearby path where footprints and wagon tracks are clearly visible. This spot is far from ideal so I walk further into the wood. Not far off there's a village which looks friendly insofar as I can tell from a distance – no vehicles indicating the presence of the military are to be seen.

We are resting when a farmer approaches our camp with his herd and drives it into the wood close to us. Some cows and sheep also make their way into the wood so that we are literally surrounded by them. In vain we try to keep them away from our hiding place, hissing at them and making other disconcerting noises which the farmer overhears. Slowly he comes towards us and, to our astonishment, without being asked and without a word, he hands us a crust of bread and then goes back to his herd with a friendly smile. I guess he already knew who we were and this was not the first time he had encountered fugitives like us.

We hope he won't mention our presence in the village, and we are concerned when, a little later, we hear several shots, first at a distance but coming closer. Through the twigs we observe two civilians armed with rifles who we presume are partisans. They move right up to us and stop on the path only 5m away. We sit there petrified, and then I whisper to Georg: 'Should we run?' He shakes his head and so we refrain from doing the one thing that might have saved us, namely jumping up suddenly and running off as quickly as we can through the wood. Then perhaps with a lot of luck we could have found somewhere else to hide. But something stops us from trying this and we stay where we are, awaiting capture with equanimity. It seems to us inevitable – we think we have reached the end of our adventure.

It looks like they are going to shoot us as they take out loose cartridges and start slowly and clumsily to fill their magazines. They have – like the two partisans in the village in the Nalibocka forest – German 98 K carbines which hold eight shots. Automatically I count the cartridges as they slot them in. The carbines are pointed towards us as they load the magazines. The men don't say a word – they don't even order us to come out of our hiding place. Shoot then at last, you dogs, I say to myself, hoping that it will be short and painless, and Georg is certainly thinking the same thing.

Now they load – we hear the metallic clicks of the gun locks – and expect them to fire at any moment. But then the unbelievable happens – they swing their carbines over their shoulders and, looking past us into the trees, they walk cautiously forward and vanish into the wood. We glance at each other perplexed, hardly able to believe that we are still alive. Georg is the first to recover his power of speech and, fully understanding what had just occurred, he says to me: 'Man, if we get home in one piece and tell them everything that happened here, no one will believe us.'

Once we have recovered our senses we consider what had happened.

'I thought the farmer had betrayed us – that he only gave us the bread to make us feel secure', says Georg.

'He must have realised that we are unarmed, as otherwise the two of them would not have stopped in the open only a few metres away', I interject.

'We could have had pistols', remarked Georg astutely.

'If I had had one then the two of them would have been blasted away', I say.

We were lucky the episode hadn't ended in that way, especially as it is possible the two men weren't partisans but villagers who by chance had paused to load their guns near our camp. Firearms probably wouldn't have been much use in this situation anyway, and many of the people we'd met had been friendly and had been glad to help us – we hadn't needed weapons to threaten them. The situation had been potentially explosive, but we had survived intact. I was reminded of the saying 'Man proposes; God disposes'.

2 August

We continued our march and soon came to the Lithuanian border. We made good progress in the starry night until we spotted the outline of some houses in the moonlight. We reckoned the settlement was a small one we could get through quickly so we went straight in. With growing unease we realised there were many more houses than we had expected. Could this be the big town of Aschmena on the Oszmianka, and was it occupied by the Soviets?

Listening intently, we halted. We could hear running water from a river. It is too late for us to turn round and, if we had done so, it would have seemed suspicious, so we went on slowly, hoping we look like two tired inhabitants on their way home. Our hearts were beating fast, but eventually we reached the last of the houses and the river.

There is the bridge. Anxiously we observe it from the shadow of a house. Everything is dead quiet, no movement whatsoever, no sentries to be seen.

'Let's go carefully across', I whisper to Georg. 'If someone calls out, jump straight into the water!' Completely silently we creep on tiptoe over the wooden planks, as we did at the Little Beresina, and reach the other bank unchallenged.

'That was lucky,' says Georg quietly, 'but it's strange the bridge isn't guarded.'

Right behind him, however, there's another small house, the last one in the village, which we have got to get past.

'Look!' he says, and points in surprise to a figure sitting immobile on a bank near the door of the house.

'He's not moving', I answer perhaps a bit too loudly, convinced that one of the people from the house is sleeping off his drunkenness. But the man suddenly wakes up, lifts his head and looks at us in a sleepy and completely harmless way. Just then I spot behind him on the bench a machine pistol which glints in the moonlight. We realise he must be the bridge sentry.

'Quickly, let's get out of here!' I call out and we turn and run as fast as we can through a nearby cornfield. We leave obvious tracks and expect at any moment to be followed and shot at, but nothing of the sort happens. Apparently, the good man has fallen asleep again.

This reminds me of the episode at the Drut and the 'Red Poppy' song, originally an old Silesian Christmas carol, which began: 'Sleep well, you child of heaven'. The thought of it makes me laugh, which Georg simply cannot understand in this situation. Annoyed, he turns towards me, making a scathing remark. I sense he's had enough – he is on the point of wishing to be recaptured or shot. At that moment, behind us, we hear a few isolated shots and, to ease the tension, I say, 'That chap was certainly slow to react.' We go on then, without further comment.

3 August

Relieved at having crossed the river without getting wet, we keep going and come to a marshy area full of moss-covered mounds, like giant molehills, which are so close together that we cannot avoid them. We are forced to walk cautiously on top of them, balancing and often slipping off. This is a really painful exercise for us with our sore feet and it is risky too because, if one of us falls and injures himself, it will be very difficult for us to go on in the dark. Our foot wraps are soaked through and constantly coming apart, and they have to be rebound each time.

Eventually we manage to get across this peculiar ground and reach a stream. It is much too wide to jump over and, using a branch as a measure, we find out that it is at least a metre deep. Tired by the difficult march through the swamp, we first sit down on the bank and rest a little, but our feet are so wet and the morning is so cold that we soon start up again. We head along the bank in the hope of finding a narrower place where we can get across, but without success.

At dawn we approach a solitary farm alongside the stream. Before we get there a woman opens one of the windows and sees us. Visibly shocked, she points in the direction from which we have come from, towards Oszmianka. '*Ruski!, Ruski!*' she calls out as a warning. With gestures we manage to calm her down, telling her we know that the Russians are there.

We enter the house and sit down at the table in the very neat living room. Without being asked she brings us as much milk as we want and half a loaf. Shortly afterwards her husband appears and, as both of them know a bit of German, we can converse well. Angrily they tell us the Soviets have driven all their cattle away. They had been there two days ago and slept in the barn. We are worried to hear this, but at the same time pleased not to have arrived any earlier. The Red Army had advanced so rapidly that their supplies hadn't kept up with the troops so they were requisitioning food in the occupied areas.

The farmer's wife still cannot grasp that the Bolshevists are now back in the territory. 'Oh God, my God,' she says, 'The Russians are bad people, Germans good, very good – when are the Germans coming back?'

'Perhaps in a fortnight or three weeks', I reply to calm her down. I am sorry for her.

Visibly relieved, she says, 'Yes, in a fortnight? Oh God, my God, in a fortnight!'

Immediately I reproach myself for having given rise to such completely false hopes.

Then her husband lets loose his feelings, raising his arms and clenching his fists: 'Ruski, shit! Shit!' he says.

He is referring to the cruel fate of his compatriots and the loss of his animals, especially the valuable cattle, during Soviet rule. Also perhaps he was remembering how Lithuania was liberated by German soldiers in December 1917 along with Lettland and Estland. Understandably the local people disliked the Soviets and were much more sympathetic towards the Germans, even when on 22 March 1939 the incorporation of the Memel area into the German Reich was not immediately put into effect. According to the Treaty of Versailles, regardless of the ethnic make-up of the Memel area, it was separated from Germany. It was then annexed by Lithuania on 10 January 1923 and this change was sanctioned by the League of Nations in the Memelland Convention of 8 May 1924.

While we have been talking the sun has risen so we say farewell, thanking these friendly farmers for their hospitality. To our final question about whether there is a bridge nearby, we are told there is a plank over the stream which we can use. Once we have crossed we find a wood where we can lie down and rest without being seen. If we had known who had stayed before us in the barn we would have kept our distance and missed out on a pleasant encounter.

4 August

We lay down to rest on the damp floor of the wood but, as so often happened, we could only manage unsettled sleep. Georg talked several times in his sleep, making me jump up in shock each time and tell him to keep quiet. I too dreamt about all sorts of disturbing things. I found myself at the Freiburg station in Western Breslau which had already had been declared a fortress and six months later was surrounded. At the moment, though, this was only a dream. In it I climbed into a car at the station in order to drive into the town centre. Suddenly a large truck came towards me full of Red Army soldiers, who promptly jumped off and began shooting at the windows of my car without hitting me. Then I ran through an arcade and sensed I was being followed. Without turning round, I ran off like lightning and came to a dark tunnel, and behind me I heard the sound of steps getting closer and closer. I felt an ice-cold hand on my neck, fell to the ground with a loud cry – and woke up.

Alarmed I get up and quickly establish we aren't in danger. Georg rests peacefully next to me, but the crazy dream has so upset me that I can't get to sleep again. The sensation of the ice-cold hand on my neck was caused by the cold, damp, moss-covered hump on which I had laid my head. The sooner we can get out of this disturbing situation the better.

Not far from us something moves in the trees, coming closer, but then we breathe a sigh of relief, as it is only a few cows and sheep being driven through the wood by two youngsters who haven't seen us. It seems that daily life here has returned to normal and the country people have resumed their usual tasks. Unfortunately for us this means we must be a long way from the front line.

The rest of the day passes without incident. The stars shine clearly that night so we can set off again on our march. We come to a small farm which looks so inviting we decide to pay it a visit. After several futile knocks, an old woman opens a window with a grumpy gesture. She doesn't say a word when we ask for food, but gives us a piece of bread and immediately bangs the window shut again. I can understand she was unhappy about having her sleep disturbed but was surprised too because we expected to be received in a friendly manner.

At the next house the whole family it seems is sitting at the table, even the grandparents, although it is almost midnight. Unexpectedly one of the sons speaks rudimentary German so we can talk easily. At once we hear encouraging news – recently German parachutists landed nearby. What a thought – perhaps we would come across them today. They would be 'Green Devils' wearing regular uniforms and with the best weapons, not pathetic figures like us. They may have a special mission in the area, possibly something involving our new friends. We imagine their initial surprise and mistrust when they see us, not recognising us as German soldiers until we tell them what has happened to us.

We can hardly wait to finally get away but, before we can go, something wonderful happens. The farming family had been looking at us with obvious sympathy since we had arrived and now the farmer brings Georg, whose footwear consists of cloth bound up with wire cable, a pair of old but well-maintained leather boots, which he is overjoyed to accept.

As is sometimes the case, this good deed, which is received with so much gratitude, prompts another, and so he is also given a jacket. This gift will make such a difference for throughout our flight from the camp in Volozyn he has only been wearing a thin shirt. Now he is fully equipped for the challenges that lie ahead of us.

I don't envy him the beautiful boots, as I could not put them on because of the state of my feet. My over-sized rubber boot, when stuffed with foot wraps, is a good fit and has caused me hardly any discomfort so far. As for the covering of my other foot, I have got used to it – the well-worn peaked cap works well when bound up carefully with cable and is easy to adjust. It is damp, too, which cools my foot.

The good people in the farm have taken such care of us that I cannot thank them enough and, when we get up to go, they bid us a moving farewell. The grandmother blesses us, laying her hands on our shoulders, and the goodness evident in her eyes is difficult to describe. Reinforced in every way, we leave this extraordinarily friendly house, thank everyone there profusely and start out on the search for our parachutists.

5 August

At the next opportunity we ask for more information about the parachutists, and our high expectations are blown away like a soap bubble. We hear that the crew of an apparently damaged or defective German aircraft had jumped out with parachutes and hidden in a wood. So probably they have already broken out and are heading back towards the German lines just as we are. But of course they will be in better physical condition than we are so long as they weren't injured when they landed and they will have better equipment. In the end we have to abandon the time-consuming search for them. Contact with them would have been so encouraging for us, and we might have acquired some useful equipment from them, a compass perhaps and a pistol for extreme emergencies. But this turned out to be wishful thinking.

6 August and Afterwards

Most of the following days passed without incident so I won't describe them in detail – I'll concentrate on the important events.

For example, we gather that only a few hours before five German soldiers had been provided with food and had gone on to a place nearby; if we hurried, we could perhaps catch up with them. We suspect this is another version of the story about the parachutists as exactly five men are mentioned, but we realise that we were far from the only German soldiers who were trying to get back to the West.

We were then told to go along a road – which fortunately ran in the direction of our march – for about 2km to a village, and so we set off on our way, walking carefully in roadside ditches, as it was already quite light and we didn't want to be seen.

We were excited about the thought of meeting fellow fugitives with whom we could talk about our experiences and perhaps even march on together, but anxious too. 'They must be still there, perhaps hiding out in a barn during the day', said Georg. 'Wouldn't it be wonderful if we could join them', I reply. Just then the village becomes visible in the morning light. We stop for a moment, weighing up the situation, then approach the nearest house.

When we knock, a young man immediately opens the door. Without a word, he also opens the door to the living room, at the same time making a gesture which indicates he has a surprise for us. And what a surprise it was! There sitting in the room are the five soldiers. They jump up, visibly alarmed, but instantly they see that the two figures in the doorway are not Red Army soldiers. At first they are speechless with astonishment, but then the first questions come and we give them a brief account of our journey, and they listen sympathetically, sometimes shaking their heads in amazement.

These comrades – an NCO and four private soldiers – make a good impression as they haven't been taken prisoner so they have almost all their equipment, but no weapons apart from the NCO's pistol. When we discover that one of them still has a compass we cautiously ask whether we could join them. We can't take this for granted because it would be difficult for five men to get through the Russian lines and even more risky for seven. But we still hope they will allow us to go with them.

For us the compass is the most important thing. Until now – with a few exceptions – we have orientated ourselves under a clear sky using the Great Bear, but we are not confident we can use the same method successfully as we go on through thick woodland.

We are grateful when they agree that we can accompany them, and we introduce ourselves, using our Christian names. Our ranks – as I've already mentioned – no longer play any role and no one asks me why I am wearing overalls without any badges of rank at all. Our new travelling companions escaped, like us, from the Minsk cauldron and belong to various divisions which shows how chaotic conditions were during the withdrawal and the various attempts to break out. All of them served in divisions that were usually led by provincial commanders. Fritz comes from Brandenburg, Gustl from Bavaria, Albert is, like Georg, a Würtemburger, Anderl is from the Sudetenland, and Fred, the NCO, from Thüringen.

On the following day Fred leaves our group when, much to our surprise, we come across three soldiers from his regiment who immediately recognise him. Both sides are joyful at this unexpected meeting and so we completely understand when he goes with them. We wish each other all the best and then we continue, six of us now, without any weapons.

All of us have broken off branches to make knotty walking sticks. We have also used strips of cloth to form rough straps so we can carry our two sacks of supplies like rucksacks, which lightens the load and leaves our hands free. And so, equipped like this, we walk on like tired wanderers through the countryside.

The next time we stop to stock up our supplies, we ask the friendly and helpful housewife if she has a map of Lithuania and she tears one out of an old school atlas. This map is really useful. It has a scale of 1:1,000,000 which makes it possible for us to find our present position. We can also work out the distances to various places and see the routes of roads, rivers and railway lines. We discover that soon we will have to cross the Vilna–Lida railway line which runs nearby in a north–south direction. Then we will enter the area where two weeks earlier we had expected to find a firm front line. Now, of course, our best hope is that the front line runs along the Memel which is about 100km away.

From what we can gather from our map, there appear to be no particular points along our route where concentrations of Russian troops might be expected, but for a long distance there appear to be no settlements, and we soon find out why.

We cross the railway line and approach a sparsely inhabited landscape known as Rudniki forest. It reminds me of the steppe-like grassland of the Hungarian plains and of a lovely song sung by Sarah Leander with her characteristic dark intonation.

The area gets its name from the only large town in the area, Rudniki, which we see from the map lies about 10km away on our line of march. Since the Russian military will certainly be found there, we must avoid it. Our fantastic map has already paid for itself!

In front of us in the moonlight is the outline of an unusually large wood that is too wide to go around without losing lots of time. It is too dark for us to tell how extensive it is, but fortunately we now have a compass so we should be able to find our way through it to open country on the other side. We know that shortly we should reach the steppe-like grassland of the Puszta.

When we are inside the wood there is more light than we expected and there is only a bit of undergrowth so we make good progress, especially when we come across a narrow path that goes roughly in the right direction.

The hours pass quickly, but the wood does not come to an end. At dawn we keep on going because it is easier to find our way in the light and there is no hint of danger.

Time passes quickly and still there are only trees as far as we can see. Finally, when we are tired and still surrounded by trees, we look for a place to rest for a few hours. 'It looks like we are going to have to spend some time in the Puszta', says Albert looking at the map. None of us realise that a march of at least 30km through the wood lies ahead of us, during which we will not come across a single settlement.

Until now we hadn't walked for long through woods and we'd done it in daylight, but now we decide to risk it as we want to leave the area behind as soon as possible. 'At least there are no partisans here', says Fritz. But then we get a shock. In front of us, in the middle of a small clearing, we see without apparently ourselves being seen ourselves, a man armed with a rifle on sentry duty. He is wearing a light grey military jacket with gleaming copper buttons similar to those on my drill uniform. At first we keep absolutely still and watch this odd-looking character. He doesn't look like a partisan, at least not like those we've seen before, so eventually we approach him slowly to find out who he is.

To our surprise he isn't alarmed to see us and there is nothing threatening about his attitude. It seems he has been waiting for us here. He had noticed us some time before and had taken us for harmless wanderers with our knotted sticks and rucksacks.

Once we get close to him, I see that his uniform buttons are stamped with the Polish eagle. He speaks a bit of German and Anderl speaks a few words of Polish, so we can converse quite adequately. We discover that here in this vast woodland there are Polish partisans – or perhaps we should call them resistance fighters – who, just like the Lithuanian partisans under Juozas Jakavonis, are carrying on a guerrilla war against the Soviets. They are also looking out for possible recruits.

To the question whether there are Russian military in the neighbourhood, he tells us that in Rudniki, as we had expected, a group of soldiers with two T-34 tanks are stationed and their task is to control the woods, though until now they have seldom come near. 'The Russians are scared in the woods', he says disdainfully, and that one can understand, as a tank can easily be shut in on one of the few tracks that are wide enough to be useable. I remember the fate of the Soviet tank driver Vera Proschina who was well known for her inflammatory speeches. In a wood her T-34 was hit by a Panzerfaust fired by a resistance group, and she met a sad end.

When we ask our Polish friend about the size of the wood, he replies: 'You have many kilometres to go before the end.' 'How many?' Georg asks, wanting to know exactly. The man isn't good at figures, so instead he raises his hands three times – so the answer is 30km. Now we understand why this land is described as '*Puszcza*', a wilderness.

After taking in this discouraging news we say goodbye to him and continue on our way. Since such a long journey through the woods lies ahead of us, we decide to march only by day. This will be easier for us than travelling at night – we should be able to find our way – but we will have to move with great care because there is a chance we will meet unfriendly local people. This slows us down and we also have to keep stopping to check our direction with the compass.

As we want to avoid the risk of going into villages, we must save our scanty rations and as far as possible make do with berries and mushrooms. In the woods there are plenty of berries – blueberries, blackberries and cranberries. Whenever possible we rest by streams where there is clear water to quench our thirst and refill our flasks.

I take the opportunity to search for mushrooms which grow so well here that there is a good supply. Using fresh water from the stream, we then cook a splendid soup. At first the comrades are quite sceptical about the mushrooms – they didn't know much about them and had collected inedible ones – but I am confident. My knowledge came from my father who had taken me and my sister to collect mushrooms when we were young; he loved nature and, as a pharmacist, he could identify the different kinds. He told us not pull the mushrooms out of the ground, but to cut them just above the ground in order not to lose the flavour, and here in the Puszcza Rudnicka we pick them with the same care, using a pocket knife belonging to one of our new comrades (mine and Georg's had changed owners in Volozyn).

Then we go on through the wilderness. Several times we come across recent signs of fighting – hastily dug shallow foxholes and incomplete trenches which show the defence didn't last long. At a crossroads we come across empty tin cans labelled ham and eggs, meat and vegetable stew, corned beef, etc., all from the firm of Oscar Maier in Chicago. These must have been supplied to Uncle Joe – Joseph Stalin – under the Lend-Lease programme of 1941. We take a close look at the cans and try to work out what the contents would have been.

Again and again we study the map, searching for the best places to rest and for places that will be risky and should be avoided. We are aiming for the Memel which represents the next serious obstacle and our goal – we are longing to get there but know it will be dangerous for us when we do.

In any case we must get over the river because, wherever the Russian offensive has been stopped, it must be somewhere on the west bank. Our immediate concern is to find our way through the difficult terrain we have in front of us. According to our map we must cross about 15km of woodland in order to reach the Mereczanka, a large river running in a south-westerly direction which we can't avoid. In this uninhabited area there won't be a bridge so we hope the river won't be too deep to wade across. Further on we will have cross the Vilna–Grodno railway line, which again we can't avoid, but by then we will have finally put the *Puszcza* behind us.

Once we have studied the map, we engage in another intensive louse hunt which we can carry on undisturbed in these quiet surroundings. Some of us have more of these wicked creatures to deal with, especially Georg who seems to have blood that is particularly attractive to them – at least that is what we think.

Afterwards we come to a small lake surrounded by trees which looks just right for a refreshing – and urgently required – bath. Without hesitating we decide to do this, thinking no great risk is involved. We haven't had a chance to get out of our clothing for such a long time and we need to wash, and Albert even produces a piece of soap – no one else has any. For a short time we swim around and briefly it feels like we are on holiday. We would have liked to wash our clothes in order to get rid of the lice, but since we can't afford to wait for them to dry we have to put them back on after our swim and this puts a damper on things.

We have already spent four days in the Puszcza Rudnicka and, apart from the Polish guard, haven't met anybody. But when we reach the Mereczanka, which is as wide here as the Little Beresina, we hear some shots behind us so immediately we climb fully dressed into the water. As the woodland path continues on the other bank, we come across a ford where the water only rises to our thighs. However, the current in the middle is so strong that I was turned round twice on my own axis without losing my balance or my rucksack. All of us emerge half-dry on the other bank, shake the water out of our boots and continue our march. In several places we discover clear traces of tank tracks and in narrow stretches the trees on both sides have been smashed down. Everywhere there are destroyed or discarded items of equipment, among them empty boxes and cartons with English labels. So many abandoned things seem to indicate that the resistance didn't last long here.

Nearby there must be an airfield – perhaps near Olkieniki, a large town shown on the map on the edge of the woodland – because one after another aircraft are diving down to fire with their machine guns apparently at the same target. I can clearly hear their engines as they go in, then climb back into their formation. As a precaution we alter our direction of march in order to avoid them.

The aircraft remind me of the devastating aerial attacks on the Minsk cauldron during the breakout attempt. At that time, I was expecting I would quickly get back to our own lines, but since then I've spent five weeks escaping across the countryside and I am still not sure I will get there in the end.

As we progress through the woods we find pamphlets the Soviets have dropped for the retreating stragglers like us. Their text is written in impeccable German and I wonder if they have been produced with the help of the Nationalkomitee Freies Deutschland which frequently broadcasts loudspeaker propaganda at the front. In the pamphlet I read: 'To German officers and men who have concealed themselves in the woods – you will not get through, you are lost. Come out voluntarily and give yourselves up. You will be well treated and get plenty to eat.'

Needless to say, this does not appeal to us. We haven't struggled through the countryside for weeks only to be lured out of the woods by the promise that we will be 'well treated' in captivity. As for food, we are getting along well enough with the help of the well-meaning local people, and we know that in Siberia, or wherever the Soviets send us, we can hardly expect tasty mushrooms! Nevertheless, we are delighted with the leaflets and collect as many of them as we can find because they make good toilet paper. Until now we have had to make do with large leaves from the woods and fields.

At nightfall we emerge on the far side of the vast woodland and are able to keep going at night. With great caution we cross the Vilna–Grodno railway line which goes on to Warsaw via Bialystok. The tracks have not yet been switched to the wider Russian gauge, perhaps because this stretch runs in a north–south direction rather than east–west to the front line, and anyway the Red Army has acquired a number of trucks from the USA for its supplies, so it doesn't depend on the railways.

At dawn we come to a narrow river that is not shown on our map. Apparently it is a minor tributary of the Mereczanka, but it is a major obstacle for us because the river bank is so swampy that we can't reach the water without taking serious risks. In the growing daylight we don't dare to make the crossing and instead seek shelter in a nearby wood. This is a precarious position for us to be in because we can be trapped on this side of the river or we can be forced back from it. During our journey we have learnt a lot that can't be found in any training manual.

This time, once again, we seem to be lucky. We spend the long day undisturbed and leave the wood as night comes on, hoping to get over the river more easily further along. Soon we find a spot that looks promising, and not far from the opposite bank is a small village where we can get supplies. But when we reach the river bank we see a woman who waves us away, calling out: 'Go, go! – Russians, Russians!' Immediately we turn and run back towards the east, then make a wide detour before returning to our line of march. We don't come across the river again – somehow we must have gone round it during our flight.

We go on towards the Memel, which we estimate is about 50km ahead of us and can be reached in about a week if conditions allow. According to our map, our route doesn't go past any big towns. The area is apparently lightly settled and no further rivers or railway lines are shown. Nevertheless, we know we must continue to take great care and can in no way relax just because the last days of the march have been so free of problems. Gradually we are approaching the presumed front line and it is possible that troops are stationed deep in this hinterland.

As we replenish our supplies in a house, we learn from the occupants that unrest has broken out in Germany. Hitler has been seriously wounded and a number of generals have been shot. The Allies are standing in front of Paris and the Soviets are on their way to Warsaw. We simply cannot believe all this and assume it is based on propaganda or rumour or on false stories like the one we had heard recently about the parachutists. But what if it were true? We are worried and want to know what the situation really is. 'There must be radios here in Lithuania', says Georg and Anderl suggests we should look out for aerials on the roofs. There aren't many of them, of course, because the Soviets have confiscated the radios.

Russian bombers and fighters are constantly flying over us in a westerly direction, squadron after squadron. They look scornful to us, with the red stars on their wings, and give us a feeling of inferiority and helplessness. We sense we have been abandoned. There is still no sign of a front line.

'We should hear gunfire by now', says Fritz, but soon we discover why we don't. In a village we ask where the front line is.

'The front? Oh, on the German border', we are told.

'No, that is impossible, it cannot be true! The Soviets on the German border!'

Unfortunately, this turns out to be the case. Two major cities were taken by the Soviets a fortnight ago – Marijampolė, 40km from the East Prussian border, on 31 July, and Kalvarja, 30km further on, a day later. It looks as though resistance on the Memel didn't last long and now the Red Army is standing at the door of East Prussia. This shattering news means we have at least 130km further to go. This will take us more than two weeks, and then we will have to find our way through the Russians at the front line. We can only hope they will come to a halt at the border as they will need time to prepare for their offensive into our territory and surely they will also need to consolidate their position after an advance of more than 600km.

One ray of hope is the knowledge that we will not have to cross the Memel in the no man's land between the two front lines, which would be very dangerous. Yet, we reckon the Soviets will maintain a close watch on the west bank as that is a good place to catch fugitives like us.

Using the map, we try to work out the best place to cross the river. If we maintain our present direction we will pass between the towns of Olita (Alytus) and Punia, which are about 10km apart. This route looks promising because the course of the Memel is straight here; what we must avoid are the two enormous serpent-like loops north of Punia and the smaller one south of Olita where we might have to cross the river two or three times which would make the risk of running into a patrol even greater. Without our priceless map we wouldn't have known about these places and our journey would have been much more difficult.

Yet again we seem to be a such a long way from our destination. We have to renew our determination to keep going despite the distance involved and the time the march will take. All our energy will be required, and we will have to ignore the prospect that all our efforts may be in vain. It is not surprising then that many of us are visibly downcast and listless when we set off again and we don't look out for danger in the same way as we did before.

'Once we get the Memel behind us, it shouldn't be too far to the German lines', I say in an attempt to lift everyone's spirits, and gradually the alertness and resolution of our group revives.

During the long hours when we have to hide during the day we have ample time to discuss our further progress, in particular the crossing of the Memel.

'Perhaps we can find a canoe', says Anderl.

'Certainly that would be best – then we can all get over dry. What a break that would be', Fritz replies.

'We ought look for ropes and then make a raft', I say, but Gustl dismisses this.

'Where would we get the wood for it – we can't saw down trees,' he says, 'and with six men we could never get everyone on.'

'If we swim across, we will have to leave some stuff behind', Albert observes, and he's right – we need to consider this because, once we've crossed the river, we will still have a long way to go.

'But if the water is not too deep, we may be able to wade through it like at the Mereczanka', says Fritz.

Georg is doubtful about this.

'Yes,' he says, 'and then, if there are sentries on the other side, we will be taken immediately.'

'Anyway,' I say, 'we must get ropes or cords so that we can tie things on our heads, at least the most important things. We will have to do this whether we swim or wade.'

We decide we will have to wait and see how things turn out.

At dawn, since we couldn't find a wood to hide in, we go into a barn in the next village and conceal ourselves in the hay. Two young farmers come in and start working with their pitchforks right next to us. They soon discover us, nod to us with no sign of shock and smile as if our presence is no surprise.

As the day goes on my comrades become increasingly nervous and, after much discussion, they decide to wait until they are more confident about making the crossing without being seen. I don't know what to do – should I stay with them or go on alone? Then I realise I may not get the chance again and decide I must attempt the crossing at once.

Quickly I calculate how long the moon will be covered – for about 5 minutes, I reckon. In that time I must get to the side of the lake. Then I can conceal myself behind the thick willows and remain under cover and figure out what to do next. I wait till the cloud covers the moon, then very carefully crawl into a dip which metre by metre becomes shallower until finally I'm exposed on the flat meadow. Behind me I hear the voices of the sentries and I fear they have noticed something. Then there is the metallic click of rifle bolts. I guess they have spotted me, but nothing happens. In such tense situations one always feels one is the centre of attention. Go on, go on, I say to myself. The cloud has already gone across half the moon. Then I see in front of me a row of small box-like humps, one behind the other in a chessboard pattern, half a metre apart – mines, damn it! They are buried in the ground with a projecting wire slanting out to one side, and they will go off at the slightest touch. I must get through as there is no going back, and so I wriggle my way past the mines without knocking against any wires. Once again, I have been lucky, especially as the guards were distracted.

Quickly I complete the last metre to the lakeside and, immensely relieved, conceal myself behind the willow bushes just as the black Zeppelin-cloud allows the full moon to shine again in all its glory. Then, as suddenly as it came, it vanishes without trace. I couldn't have had more luck. Although many challenges lie ahead of me, I am now much more confident about getting through the Russian front lines intact and without running into the enemy. The next phase of the escape, though, requires the greatest caution and I realise immediately that I am faced with another problem.

In the lake there is a line of reeds which I won't be able get through without making a loud rustling sound that would certainly be heard 50m away on the front line. I decide the best thing to do is to swim along a bit to a spot where I will be less likely to be seen in the water which is gleaming now in the moonlight, so in the cover of the willows I very carefully begin to strip off. Even at a distance the small rings made by fish when they come the surface are easy to see. Since a naked body will be conspicuous in the moonlight, I keep on my long underpants and grey pullover and hide everything else in the bush next to me, covering the dirty white overalls with the dark uniform socks. The scraps of bacon in the pocket of my overalls I am happy to get rid of, but it isn't so easy to say farewell to my battered rubber boots which have served me so well.

When I'm fully prepared and ready to go, at just the right moment, wild shooting starts a few hundred metres away. Green and red tracers fly here and there, flares climb high and the sound of several machine guns echoes through in the wood. There is so much noise that I ought to be able to slip through the reeds without attracting attention. I climb down into the lake and, although I sink into the mud, I work my way quickly into the reeds until I look out across open water with only my head sticking out.

Once the sound of firing has died down, I search for a suitable place to swim across. About 300m away a wood on the bank casts shadows on the lake which may allow me to cross safely, and I decide to try my luck.

As the reeds stretch along the bank without any gaps, I can swim beside them without being seen. To avoid splashing, I swim using short strokes of my arms and without moving my legs. I know that, behind the reeds and the bushes on the bank, on an open field between the two woods which are less than a 100m apart, is the Russian front line. After very slow and exhausting effort I reach the shady area in the lake without being spotted. There I turn 90 degrees and, swimming in the same cautious way, I cross the last 300m. Beyond the bank, in the moonlight, I can see the ruined church tower of a village.

As I get closer, metre by metre, my excitement increases and I feel stronger, then, when I'm still a long way from the bank, unexpectedly I feel the bottom of the lake under my feet and carefully, but happily, I wade through the shallows. There is another belt of reeds here which I have to cross to reach firm ground. I still can't really believe I am so close to my goal. Isolated shots can be heard, accompanied by green and red tracers, and I am sure I must be near the German front line.

Tense, not sure what will happen next, and shivering with cold in my soaking clothes, I look around and see what appears to be a narrow path, a black band in a trench which I later realise is a way through a minefield. But I don't dare to jump down into it because it occurs to me a Russian outpost or supporting position might be at the other end. I've become so apprehensive that I consider every possibility, however unrealistic or illogical.

Then, a few metres away, I see away something sticking up from the trench – a sentry post. A sentry is standing there, but I can't tell which army he belongs to. Although his steel helmet flashes in the moonlight, Russian helmets, especially at night, are not easy to distinguish from ours. I am very worried I've come across a Soviet forward position and I stay rooted to the spot. I don't know whether to go forward or back. Yet, somehow I must find out for certain, so as quietly as I can I call out: 'Hullo!' There is no reply. Perhaps he has fallen asleep.

So once again, a bit louder, I say: 'Hullo, are you . . .'. Immediately the dark figure swings round, pointing his carbine at me, and shouts: 'Halt! – Password!' Like lightning, I raise my arms high and shout so loudly that even the Ivan over there must have heard: 'Don't shoot, don't shoot, I'm German, German!'

Despite this, he keeps his weapon aimed at me and doesn't let me into the trench – he's worried I'm a Russian trying to trick my way into the German positions. But then other sentries rush up including an NCO, who quickly recognises I'm not Russian and calls out to me: 'Quick, man, come in!' Immediately I take a big jump into the trench and fall on his neck.

I want to lose myself in indescribable happiness, but I can't. I can scarcely breathe, my voice croaks in my throat. My comrades clap me on the back and wait for me to calm me down, but I feel as if I've lost my senses. I am so overwrought that I scratch at the trench wall and it is only when I feel the sand between my fingers that I know for sure I am no longer dreaming. So often I've dreamt of this moment, and so often when I've woken I've been disappointed by the bleak reality. But now the dream has come true.

The realisation that everything I had gone through during the last weeks and months, in such awful conditions, had not been in vain was overwhelming. I had won my life back, although the wretched war hadn't ended.

The NCO takes me to his bunker and along the way I shake the hand of every sentry we pass because I have to convey my joy somehow. It is long after midnight, but the soldiers in the bunker have not settled down to sleep. Astonished, they look at me, in my soaking underpants and pullover.

'Where have you come from?' one of them asks.

'From Minsk,' I reply as if it was obvious, 'from the Minsk cauldron.'

'What, from Minsk?' says another, incredulous.

Before I can say any more I spot a Wehrmacht radio in a corner of the bunker from which light music is coming – wonderful music which I hadn't heard for so long. At that moment the exceptional tension inside me begins to ease off and I find I can't keep my feelings under control. In complete turmoil I throw myself down on a field bed and cry unrestrainedly, trying to pour all the misery out of my soul. Then quite suddenly an immense peace comes to me, and I sense I'm getting back to normal.

Eagerly my fellow soldiers get me something to eat and drink. One brews coffee, another prepares bread and butter, covering it with sausage and tinned meat. Another brings cigarettes, cigars and tobacco in packets that are already open, and cartons of sweets. They pile all these things up on a stool next to my bed.

They do this quietly, without saying much. They can understand something of the experience I've gone through and they are full of the remarkable comradeship that exists on the front line. When they have finished the stool looks like a table of birthday presents, and I remember that day as if it was my second birthday.

When we get talking again one of them asks about my rank, and when I tell him they are visibly embarrassed. Immediately I say that, during the escape, we addressed each other simply by our first names and ranks had played no role. I ask which unit they belong to and the reply, which I find hard to believe, is 'the 30th', a regiment of our 18th Panzergrenadier Division which had been located in front of my observation post in the 'Dnepr Balcony', though no one I know from the division is present here.

This regiment was formed a few weeks ago by bringing together former members who had had the luck at the time of the Russian offensive to be wounded, sick, on leave or in training or for some other reason not at the front. Also there were young, fresh-faced soldiers who had been called up as replacements from the homeland.

When I was talking to the NCO I discovered I had been extremely lucky, as I had come right through the mined lane to the front line. He told me that a few nights ago, in a stretch of the front line guarded by a neighbouring company, a German soldier who was trying to get through – I immediately thought of Georg – had trodden on a mine at the same moment as a sentry challenged him. He was badly wounded and fell on another mine which killed him. Only someone who has been through the same ordeal could fully appreciate what an awful tragedy this was.

Deeply affected, I jump up and leave the bunker immediately, struggling to hide my feelings since these front-line troops know I am an officer. I simply must get some fresh air. I look up at the moon and the stars and wonder how they can still shine after such a calamity. My extreme reaction shows how emotional I had become after so many weeks under incredible presure.

Once I have calmed down I return to the bunker. I'm freezing cold and, after I've removed my wet, dirty, lousy clothing, my comrades bring me a warmed woollen blanket. I want to stretch out and sleep, but sleep doesn't come because much too much is still going through my head, especially what had happened in the final few hours before I had landed in the German trench.

I think of how lucky I had been to come across the spit of land which gave me such a good opportunity to get through the Russian lines, then of the long stretch of black cloud – the only cloud in the sky – which hid the moon, and of the enormous risk I'd run as I crossed the Russian mine field. And then, at just the right moment, the noise of fighting had enabled me to go unmolested through the thick reeds and the shadow of the wood on the lake that had concealed me as I swam. Finally, I had stumbled along a pathway through the German mines – otherwise I couldn't have made it.

But, after surviving so many extraordinary episodes, I couldn't very well speak simply of being lucky. I remembered a line from the Bible, as follows: 'See, I am sending an angel ahead of you to guard you along the way and to bring you to the place I have prepared.'

Epilogue

T he following day I hoped to celebrate Georg's 19th birthday with him, but he hasn't turned up and nothing is known of his fate. Only a few of the German soldiers caught behind Soviet lines got away with their lives and were transported to prison camps and, if Georg was one of these, he must have died there without leaving a message behind.

Nor do I know what happened to my other four comrades. We had not been able to exchange addresses, so all I can do is hope that some of them were fortunate enough to reach their goal. Later research shows that only about 5 per cent of all returning combatants reached the German lines again.

With hearty thanks I say goodbye to the soldiers in the bunker who had looked after me so well and in such an understanding way, then I went to eat with the officers of the regimental staff. The meal is held in the cellar of one of the few surviving houses in the village, the atmosphere was really friendly, and I tell them all about my experiences. Everyone there is well aware of the gravity of the situation, with strong Russian forces so close to Germany. As I said farewell and climbed into the VW-Jeep that took me to the East Prussian border near Neidenburg, I knew that many of them would gladly have exchanged places with me.

The 4th Army's collection point for soldiers who had come through the enemy lines was based at Neidenburg and there I could tell my worried family what had happened to me. It was a wonderful drive in radiant sunshine with a clear blue sky, past woods that were beginning to take on their autumnal colours and between undulating fields of corn ready for the harvest. It was a picture of the deepest peace, and I delighted in the knowledge that at last I wasn't constantly surrounded by danger. The people we encountered gave us a friendly wave, but in many of their faces I sensed their anxiety, and the east wind carried the rumbling sound of firing from the nearby front line.

At Niedenburg I expected to stay for a few days to answer questions about my escape and the catastrophe of our defeat, and I wanted to find out about the fate of so many comrades who were missing or had been killed or captured.

Also at Niedenburg individuals who were members of the notorious National Committee for a Free Germany had to be identified – they had been smuggled into our ranks by the Soviets in order to sabotage our withdrawal.

Anyone who is – usually unfairly – regarded as suspicious has to undergo further interrogation and is kept under guard in a quarantine camp at Lisa near Posen in Poland, and they may not contact their close relations. Frequently detention in this camp lasts for several months and soldiers who have taken great risks on their long journey home are understandably embittered by such treatment – they don't feel free in this camp. It is also incomprehensible that soldiers who have been detained have to apply in writing for their release. If they don't, they may be completely forgotten and will never see their homeland again.

Luckily I was interviewed by a second lieutenant on the staff at Neidenburg who was so convinced by the authenticity of my report and impressed by me that he assured me, clapping me on the shoulder, 'I will see to it that you go home immediately.' So I only spent a day there.

The last stop on my way home was in the reserve hospital in Świdnica near my hometown of Freiburg, Silesia, where I had an emotional reunion with my mother and sister, especially so as my father had died shortly before. During the stay in the hospital my wounds – and my feet – finally healed and my weight went up from 45kg to normal. I had a lovely time as the doctors as well as the nurses were so concerned with my well-being.

Shortly before my release I was offered the choice of promotion to lieutenant in the reserve or a four-week special leave. Immediately I replied 'special leave' and in that time I made notes about my experiences which eventually became the text of this book.

When my leave finished I discovered I couldn't re-enter my old artillery regiment which had been reconstituted after so many losses in the Soviet Union. Since I had been a prisoner of war – even though for a short time – I could no longer serve on the Eastern Front. Instead, I was allocated to Artillery Regiment 102 which was based in the West.

Its solicitous commander, Colonel Hofer, employed me on the regimental staff as orderly officer after he had learned of my Russian adventure. Later, during a reconnaissance, I was captured by the Americans and, after an abortive attempt to escape from a transport train on the way to the Attichy camp in France, I was there at the end of the war.

After the war I didn't return to Silesia, but fifty years later I went to Freiburg, which is now known as Świebodzice, and found our old Adler chemist shop which goes by the name Apteka Franciskanska. Naturally the brass Prussian eagle which hung over the entrance on the corner of the building is no longer there – one could say that he freed himself and flew away.